Graduate Students at Work

Rethinking Careers, Rethinking Academia

Joseph Fruscione
Erin Bartram
Series Editors

Graduate Students at Work
Exploited Scholars of Neoliberal Higher Ed

Edited by
Tessa Brown

University Press of Kansas

© 2023 by the University Press of Kansas
All rights reserved

Published by the University Press of Kansas (Lawrence, Kansas 66045), which was organized by the Kansas Board of Regents and is operated and funded by Emporia State University, Fort Hays State University, Kansas State University, Pittsburg State University, the University of Kansas, and Wichita State University.

Library of Congress Cataloging-in-Publication Data

Names: Brown, Tessa, editor.
Title: Graduate students at work : exploited scholars of neoliberal higher ed / edited by Tessa Brown.
Description: Lawrence : University Press of Kansas, 2023. | Series: Rethinking careers, rethinking academia | Includes bibliographical references and index.
Identifiers: LCCN 2022024376 (print)
  LCCN 2022024377 (ebook)
  ISBN 9780700635245 (cloth)
  ISBN 9780700634071 (paperback)
  ISBN 9780700634088 (ebook)
Subjects: LCSH: Graduate teaching assistants—United States. | Graduate students—Employment—United States. | Universities and colleges—United States—Graduate work.
Classification: LCC LB2335.4 .G73 2023 (print) | LCC LB2335.4 (ebook) | DDC 378.3/65—dc23/eng/20220713
LC record available at https://lccn.loc.gov/2022024376.
LC ebook record available at https://lccn.loc.gov/2022024377.

British Library Cataloguing-in-Publication Data is available.

Printed in the United States of America

10 9 8 7 6 5 4 3 2 1

The paper used in this publication is acid free and meets the minimum requirements of the American National Standard for Permanence of Paper for Printed Library Materials Z39.48-1992.

To the former student, staff, faculty, and community members of THE General Body at Syracuse University,

and to all workers fighting for their lives

"Universities will never love you."
—Eve Ewing

Contents

Introduction: Graduate Students Are Hyper-Exploited   1
   Tessa Brown

PART I: LABOR AT THE MARGINS
Interlude 1. "Levels to This Sh*t": Layers of Graduate Student Labor   29
   Khadeidra Billingsley

1. "I Have to Go Wherever There's an Opportunity": Graduate Students' Experiences of Placelessness and Writing   33
   Charlotte Kupsh and Zoe McDonald

Interlude 2. Invisible Marginalization in Academia   54
   Samah Elbelazi

Interlude 3. Invisible Labors and Entangled Emergence   57
   Andrew Hollinger

2. "Like I'm 'The Man'": Graduate Student Administrators' Experiences   60
   Talinn Phillips, Paul Shovlin, and Megan Titus

Interlude 4. The Ethics of Progressive Internships   86
   Meagan Gacke-Reed

3. "It's Dangerous to Go Alone": Explorations of Unbalanced Labor and Mentorship in a Blended Learning Doctoral Program   90
   April Cobos and Megan Mize

PART II: THE LABOR OF TEACHING AND RESEARCH
4. Will This Take Me Anywhere? Investing Time in Graduate Student Teaching   119
   Elliot Shapiro

x | Contents

Interlude 5. Establishing *Ethos* for a Translingual GTA—
The Unwritten Labor   137
Anis Rahman

5. Learning to Teach, Teaching to Learn   141
Sara Austin and Kelly Moreland

Interlude 6. Mothering and Laboring as a Graduate Student
and Teacher   167
Alma Villanueva

Interlude 7. Parenting while Researching? It Takes Support,
Kid-Friendly Systems, and a Lot of Luck   170
Jacqueline Kory-Westlund

PART III: THE LABOR OF "PROFESSIONALIZATION"
Interlude 8. The Professoriate Is a Job   175
Sarah Welsh

6. Scholar-Selves in the Managerial University: The Hidden
Labor of Disciplinary Identity Formation in the Doctoral
Journey   178
Adam Haley

Interlude 9. Ethically Honoring Graduate Student Expertise
through Joy Projects   208
Jaclyn Fiscus-Cannaday and Allison Hutchison

7. Chinese Doctoral Students' Perceptions of Employability in
the United States: Cultivating Preparedness for a Challenging
World   213
Xueshuang Wang, Weiyan Xiong, and Huiyuan Ye

PART IV: ORGANIZING LABOR
Interlude 10. Paying to Teach: A Profile of California State
University System English Department Graduate Teaching
Associate Programs   237
Martha Althea Webber

8. "Fees Are Wage Theft": Graduate Labor Unions Confronting
   the Neoliberal University   241
   Jonathan Isaac

Interlude 11. A How-To Guide for Combating the Invisibility of
   Graduate Student Parents   264
   Alex Hanson

9. "We'll Be Taking This with Us": Relationality and Idealism in
   Three Graduate Union Locals   268
   Anicca Cox

Afterword: Striking for a Safer Campus Community   291
   Kalena Thomhave and Matt Sehrsweeney

About the Contributors   295

Index   301

Graduate Students at Work

Introduction
Graduate Students Are Hyper-Exploited

Tessa Brown

This is a book for graduate students, prospective graduate students, teachers and administrators of graduate students, and nonacademics who employ current or former graduate students. Its goal is to peer through the mist of jargon that shrouds the labor practices of academia so that we can see more clearly the millions of misclassified and underpaid workers who do the difficult labor of making this industry work: custodians, groundskeepers, food-service workers, support staff, undergraduate athletes and residential advisors, researchers and librarians, non-tenure-track (NTT) lecturers, and—the subject of this volume—graduate student workers. The pieces in this volume illustrate through reflection and research the significant expertise graduate students are asked to enact in their jobs as teachers, researchers, and administrators. At the same time, these essays draw connections between the labor conditions of graduate student workers and other workers navigating poverty wages, labor migration, insufficient benefits, safety risks, and harassment and discrimination around lines of race, gender, ability, and citizenship—the most important connection perhaps being the possibility for organization and unionization to fight for better working conditions for all. As the COVID-19 pandemic continues to transform our world and our work conditions on and off campus, the authors in this collection offer concrete and prescient commentary on strategies for recognizing and improving working conditions in higher education and beyond.

Indeed, the pandemic offers a critical moment to frankly face the essential labor that graduate students do within universities. Besides highlighting graduate students' key role in advocating for campus safety during the pandemic, the discussion here is also meant for prospective graduate students, since applications are rising, as they often do (along with student debt) during times of economic recession (even as undergraduate applications are dropping, bucking the usual trend [Pew Charitable Trusts 2021]). While graduate student and academic labor organizing was already on the rise in 2019, the pandemic raised the stakes for all workers, including academic workers. As teaching and research assistants working with undergraduate populations and others, graduate student workers faced many of the same ironic challenges as other "frontline" workers under COVID-19—lauded for their "essential" interfacing with the public even as they were among the lowest-paid workers in their hierarchies, with little control over their working conditions. Like other essential, frontline workers, graduate student laborers have little power to voice their concerns to those with decision-making capacities. And like other workers, it has often been through collective action, sanctioned by a union or not, that graduate student workers have demanded and received the information, accommodations, healthcare, time off, and proper protective equipment they need to do their jobs and keep larger organizations from collapsing.

Thus, the time is right for this volume, the first edited collection that focuses exclusively on graduate student workers' experiences, expertise, and exploitation. With particular (but not exclusive) attention to graduate workers in English and composition, these articles and short essays speak to the particularities and the universalities of graduate student labor in these fields and beyond. The collected authors here, current and former graduate students—who finished their degrees and didn't, who stayed in academia and left—address graduate student workers' developing expertise as teachers and researchers and their status as marginalized workers managing labor migration, jockeying for employment, and organizing for better conditions. In order to attend to the wide variety of graduate student experiences, this volume includes full-length research articles as well as shorter personal essays and case studies that focus on individual experiences or locations. Including these essays allows this volume to highlight more graduate student voices, including of those who are not directly researching graduate students or who had something to contribute but did not have the time or the resources to write a full-length article. These short essays, which often speak of multiple marginalizations (especially as student-workers who are of color, foreign nationals, or parents), cast light on the additional labor—seeking accommodations, pursuing change on campuses, managing an intense cognitive and emotional load—that marginalized graduate student workers perform while seeking to receive their education and do their jobs.

This volume focuses on graduate students who are employed by the colleges and universities where they are matriculated and who are referred to throughout as graduate student workers. But graduate students are a much larger category, all of whose members produce surplus value for their institutions—whether through their labor as underpaid workers replacing higher-paid staff positions, or through their tuition, which has been rising for the past five decades as state divestment from education has pushed costs onto students, often financed through loans. No longer a medieval guild, higher education is rather a huge, modernized industry full of workers with confusing and overlapping classifications, many of which help this industry, with its sophisticated, diversified revenue streams, get its labor on the cheap. As state funding fades, universities have diversified their business models, collecting funds through tuition (often paid through federal grants), alumni and other donations, hospital fees, research grants (including lucrative Defense Department grants), and athletic revenues. At Stanford University, where I most recently worked, only a small portion of the earnings of the university's $30 billion endowment is put toward campus costs every year. The remainder is reinvested into the endowment's diversified investment portfolio by the Stanford Management Company, giving credence to the line that Harvard and other peer institutions are "hedge fund[s] with a university attached" (Weissmann 2015)—which don't pay taxes on their earnings.

The industry we call academia is huge. In the United States, it spans over four thousand universities, colleges, and community colleges (Moody 2019). In 2017 there were three million domestic graduate students, including those in master's, doctorate, and professional degree programs, 426,000 of whom were foreign nationals (NCES 2020)—though that representation has been shrinking rapidly since the advent of the Trump administration and throughout the pandemic (di Maria 2020). Although doctoral education has long been framed as a direct route to the professoriate, tenure-track jobs have been steadily disappearing, with undergraduate instruction increasingly supplied by NTT instructors, including part-time adjuncts and graduate student instructors, even as tenure track positions' workloads are rising. Between 1969 and 2020, the percentage of instructional staff on the tenure track at US colleges and universities collapsed from 78% to 33%; over a million college and university instructors teach off the tenure track (Petersen 2020). In 2014 "part-time instructional staff positions [made] up nearly 41 percent of the academic labor force and graduate teaching assistants [made] up almost another 13 percent" (AAUP 2016). Non-tenure-track jobs range widely in stability, opportunities for promotion and growth, and access to living wages and benefits, and the category's growth has opened many stable new NTT positions that have themselves become a locus of collective organizing. While tenure-track faculty numbers increased by 4.85% between

2005–2015, graduate student employment rose by 16.7%, and numbers of adjunct faculty rose by 21% in the same period (Kroeger et al). In 2012 the Economic Policy Institute (EPI) reported that "the average graduate student is 32 years old"; 12.1% worked as graduate student assistants, including 57.9% of doctoral students outside the field of education (Kroeger et al. 2018). These trends resonate beyond academia, as workers across sectors do the same jobs for less pay and fewer benefits than our parents did a few decades ago.

Graduate students are exploited by their employing institutions not just by virtue of working for poverty wages but also because they take on debt to cover rising tuition costs amid state, federal, and local divestment in higher ed. As the professoriate has shrunk, graduate school offerings have also diversified to offer a range of preprofessional programs, including many master's degrees and pre-professional (as opposed to pre-academic) doctoral degrees. As of 2011–2012, 73.3% of graduate students held educational debt, and the average debt among them was $77,700. By 2015–2016, the average debt of those completing doctorates was over $100,000 (NCES 2018). Despite this huge debt, about half of doctoral students do not finish their degrees (Grasso, Barry, and Valentine 2009). And, although this volume focuses on graduate student employees at public and private nonprofit universities, graduate student debt is growing most rapidly at private for-profit universities, where 71% of those who achieved master's degrees, 76% of those who achieved a professional doctorate, and 90% of those who achieved a research doctorate graduated with student loan debt, at an average of $90,300, $160,100, and $221,800, respectively (NCES 2018). While these essays focus on graduate student workers, we must recognize that part of the way graduate students writ large produce value for universities and the wider economy is by taking on huge amounts of student debt. Further, the evaporating promise of tenure-track or other livable positions for academics means that graduate students graduating with six-figure debt are increasingly unable to repay that debt from the career field in which they've been trained. As the movement to cancel student debt has emphasized, student debt is disproportionately held by women and people of color, with Black women holding more debt than other group (AAUW 2018). And as Tressie McMillan Cottom discusses in her landmark study of for-profit education, *Lower Ed* (2017), students are invited to think of student loan debt as an investment, when it is more properly understood as a liability—as real debt whose repayment is in no way guaranteed.

As neoliberalism shrinks opportunities for all workers, graduate students who stay in or leave academia look forward to careers as precarious

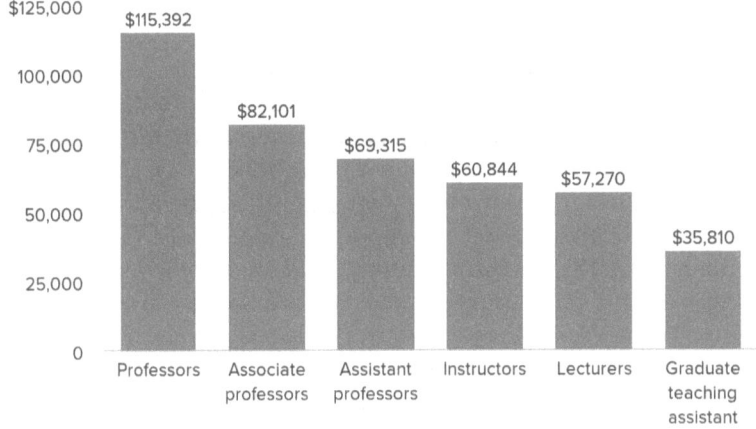

Note: Salary data by academic rank are in 2015–2016 school year dollars. Graduate teaching assistant salary data are in current (May 2016) dollars.

Figure I.1, Average salary of instructional staff, by academic rank, 2015–2016 school year. Courtesy of Economic Policy Institute.

and exploited laborers. No longer satisfied by the future, graduate students (as well as other university employees) are increasingly organizing for labor rights *now*. A 2018 report from the EPI on the state of graduate student employee unions compares graduate student workers' salaries with those of other academic instructors and researchers in order to understand increasing moves toward graduate student unionization (discussed more extensively in this volume's closing section, with key articles by Jonathan Isaac and Anicca Cox). The EPI report compares graduate student compensation with that of NTT and tenure-track positions, noting that "graduate teaching assistants have dramatically lower compensation than faculty, so they are much less costly for universities to employ."

In this chart (figure I.1), graduate teaching assistants' 2016 mean annual salary of $35,810 is positioned alongside the mean annual lecturer salary of $57,270 and assistant professor salary of $69,844 to gesture at the meager wages of graduate students. But only the most highly paid graduate student researchers and teachers I've known—those doing sought-after research at the highest-tier institutions in expensive locations—have had their pay exceed $30,000 annually.

When I was a doctoral student in 2017 at a Research-1 (R1) institution, my take-home salary as a graduate student instructor was about $17,000 a year. In an informal poll of my network of graduate student workers, many of whom also teach and study at R1 institutions, reported take-home pay between 2011 and 2019 was between $11,000 and $30,000. A dive into the source tables for these data doesn't fully clarify the provenance for these salary numbers but may indicate an explanation for them: "Annual wages have been calculated by multiplying the hourly mean wage by a 'year-round, full-time' hours figure of 2,080 hours; for those occupations where there is not an hourly mean wage published, the annual wage has been directly calculated from the reported survey data" (US Bureau of Labor Statistics 2018). Yet most graduate student employees are not paid their wage for a full forty hours per week; rather, they are .5 or even .3 FTE (Full Time Employees). At a hypothetical .5 workload, the average graduate teaching assistant as described by the EPI—close to thirty-two years old, teaching two to four college courses per year or doing professional-level research—would take home $17,905 a year. And let's be clear: graduate students are paid for part-time work, but they are kept busy full-time. When I was a .5 FTE graduate student instructor as a doctoral student, I taught three classes a year, which is what I was paid $17,000 a year for; I was also enrolled in two courses a semester, while additionally conducting my own research. There was no time, nor was there expected to be, for me to supplement my ostensibly part-time job with other work (although members of my cohort, especially those with children, found ways to do so—whether tutoring, editing, or taking restaurant jobs, as contributors Khadeidra Billingsley and Adam Hollinger also discuss.) It is an unassailable truth of graduate student work that graduate study is a full-time job, paid at half-time wages. So, if you're looking at that chart above, take that last column on the right, and cut it in half.

While my story is one of relative privilege, a decade studying and teaching off the tenure track has positioned me as downwardly mobile relative to my family and college peers. At twenty-three, my fully-funded master of fine arts in creative writing felt like a luxurious gig: in the first year of my program, I served as the teaching assistant for one course each semester, helping a tenure-track professor manage their courses, hold office hours, and grade papers. The following year, I became an instructor of my own classrooms (the "instructor of record"), teaching one course of freshman composition each term, to twenty-two frosh. For these services I received a tuition waiver plus annual wages of about $17,000 a year. I then worked for two years as a full-time lecturer at that same institution, earning in the low $30,000s annually—I was rich! When I returned to graduate school two years later for my PhD, matriculating at age twenty-seven, I was back to earning under $20,000 a year—this time teaching three classes a year, taking a full course load, and conducting research.

My last position as an NTT, full-time lecturer is more stable than the situation of many people teaching off the tenure track—lives often characterized by teaching multiple courses at different campuses with no benefits, no office, and no security. I had benefits, but not the privilege of teaching at the level I was trained for—and certainly not the access to salary, housing and childcare stipends, and research leave enjoyed by those designated "faculty" at that institution. And I navigated these economics with privilege—I am a white, cis, able-bodied US citizen who speaks a privileged variety of American English. Most crucially, my family is economically stable and didn't need my financial support, and I don't have children of my own. Of course, I mustn't discount the gendered battles I've faced: my time as an undergraduate, master's student, and PhD student was shaped and slowed by encounters with sexual predators and administrative bullies (Brown 2018), situations that were worsened by the unclear boundaries and governance that classification of graduate workers *as workers* could have improved. (Hence the increased importance that sexual misconduct grievances are taking in graduate student organizing nationwide [Jaffe 2018, Fink 2019].) In her classic study of the economics of literacy across multiple generations, Deborah Brandt (2001) suggests that literacies, like other forms of currency, experience inflation. My experience moving between graduate school programs and full-time, NTT teaching jobs suggests to me the inflation of the value of my degrees. When I finished my MFA, I became a full-time lecturer in Michigan. After my PhD, I became a full-time lecturer in California. While my salary went up significantly, the differences in cost of living by place and time meant that my standard of living actually went down between the Bay Area today and Michigan ten years ago. When the value of degrees is inflated, the potential earning power of one degree goes down and you need another just to stay afloat at the same level, not even to climb.

At the same time, the collapse of tenure-track jobs has pushed the expected research production of tenure-line academics—the *work* of academia—onto graduate students and NTT instructors. Laboring under an intensifying mythos of meritocracy, aspiring professors continue paying labor into academic publishing in hopes of making it into a tenure-track position, or even just to express what they know. I remember my doctoral advisor explaining to me that academic journals didn't pay writers or editors, and academic presses barely did, because his and others' tenure-track professorships were understood to pay for their research time, editing work, and other non-teaching labor. But as tenurable positions evaporate and more academics work as graduate students and teaching-track instructors, this rationale collapses. In my experience, I needed published, peer-reviewed papers to even apply for a job like his—and many of my colleagues, including contributors to this volume, not only conducted and published research but also edited journals, coauthored books, and administered entire programs while they were graduate students. As academia shifts away from the tenure model, the whole structure of academic publishing is called into question.

This volume's particular attention to teaching, writing, and rhetorics is shaped by my training and experience in a range of English and composition departments and programs. An unwanted stepchild of English departments, composition emerged as a subfield shaped by the labor demands created by college writing courses, and its development into a discipline of its own has spawned a meta-inquiry into academic labor practices. Historian of composition James Berlin (1987) recounts how assessment and low-pay labor intersected at the invention of composition as a field in the aftermath of Harvard's institution of an English-language freshman entrance exam in 1878. The advent of the exam created a new need for English education, until then a vernacular that wasn't tested at all, unlike Latin or Greek. Tests shape how we teach and learn; once Harvard created the test, faculty discovered—or invented—students' low proficiency in English, the language students spoke fluently every day but rarely studied or wrote. English preparatory curricula sprang up at the high school level, and colleges created new freshman English courses for those who did poorly on the test—courses in which students wrote reams of papers that needed to be graded. The "monumental task" of grading papers (Berlin, 22) inaugurated composition's need for nonprofessoriate paper graders around whom an endless effort would be waged to "cut costs" (23). From its inception, composition's tenuous place in higher education has highlighted tensions between the relative value of research and teaching; the social constructions of access and excellence; and the costs of teaching labor and its real value to the university bosses.

As required composition courses have expanded across higher education, composition has grown as a field that studies teaching, research, and university management. Its expression across myriad types of programs and departments, each with its own unique approach to staffing and managing huge undergraduate writing programs and growing graduate programs, has deepened compositionists' autoethnographic interest in our own labor and its contexts. The continued reliance of composition on underpaid, misclassified graduate and adjunct teaching labor means that many of us in this discipline have an intimate familiarity with university labor and management practices at their most exploitative. This knowledge is a valuable contribution to academics organizing for more dignified work conditions across the university. Although not all the writers in this collection share this theoretical framing, composition's inquiry into its labor practices has often engaged a Marxian materialist framework that sees exploitation occurring via the "relations of production" between workers and those who own and trade in the fruits of their labor (Marx qtd. in Schell 2012, 125). This tradition shapes the work of colleagues like Bruce Horner, whose *Terms of Work for Composition* (2000) emphasizes the inherent tensions in composition's liminal position in the academy, arguing that more truthfully theorizing our discipline and the work we do in it demands interrogation of the real "work" that compositionists do, beyond the cultural myths that narrativize that work. And our work is extensive, including that by graduate students: in departments, programs, and within English departments, graduate students in composition and rhetoric serve as instructors of record for undergraduate composition courses, tutor in writing centers, and serve in administrative roles managing large undergraduate writing programs, composing and responding to documents in a dizzying array of genres.

Composition's wide variety of institutional locations has strengthened its ability to understand this institution that depends on us, yet can never quite find a place for us. As cross-disciplinary compositionists draw on methodologies from the humanities and the social sciences, our available methods of rhetorical analysis; historical recovery; and classroom, institutional, and autoethnographies position us to deeply interrogate the material and discursive behaviors of the universities where we work. Meanwhile, collections like Seth Kahn, William Lalicker, and Amy Lynch-Biniek's *Contingency, Exploitation, and Solidarity: Labor and Action in English Composition* reflect compositionists' prescient attention to the "new faculty majority" (Schell 2017, ix) of those teaching off the tenure track. Compositionists' uniquely and consistently diverse experiences of academic labor allow us to hold a mirror up to the wider university, illuminating its systems of labor classification, management, work assignment, and subject formation. Our rhetorical studies of mass culture and its constitutive effects on individuals and communities key us into the complex ideological processes of identity formation (discussed by contributors to this volume like Charlotte Kupsh and Zoe McDonald, Sara Austin and Kelly Moreland, and Adam Haley).

Thus, it's no surprise that one of the most clear-eyed analyses of academic labor misclassification and value production comes from a fellow compositionist, Marc Bousquet, whose 2008 *How the University Works* is a touchstone for this volume. While much research on graduate student labor asks how graduate students can maximize their potential for success on the "job market" for tenure-track positions, I find myself turning to Bousquet, who positions contemporary academic labor practices as one more facet of the "bonanza in global capital's voracious quest for low-cost, underregulated labor" (27) that we know as neoliberalism. Neoliberalism describes an economic and cultural movement away from mid-twentieth-century levels of public and private benefits, whose emergence in the United States I and others have theorized as the decentralized white power structure's response to desegregation (Brown 2019, Ferguson 2012). Over the last half century, neoliberalism has systematically dismantled protections for America's middle class through multiple mechanisms, including the state deregulating the financial sector and divesting from public goods including schools, healthcare, and public transit; the private sector abandoning its workers through factory closures, off-shoring of jobs, and the gutting of pensions and worker protections (a trend that continues through the tech industry's production of the gig economy); and the rise of cultural propaganda that still works to convince people the world over that we are individually responsible for our own successes and failures—a fiction which the COVID pandemic has seriously punctured, though not yet destroyed.

Ever the materialist, Bousquet disabuses us academics of our guiding metaphors, recasting academia in the stark light of reality: as a multibillion-dollar industry comprising some of the richest institutions in the world, that for some suddenly strange-appearing reason, does not pay taxes. Bousquet's work is demystification, the anthropologist's job of making the familiar seem strange. Graduate students are taught that we are trained as teachers and researchers in order to be competitive on the academic "job market," an annual process in which all the graduating PhDs *in the world* apply for a few dozen tenure-track positions hiring in their very specialized disciplines and subfields. Materialism allows us to see the workings of economics in culture (see Schell 2012 for a fuller discussion): with few positions available, we all have been taught that we have to work harder, publish more, take on more of the committee responsibilities we call "service," in order to be competitive in an ostensibly meritocratic labor market. Bousquet deconstructs the language of the "job market" altogether, dismissing the hegemonic narrative that the "jobs crisis" is a failure in the system's proper workings to prepare graduate students for careers as tenure-track (what Bousquet calls "tenurable") professors. From Bousquet's perspective, this fiction "disables the practice of solidarity and helps to legitimate the tiering of the workforce" (20). To Bousquet, the system is not broken, but functioning as designed; *to the university*, he argues, the point of graduate students is not to train them for future work but rather to extract value from them, as tuition or laborers, in the present. "Graduate schools admit students to fill specific labor needs," Bousquet writes. "Universities that have cut their graduate employee rolls have consistently preferred to make other flexible arrangements, hiring part-timers or nontenurable lectures and not new tenurable faculty" (20). Although his language is harsh, I find solace in one of Bousquet's most ruthless, and grossest, metaphors: excrement. For many graduate students, Bousquet reminds us, their graduation from their program will mark the *end* of their academic career, not the beginning. Increasingly, he says, "the holders of the doctoral degree are not so much the *products* of the graduate-employee labor system as its *by-products*" (21). We "feel 'treated like shit,'" he goes on, "without [perhaps] grasping the systemic reality that [we] are waste" (26). As depressing as this sounds, it means that we are also the "persons who can perform acts of blockage" (26–27)—who can organize and act to disrupt this system designed to sideline us.

In late 2019 untenable working conditions like these sent the University of California-Santa Cruz students into a wildcat strike in one of the most expensive housing markets in the country. Attention to this action highlights the low pay, essential work, and dishonest rhetorics that characterize graduate student work—and underwrite graduate student organizing—in the United States today. As COVID first emerged abroad in December 2019, students at the University of California-Santa Cruz began a sustained fight against their administration. The ensuing wildcat strike (that is, a strike unsanctioned by their union) demanding a Cost of Living Adjustment (COLA) reflected a significant escalation by graduate student labor. It also marked an escalation in the administration's response. In a city south of Silicon Valley where median rents approach $3,000 (Rent Jungle 2020) yet graduate student salaries are $2,434 a month or $18,000 in take-home pay per nine-month year (Gilich and Boardman 2020), graduate students rejected their United Auto Workers (UAW)–negotiated contract and launched a grade strike at the end of the fall term that began with a refusal to enter student grades and escalated its tactics into 2020. In his coverage of decades of graduate union organizing, Bousquet remarks that "in organizing campaigns, the suppression of labor knowledge by administrations can take the form of nonrenewal of the fellowships and assistantships of organizers, as well as punitive recommendations by advisers—even, occasionally, expulsion" (31). But the University of California's response was stronger than Bousquet could have anticipated, as system President Janet Napolitano sent police to quell the emerging teaching strike; later, eighty-two graduate students were fired from their TA positions for refusing to submit fall 2019 grades.

After several months of activism and in the context of the onset of the COVID-19 pandemic, these fired workers' health insurance was reinstated in March 2020—and activism continued for another year to have them reinstated to their jobs as well (UAW2865 2020; Pay Us More UCSC 2020). Meanwhile, as campus faculty signed petitions and forwarded resolutions in solidarity, graduate students across the University of California (UC) system struck for their own COLAs. In March 2020 97% of graduate students across the UC system voted for the UAW 2865 to "reopen contract negotiations and to fight for COLA across the state" (Pay Us More UCSC 2020). The ongoing strike was disrupted by shifts to online teaching brought on by the pandemic, which itself raised further concerns to organize around. The use of militarized police to attack student protesters, the wildcat strike tactic that rejected the validity of the union bargaining process, the widespread circulation of a petition for faculty at other universities to boycott all UC campuses until the COLA was approved, the UC's status as the third-largest employer in California (Council of UC Faculty Associations 2020) and its management by Janet Napolitano, Barack Obama's Secretary of Homeland Security from 2009 to 2013—these all point to the significant consolidation of state and educational power in the interest of protecting the availability of cheap labor for capital, including at universities, and the growing solidarity of academic workers in response.

A letter from the dean of UCSC's Division of Physical and Biological Sciences, Paul L. Koch (2020), illustrates the complex of ideologies, misclassifications, and extraordinary labor needs that shape graduate student working conditions. Sent in March 2020 as the grade strike entered its third month, the letter is a piece of public relations meant to reassure readers about the smooth functioning of Koch's division and to persuade the graduate students in his chain of command—in tones ranging from the supportive, to the patronizing, to the gaslighting—to get over the firing of eighty-two colleagues, accept small improvements to their current compensation, and "[meet] their commitments to our undergraduates and the educational mission of the campus." While the letter's reflections on its author's own near-participation in a wildcat strike in the 1980s are fascinating in their denialism, and its framing of "the violence that developed between protesters and police" equivocates, most relevant here is the dean's defense of the fundamentals of the strikers' existing pay scale. He writes:

> The issue the graduate students are trying to address is real . . . Year after year, at the state and local level, we fail to address the need for affordable housing. Yet I believe the solution demanded by the strikers, a change in their salary that would lift them out of housing burden (defined as a salary that would have them spend no more than 30% of their income on housing), is flawed. Graduate students (either TAs or graduate student researchers [GSRs]) are halftime employees, and they are trainees, not professionals in career positions. There is no reasonable salary that the UC system can offer *a trainee working half time* that will lift them out of housing burden in a market like the one in Santa Cruz. Doing so would dramatically distort the hourly wages of graduate students relative to other full time, career employees. And, sadly, none of those career employees (or their dependent children) enjoy the benefit of a tuition waiver along with their employment, as graduate student TAs and GSRs do. (Koch 2020, emphasis added).

Koch's dismissal of graduate students as "trainee[s] working half time" is key to our understanding of graduate student working conditions. This subtle dressing-down is meant to put graduate students in their place, to remind them of their lack of expertise and certification compared with their managers on the tenure track, and to imply that of course a part-time job cannot and should not pay rent in Santa Cruz. There are two sleights of hand here. The first, as I discussed above, is the idea that grad students are working half time. Koch's logic conveniently elides the truth that graduate students are expected to live in Santa Cruz on the money the university pays them, and nothing else. So how are they supposed to live? Koch positions graduate students' tuition waivers as a benefit to which they should be grateful—part of their income, even, though they certainly can't apply it toward their bills. But enrollment in courses is part of the condition for the part-time work. It is simply dishonest to frame graduate student workers as "part-timers" when coursework constitutes the other half of their full-time labor, the half for which they are never, at least in the United States, paid. Perhaps they should be paid for it, as in Denmark (Noack 2015).

The second sleight of hand, the claim that the striking graduate students are "trainees," is a familiar refrain from professors on the tenure track justifying the exploitation of graduate student workers. Entry-level workers in all industries are, in some ways, "trainees," lacking the expertise of their superiors; yet, as Bousquet points out, an entry-level worker in accounting or law often earns as much as a humanities professor "at the end of a career covered in distinction" (42). In fact, graduate student salaries pull down the wages of the entire hierarchy above them, especially in the humanities, the research area disproportionately populated by women (Bousquet 42). Koch's reliance on the language of apprenticeship reinforces the fiction that there is an assured future of economic stability and success in which the opportunity costs of training will be recouped. Yet the data simply do not support this view. Koch closes his letter by endorsing the existing administrative proposal for an increased housing stipend, small salary increases at the department level, lobbying for state investment in higher education, and the development of "a Joint Senate-Administrative Graduate Education working group" and a "standing committee that advises the Chancellor on graduate education"—mirroring Bousquet's discussion of such standing committees as a stalling tactic for academic labor (74–75). Koch's conclusion, with a slap and a bear hug, reinforces the myth of future stability for graduate student workers—except, of course, the fired ones:

> As the consequences of graduate student dismissals sink in, the next weeks and months may be tough. I thank you all for contributions that have made our division a *research powerhouse and an engine of upward mobility*. I'm confident we will come out of this crisis better supporting our graduate students, who are so critical to that success, and better supporting others in our campus community who are struggling with the cost of living in Santa Cruz. (emphasis added)

Three years of pandemic discourse about "essential workers" has now prepared us all to critique these lines. "Upward mobility" for whom? And if graduate students are "so critical" to the university's "success"—defined by that mobility and by its research "power"—why does this letter, at its core, dismiss their demands for a living wage?

Dean Koch's insistence that UCSC is an "engine of upward mobility" is delivered with remarkable earnestness, given the context of student workers being fired as they organize for living wages to keep them from potential homelessness. In her study of graduate students teaching composition, Allison Laubach Wright (2017) explores the tension between universities' "brand of excellence" (266) and the realities of their employees' work conditions and their students' learning conditions. Wright argues that graduate student labor is invisibilized by Tier 1 universities as they cultivate a "brand of excellence" (266). This "excellence" depends on graduate student research and teaching to function and yet would be undermined by publicly acknowledging the extent to which undergraduate courses are taught by graduate student teachers. Wright draws special attention to "English departments, where four-year universities have graduate students teaching the labor-intensive first-year writing (FYW) course while minimizing both the presence of the course and the work of the graduate students" (266). She continues with a case study of one English department:

> Even though FYW courses make up around 70 percent of undergraduate courses offered [by the Department], those courses appear as two or three entries in the course catalogue, where they are taught by "STAFF" rather than a named individual (Slevin 5). At large research universities, FYW courses are generally taught by graduate students, whose names are absent from the course history of the university. (266–267)

Wright's analysis reflects the ways graduate student labor is intrinsic to the functioning of the university yet is erased when convenient. Like the deceptive claims of gig companies like Uber and Instacart, which brag about the desirable flexibility of working for them when that flexibility equates to below-minimum wage labor with no benefits (Reich and Jacobs 2019), Koch's letter is an exemplar of the contradictory discourses of the university, which celebrate the value it brings students while actively impoverishing them.

More broadly, universities' claims to "excellence" are omnipresent in their institutional communications today. A critique of this term has made its way to the sciences, where researchers are pushing back against it as an empty signifier that projects false values of competition and scarcity into research (Moore et al. 2017; *Nature* 2018). But critical theorists writing in the tradition of Black studies offer a richer genealogy of the term, situating the emergence of "excellence" in the context of neoliberalism's rejection of race in the aftermath of the civil rights movement. My own research on the emergence of neoliberal regimes at the City University of New York (Brown 2019) demonstrates how that system's post–civil rights agenda to admit and educate large numbers of poor, Black, brown, and immigrant students was undermined in the mid-1970s by the imposition of tuition, the embrace of standardized testing, and the firing of NTT faculty of color who protested these changes with students. For critical theorists of race, gender, labor, and transnational capitalism, we understand the last fifty years' decimation of the gains of the civil rights movement as a "unified front in social policy" (Kynard 2013, 230). These widespread policy shifts have been accompanied by rhetorical innovations that use bureaucratic jargon to occlude obvious, measurable decreases in quality and protection of life for poor people, people of color, and LGBTQIA+ people across normalized or reified metrics in health, education, professional attainment, residential segregation, wealth, income inequality, and even mortality. Roderick Ferguson (2012) characterizes race-blind discourses of excellence as themselves another "technology of power" (83) that universities like CUNY used in the 1970s to recreate racially determined outcomes post–civil rights, while avoiding race-based language. Arguing that "excellence arose out of the interface between the academy and the federal government" (83), Ferguson uses a close study of June Jordan's writings from the CUNY Open Admissions period to locate "efficiency, competence, and excellence" as Vietnam-War-wrought neoliberal values that, when applied to a newly diverse CUNY student body, reproblematized the presence of Black and Puerto Rican students and positioned *access* as an antagonist to *excellence*. In Ferguson's reading, "excellence" is an empty signifier and a rhetorical hallmark of neoliberalism, a technology writ in language that was invented to allow universities to reinscribe racialized exclusion in the aftermath of the civil rights movement's end to explicitly racist policy.

Here is the great irony of graduate study: it teaches us to understand the world, not just through our coursework, our deep reading, and our research training but also through the impoverishment of our living and working conditions. Graduate school radicalizes us not because we are taught critical theory, but because we can't pay rent. When I was a doctoral student, my deepest education came from the fellow members of an activist collective, THE General Body, which coalesced at my institution in the fall of 2014 (see THE General Body 2015). This coalition of multiple minoritized student groups came together to reject our new chancellor's austerity regime, under which he cut services and programs for students of color, rape and domestic violence survivors, students with mental health needs, and others, unilaterally rendering the campus more hostile for a majority of its residents. Like the graduate union chapter presidents in Anicca Cox's study for this volume, as a member of this group I learned about organizing from being in solidarity with the group's other graduate and undergraduate students, staff, and faculty. Beyond learning about organizing, I learned how to critique the budgets of the entire university. As a collective, we tracked the flow of accumulated capital from the miniscule budgets of the closed rape center, the cancelled Black abroad program Paris Noir, and the bought-out contracts of our department administrative workers as they were redirected to renovations to the basketball stadium and the military-aligned public policy school—all pursued under the banner of "excellence." Living and teaching on $17,000 a year while performing well over forty hours a week of labor compulsory to my degree completion, I learned the same lesson that Bousquet says is taught in the university management simulation VirtualU, where all management decisions can ultimately be modeled by "financial flows" (76). "Designed by a former Stanford vice president" (Bousquet, 73) as a game where the only player role is a university president, the player's ultimate and underlying job is "to maintain steady revenue . . . and preferably grow revenue" (VirtualU qtd. in Bousquet, 77).

Across industries, the COVID pandemic has exposed the emptiness of corporate platitudes that celebrate "essential" workers while exploiting their labor and their lives. As droves of workers nationally have raised their voices, organized, and quit, so too in academia: recent years saw a renewed union drive among graduate students rejecting their employers' insufficient policies, protections, benefits, and remuneration for labor performed during a deadly global pandemic. Tragically, the pandemic has also augmented the discriminations endemic to our systems, as people of color, parents, and people with disabilities have been disproportionately struck by stressors, forced or pressured job loss, and threats to health and even life. Interruptions to work and research spiked particularly for female academics, especially those with children (Michalegko et al. 2021). For Black and Indigenous communities with long histories experiencing compounded environmental and medical racism, states' failures to contain the pandemic were deadly, with Black, Latino, Indigenous, and Pacific Islander people facing disproportionately high rates of illness and death, especially in Republican-run states ("The COVID Racial Data Tracker" 2021)—trends that intersected with campus politics. In Georgia, for example, the twenty-six-campus University of Georgia system followed Governor Brian Kemp in refusing to institute mask or vaccine mandates on campus. As the fall 2021 term started, faculty spoke out, demanding an indoor mask mandate (Stirgus 2021). Meanwhile, faculty at the Black women's Spelman College in Atlanta refused to teach on campus as classes began, despite the school's mask and vaccine mandates, "citing a lack of 'clear and enforceable' safety guidelines from the school administration" (Rummler 2021).

Spelman faculty's actions for their own and student safety reflects a widened role for campus organizing under COVID-19. As Kalena Thomhave and Matt Sehrsweeney discuss in their afterword to this volume, graduate student organizing during the pandemic often embraced the intersectional tactic of "bargaining for the common good," linking demands for living wages and workplace protections to Black community calls for campus police abolition, survivor and feminist insistence on revised protocols for responding to harassment and sexual violence, and additional protections for caregivers, international students, and those with disabilities. Indeed, as the pandemic expanded threats to everyone's health and safety, one could argue that the definition of "bread and butter" basic economic concerns expanded. The pandemic truly illustrated the wisdom of Black feminist organizing principles, articulated by the Combahee River Collective Statement (1977): "If Black women were free, it would mean that everyone else would have to be free, since our freedom would necessitate the destruction of all systems of oppression." The intersecting violences of the pandemic have shown us more clearly than ever that centering the multiply marginalized in our organizing—against economic, workplace, gendered, and state violence—is the path to keep all of us safe.

For me, engaging with critical scholars of race has been essential to critiquing academia and capitalism writ large, because it is scholars of anti-Blackness who identify most honestly the ways that capitalism is willing, or even designed, to exploit labor to the point of loss of life. Participating in Twitter discussions about the academic jobs crisis, sociologist Tamara K. Nopper (2019) tweeted that "the discourse about academic labor and the crisis of higher ed [is] dissatisfying in terms of racial politics" because "it does not adequately account for the premature death of so many Black academics." Like all American industry, academia is built on Indigenous lands and cheap labor from workers of color which produces grossly unequal outcomes for its participants, including death. This is why, writing in 1969 against resistance to the open admissions movement at CUNY, June Jordan framed Black studies as "life studies," scathingly rejecting any appeals to "the standards that only human life threatens to defile and 'lower'" (qtd. in Ferguson, 96). "As 'life studies,'" Ferguson goes on, "black studies, for Jordan, is committed to all possibilities of life and not simply the possibility of black lives" (109). Taking an intersectional approach to university organizing requires us to be in solidarity not just with fellow academic workers, but with all university workers and indeed, all workers fighting for *life*. We must resist the temptation to believe that our education and intelligence sets us apart from fellow workers. Instead, we should view ourselves as part of a growing, intersectional labor movement in which workers have the power to demand better for all.

The collected authors in this volume speak to the wide range of labor graduate students perform—expected and unexpected, reasonable and not. As such, the book is divided into four sections: Labor at the Margins; the Labor of Teaching and Research; the Labor of Professionalization; and Organizing Labor. Throughout the book, short essays are interspersed with the full research articles, the latter denoted as numbered "chapters."

Khadeidra Billingsley opens the volume by voicing the emotional labor of working as a graduate student, declaring, there's "levels to this sh*t." In chapter 1, Charlotte Kupsh and Zoe McDonald identify labor migration as an indelible facet of graduate student life, connecting academic labor migration to other kinds of movement for work. Theorizing groundedness and placelessness, they remind us that graduate study and research is shaped by our material locations, even if we imagine ourselves primary residents of some transcendent intellectual plane. In the essays by Samah Elbelazi and Andrew Hollinger, Elbelazi speaks of marginalizing encounters as a Muslim woman navigating a doctoral program, and Hollinger challenges normative visions of graduate students as young and unencumbered by family life, illustrating the realities of raising a family while a graduate student worker. In chapter 2, Talinn Phillips, Paul Shovlin, and Megan Titus study graduate students working part-time as Writing Program Administrators (gWPAs). Their article highlights the administrative labor that many graduate students do for the cost, to the university, of their tuition and stipend, and the ways that this labor complicates their position vis-à-vis the other graduate students they manage as well as university faculty or administrators they must work with across uneven power dynamics. In the next short interlude, Meagan Gacke-Reed reflects on how to support "alt-ac" internships that take students outside academia. In chapter 3, April Cobos and Megan Mize close the section with a study of horizontal mentoring between residential and nonresidential students in the same hybrid doctoral program. With conclusions even more relevant as COVID has accelerated online learning, Cobos and Mize's study highlights how solutions suggested by new technologies also create new kinds of labor that, without care and attention in program design, may be performed without pay or recognition.

The next section focuses on more familiar forms of graduate student labor: teaching and research. In chapter 4, Elliot Shapiro reflects on his career teaching in and administering a writing program from off the tenure track, and the ways his graduate students have resisted teaching labor as incidental or even counterproductive to their career goals. In his essay, Anis Rahman considers the extra linguistic and emotional labor he performs as an international, multilingual graduate student teaching English composition. In chapter 5, Sara Austin and Kelly Moreland consider how graduate students are tasked with becoming members of a discipline even as they are already teaching in that discipline, in their case specifically focused on graduate students working with a "Writing about Writing" curriculum. The section closes with two interludes by mothers navigating graduate school. Alma Villanueva asks us to grapple with tensions between feminist theories and the real joys and discriminations of raising a family while in graduate school, and Jacqueline M. Kory-Westlund speaks to the circumstances that supported her while raising a family as a graduate student working in an intensive research lab.

Sarah Welsh opens the third section, on the labor of "professionalization," by reminding us that being an academic isn't a vocation, it's a job. In chapter 6, Adam Haley's study of doctoral student subject formation re-roots us in theory as he considers how doctoral students must not only produce their research but also themselves, branding themselves as commodities for sale in our neoliberal academic "job market." Next, Jaclyn Fiscus Cannaday and Allison Hutchison encourage students to cultivate joy through some element of their work. In chapter 7, their study of Chinese nationals pursuing doctorates in the United States, Xueshuang Wang, Weiyan Xiong, and Huiyuan Ye engage perceptions of employability and illustrate how global movements of commerce and labor have opened labor constraints and opportunities to international doctoral students.

The volume closes with attention to the labor of union organizing among graduate students. Martha Althea Webber interrogates the costs for master's student teachers at one California State University campus. In chapter 8, Jonathan Isaac's study of the graduate union fight against student fees at the University of Wisconsin illustrates the discursive slippage between characterizations of graduate student workers as workers and as students. An interlude by Alex Hanson uses a "How-To" format to illustrate the challenges she faced advocating for parental support on her campus while a doctoral student. Finally, in chapter 9, Anicca Cox's study of presidents of three graduate union local chapters closes the volume with attention to graduate student organizing. Cox's findings that grad unions "return to a solidarity-model of labor organizing—an approach based in mutual aid and inclusion across working units" (303)—offers lessons for workers unionizing in other industries that see high turnover, labor migration, and internal diversity. Her findings suggest that graduate student workers can be part of a cross-industry labor movement that prioritizes solidarity with the most vulnerable and thinks capaciously about working conditions and worker rights, demanding roses in addition to bread. The volume concludes with an afterword from former University of Michigan student organizers Kalena Thomhave and Matt Sehrsweeney, who reflect on the successes, failures, and solidarity-building of their graduate student union's wildcat strike in 2020.

This volume begins the project of illuminating the essential labor, both expert and infuriating, that graduate student workers perform for the universities where they are employed. Graduate students teach, they research, they raise families, they organize, they learn. They go into enormous debt. They move. They become themselves, negotiating (as we all do) with social and political constraints. They navigate inaccessible and sometimes hostile institutions, with a range of results. While this volume represents an important first step in understanding graduate students' unique contributions to the universities where they work and study, we need more research on a range of issues facing students, workers and not, across the university. Studies of student workers in the sciences and engineering must interrogate how laboratory-based work, where principal investigators have enormous control over workers' environments, degree progression, and job prospects, as well as access to and control over their research products and processes, creates different work conditions with different constraints and possibilities than those focused on here. Studies of professional school students and graduates should interrogate the lived experiences and the impacts of tremendous student loan debt of those studying law, business, medicine, dentistry, veterinary and pharmaceutical science, and more. Studies of students working must also attend to undergraduate workers, whose share of campus jobs is increasing and—rarely mentioned in labor contexts—whose work as amateur athletes producing extraordinary value for universities is a historic expression of value extraction. Further studies of marginalized student workers must attend to how intersecting discriminations across lines of race, class, citizenship, ability, and gender and sexuality shape conditions for work and constrain rights and flourishing. To that end, we must continue to face how academia's unique guild-like bureaucratic structure, with tremendous asymmetries of power and narrow chains of command that mirror those in corporate, military, and policing structures, creates and perpetuates the isolated conditions for sexual violence and other abuse.

One last question remains: Should you become a graduate student? I discuss it with my colleagues, with my friends. Friends of friends email me asking for advice. When I started down this road, I thought a tenurable professorship was an inevitable destination, that if I did the work, I would get the job. Now I am more skeptical of the costs. Graduate school taught me so much—it gave me the frameworks I use here and everywhere to understand my world—and yet, as contributor Sarah Welsh reminds us, this work is also, simply, a job. And is it a good one? True, I would not trade work in academia for a corporate position spent elaborating on someone else's dreams. Yet intellectual freedom is constrained when we former graduate students cannot achieve the kind of work we were trained for. And for adjunct faculty teaching at multiple campuses with no health insurance, a steady job might be worth it, the life of the mind be damned. My advice for prospective students is to assess graduate school frankly, beyond the metaphors. What are your goals? Your financial needs? Your geographic constraints? What debt might you take on and what is the average salary of a prospective career field? Don't take your dream job for granted, but rather think critically about the costs of graduate school and the role it will play in helping you achieve your goals.

And finally, what can you do for the graduate students in your life? In your organization? Most fundamentally, pay them for their work—all their work—pay them enough to live their lives. Recognize them as academia's entry-level workers and manage them with respect. Stand up for them when harms arise, recognizing their lack of power. And, if they must organize—at least don't stand in their way.

Works Cited

American Association of University Professors (AAUP). 2016. "Higher Education at a Crossroads: The Annual Report on the Economic Status of the Profession, 2015–16." *Academe* (March–April): 1–22. https://www.aaup.org/sites/default/files/2015-16EconomicStatusReport.pdf.

American Association of University Women (AAUW). 2018. "Women Hold Majority of College Debt—and Take Longer to Pay It Off." May 21, 2018. https://www.aauw.org/resources/news/media/press-releases/analysis-women-hold-two-thirds-of-countrys-1-4-trillion-student-debt/.

Berlin, James. 1987. *Rhetoric and Reality: Writing Instruction in American Colleges, 1900–1985.* Carbondale: Southern Illinois University Press.

Bousquet, Marc. 2008. *How the University Works: Higher Education and the Low-Wage Nation.* New York: New York University Press.

Brandt, Deborah. 2001. *Literacy in American Lives.* Cambridge, UK: Cambridge University Press.

Brown, Tessa. 2018. "Literacy Narrative: Ways to Write #MeToo." *Composition Studies* 46, no. 2 (Fall): 189–191.

———. 2019. "'Let the People Rap!': Cultural Rhetorics Practices and Pedagogies at CUNY's Open Admissions, 1968–1978." *Journal of Basic Writing* 38, no. 2 (Fall): 106–143.

Combahee River Collective. 1977. "Combahee River Collective Statement." https://www.workers.org/wp-content/uploads/CombaheeRiverCollectiveStatement1977.pdf.

Cottom, Tressie. 2017. *Lower Ed: The Troubling Rise of For-Profit Colleges in the New Economy.* New York: New Press.

The Council of UC Faculty Associations. 2020. "Union and Student Letter to President Napolitano and Board of Regents." Letter, May 13, 2020. https://cucfa.org/2020/05/letter-to-president-and-regents/.

The COVID Racial Data Tracker. 2021. *Atlantic.* https://covidtracking.com/race.

di Maria, David L. 2020. "US Colleges Report a 43% Decline in New International Student Enrollment, and Not Just because of the Pandemic." *Conversation,* November 19, 2020. https://theconversation.com/us-colleges-report-a-43-decline-in-new-international-student-enrollment-and-not-just-because-of-the-pandemic-149885.

Ferguson, Roderick A. 2012. *The Reorder of Things: The University and Its Pedagogies of Minority Difference.* Minneapolis: University of Minnesota Press.

Fernández, Cristina [DrCristinaF]. 2020. Twitter post. https://twitter.com/DrCristinaF/status/122441877791635458.

Fink, Jenni. 2019. "Harvard Grad Students Union Ad: Ivy League University Has 'World-Class #MeToo Problem.'" *Newsweek,* April 18, 2019. https://www.newsweek.com/harvard-grad-students-union-ad-accuses-ivy-league-university-metoo-problem-1400762.

Gilich, Yulia, and Tony Boardman. 2020. "Facing Skyrocketing Rents, Santa Cruz Grad Students Extend Wildcat Strike. *Labornotes,* February 7, 2020. https://labornotes.org/2020/02/facing-skyrocketing-rents-santa-cruz-grad-students-extend-wildcat-strike.

Grasso, Maureen, Melissa Barry, and Thomas Valentine. 2009. *A Data-Driven Approach to Improving Doctoral Completion.* Washington, DC: Council of Graduate Schools. https://cgsnet.org/ckfinder/userfiles/files/Paper_Series_UGA_FrontMatter.pdf.

Jacobs, Ken, and Michael Reich. 2019. "The Uber/Lyft Ballot Initiative Guarantees Only $5.64 an Hour." (Blog), *UC Berkeley Labor Center,* October 31, 2019. https://laborcenter.berkeley.edu/the-uber-lyft-ballot-initiative-guarantees-only-5-64-an-hour-2/.

Jaffe, Sarah. 2018. "Graduate Student Workers Organize against Sexual Harassment on Campus." *Truthout,* July 20, 2018. https://truthout.org/articles/graduate-student-workers-organize-against-sexual-harassment-on-campus/.

Kahn, Seth, William B. Lalicker, and Amy Lynch-Biniek, eds. 2017. *Contingency, Exploitation, and Solidarity: Labor and Action in English Composition.* Fort Collins: University Press of Colorado.

Koch, Paul L. 2020. "Addressing the Graduate Student Strike." Letter to the Division of Physical and Biological Sciences, March 2, 2020. https://dev-pbsci-intranet.pantheonsite.io/2020/03/02/addressing-the-graduate-student-strike/.

Kroeger, Teresa, Celine McNicholas, Marni von Wilpert, and Julia Wolfe. 2018. "The State of Graduate Student Employee Unions." Economic Policy Institute Report, January 11, 2018. https://www.epi.org/publication/graduate-student-employee-unions/.

Kynard, Carmen. 2013. *Vernacular Insurrections: Race, Black Protest, and the New Century in Composition-Literacies Studies.* Albany: State University of New York Press.

Michalegko, Lesley, Eric Welch, Mary K. Feeney, Timothy P. Johnson. 2021. "Surveys of Scientists Show Women and Young Academics Suffered Most during Pandemic and May Face Long-Term Career Consequences." *Conversation.* December 16, 2021. https://theconversation.com/surveys-of-scientists-show-women-and

-young-academics-suffered-most-during-pandemic-and-may-face-long-term-ca reer-consequences-173321.

Moody, Josh. 2019. "A Guide to the Changing Number of US Universities." *U.S. News and World Report*, February 15, 2019. https://www.usnews.com/education /best-colleges/articles/2019-02-15/how-many-universities-are-in-the-us-and -why-that-number-is-changing.

Moore, Samuel, Cameron Neylon, Martin Paul Eve, Daniel Paul O'Donnell, and Damian Pattinson. 2017. "'Excellence R Us': University Research and the Fetishization of Excellence." *Palgrave Communications* 3, 1605. https://doi.org/10.1057 /palcomms.2016.105.

National Center for Education Statistics (NCES). 2018. "Trends in Student Loan Debt for Graduate School Completers." May. https://nces.ed.gov/programs /coe/indicator/tub.

———. 2020. "Postbaccalaureate Enrollment." May. https://nces.ed.gov/programs /coe/indicator/chb.

Nature. 2018. "Science Needs to Redefine Excellence." Editorial, February 21, 2018. https://www.nature.com/articles/d41586-018-02183-y.

Noack, Rich. 2015. "Danish Students Are Paid to Go to College." *Washington Post*, February 4, 2015.

Nopper, Tamara K. [tamaranopper]. 2019. Deleted tweet.

Pay Us More UCSC. 2020. "Campaign Timeline." https://payusmoreucsc.com /campaign-timeline/.

Petersen, Charles. 2020. "Serfs of Academe." *New York Review of Books*, March 12, 2020.

Pew Charitable Trusts. 2021. "How the Pandemic Could Affect the Rise in Student Debt." https://www.pewtrusts.org/en/research-and-analysis/issue-briefs/2021 /12/how-the-pandemic-could-affect-the-rise-in-student-debt.

Rent Jungle. 2020. "Rent Trend Data in Santa Cruz, California." https://www.rent jungle.com/averaeg-rent-in-santa-cruz-rent-trends/.

Rummler, Orion. 2021. "'Black Women Being Trailblazers': Spelman Faculty Refuse to Teach in Person as Classes Begin." *19th*, August 19, 2021. https://19thnews .org/2021/08/spelman-faculty-refuse-to-teach-in-person/.

Schell, E. Eileen. 2012. "Materializing the Material as a Progressive Method and Methodology." In *Practicing Research in Writing Studies: Reflexive and Ethically Responsible Research*, edited by Katrina M. Powell and Pamela Takayoshi. New York: Hampton Press.

———. 2017. "Foreword: The New Faculty Majority in Writing Programs: Organizing for Change." In Kahn, Lalicker, and Lynch-Biniek, *Contingency, Exploitation, and Solidarity*, ix–xx.

Stirgus, Eric. 2021. "Group Wants Gov. Kemp to Give College Leaders Local Control to Implement a Mask Mandate." *Atlanta Journal-Constitution*, September 13, 2021. https://www.ajc.com/education/georgia-professors-to-demonstrate-for -tougher-covid-19-guidelines/OYP7AURMNVAQ5AX75EAAUX7VVE/.

THE General Body. 2015. The General Body. Website. thegeneralbody.org.

UAW2865. 2020. "COVID-19 Crisis Makes One Thing Clear: We Need a COLA Now More Than Ever." March 16, 2020. https://uaw2865.org/covid-19-crisis-makes -one-thing-clear-we-need-a-cola-now-more-than-ever/.

US Bureau of Labor Statistics. 2018. "Occupational Employment and Wages, May 2018: 25–1191 Graduate Teaching Assistants." https://www.bls.gov/oes/2018/may/oes251191.htm.
Weissmann, Jordan. 2015. "Harvard Is a 'Hedge Fund with a University Attached to It.'" *Slate*, September 19, 2015. https://www.businessinsider.com/why-harvard-should-be-taxed-2015-9.
Wright, Allison Laubach. 2017. "The Rhetoric of Excellence and the Erasure of Graduate Student Labor." In Kahn, Lalicker, and Lynch-Biniek, *Contingency, Exploitation, and Solidarity*, 271–278.

PART I

LABOR AT THE MARGINS

Interlude 1

"Levels to This Sh*t"
Layers of Graduate Student Labor

Khadeidra Billingsley

As I sit in class and engage in discussion with my peers about the most effective way to get students to show up to their writing conferences, I cannot help but feel the ache in my right foot from standing and teaching in heels for six hours straight yesterday . . . and the day before. I cannot help but feel the anxiety manifest into a tension headache as I think about the rent, electricity, car insurance, and all the other past due bills that will deplete my bank account tomorrow. I cannot help but think that I would love to seek help for these ailments but I have neither the time nor the resources to do so . . . hence, Tylenol and soft-sole shoes will just have to do for today and the many other days like it that I must endure as a graduate student.

The extensive and complex hierarchical lines that separate graduate students and the administrators who hold the power to make literally life-changing decisions about our lives seem to convolute the perception of what we do and who we are. Nevertheless, we, whose reality this is, know that there are many more layers and levels to our identity and struggle as graduate students than are typically acknowledged. As evident in the experiences of my co-contributor Andrew Hollinger, which he illustrates later in this volume, when defining graduate student labor we must holistically recognize our constant exertion of financial, emotional, intellectual, and professional efforts. In order to advocate for fair working conditions, we must make visible the entirety of what our labor entails—including what it takes to manage the unique stressors that come from pursuing innovative research contributions on poverty-level wages.

Completing graduate school is not an easy feat, which may explain why only 1.5% of the US population has a doctoral degree. With most PhD programs taking between five and seven years to complete, there is an immense amount of effort that is required, first of all, on an intellectual level.

PhD students are usually identified as being high-achieving students who excelled academically in their undergraduate careers (Wollast et al. 2018). Thus, it would seem plausible that these students can easily meet the cognitive standards to which they are held. However, for many students, this is not the case. Graduate school brings with it another layer of required intellectual capability in the form of innovation and elevation, which can come as a surprise for many students. The caliber of work, reading requirements, seminars, and taught classes, as well as publication pressures, can place a tremendous strain on the brain. Nevertheless, universities and colleges seem to constantly be increasing the stakes as many institutions further incentivize success in the classroom. For example, some programs even award funding on a competitive basis determined by students' academic performance and prowess in their program, thus necessitating staying at the top of one's game at all times. Thankfully, my program does not do this, so I do not know what it feels like to be in such an environment—however, I imagine it is an intense space. Are the constant demands of us to perform in the classroom, develop innovative research, *and* teach two to three courses not enough without being exacerbated by such tension?

Due to the incongruence between the labor that they are exerting and the pay that they are receiving, many graduate students are financially strapped, requiring them to exert more effort, oftentimes outside of the classroom, to make ends meet. Although it can be frowned upon, more and more graduate students are having to acquire second and third jobs—or even four, like me—to supplement their wages. During one year of my PhD program, I worked as an instructor of two classes, a tutor, an online ESL teacher, and a writing consultant. Rogers, Eaton, and Voos (2014) assert that this choice, which is more like a necessity, could interfere with students' ability to focus and/or complete their coursework and degrees. In March 2011 approximately 360,000 of the 22 million Americans with advanced degrees were receiving some form of public assistance; the percentage of these individuals had almost tripled over the course of three years between 2007 and 2010 (Patton 2012). This "dirty little secret of higher education" (Williams qtd. in Patton 2012) would benefit from exposure, as it is important to consider how the phenomenon of graduate student impoverishment complicates the path to matriculation, especially for students lacking outside resources. The only reason why I was able to stop working so many jobs during my program was that I discovered I was eligible for military educational benefits. With more and more students having to worry about how they will financially survive another month or where their next meal will come from, we can see the formation of a layer of stress, anxiety, and exhaustion that does not fit well with the pursuit of an advanced graduate degree. This layer of labor, which is oftentimes not known or visible to school administrators, warrants our attention.

Graduate students' emotional labor may not be visible to those around them; however, it does have a profound effect on their ability to function in their everyday tasks. Writing from the perspective of a Black lesbian, S. Tay Glover speaks of how, during several moments in her graduate career, she "blinked back tears of sadness and anger" (2017, 157). For those of us who are minorities in these spaces, keeping our thoughts, feelings, and anxieties in check is a routine struggle. Pressures from faculty members, advisors, family, students, coupled with the normal requisites of life, seem to amass very quickly and can lead to feelings of wanting to call it quits. Glover goes on to describe how "the in-betweenness of being an employee and student . . . would mean an uneven load of labor and trauma" (2017, 162), a load that she did not anticipate prior to entering her doctoral program. Not only do some of us struggle with feelings of not belonging, but many of us are constantly overwhelmed with anxieties about the role that we are supposed to assume. Thus, emotional labor can become commonplace. A study by Eisenberg et al. (2007) found that 51% of students considered stress to be a normal characteristic of graduate school, yet only 36% of students who screened positive for depression were taking any medications or utilizing any form of counseling services. Surprised? I'm not.

There is a growing body of work addressing problems faced and labor endured by various subgroups of graduate students. As we galvanize and move toward negotiation of better conditions, however, we need to present a united front, which will require a comprehensive illustration of our collective struggles. As Adam Haley argues in his chapter in this collection, "the production of identity is a nexus of significant but unacknowledged intellectual, emotional, and relational labor by graduate students" (179). As another fellow contributor, Sarah Welsh, reminds us, "remember that whatever job you end up with will be a job" (177). It would take far more words to describe the full magnitude of the intellectual, financial, and emotional pains that comprise graduate student labor. For now, just remember that there's layers to this sh*t.

Works Cited

Eisenberg, Daniel, Sarah E. Gollust, Ezra Golberstein, and Jennifer L. Hefner. 2007. "Prevalence and Correlates of Depression, Anxiety, and Suicidality among University Students." *American Journal of Orthopsychiatry* 77, no. 4 (October): 534–542.

Glover, S. Tay. 2017. "Black Lesbians—Who Will Fight for Our Lives but Us?': Navigating Power, Belonging, Labor, Resistance, and Graduate Student Survival in the Ivory Tower." *Feminist Teacher* 27 (2–3): 157–175.

Patton, Stacey. 2012. "The Ph.D. Now Comes with Food Stamps." *Chronicle of Higher Education*, May 6, 2012.

Rogers, Sean, Adrienne E. Eaton, and Paula B. Voos. 2013. "Effects of Unionization on Graduate Student Employees: Faculty-Student Relations, Academic Freedom, and Pay." *ILR Review* 66, no. 2 (April): 487–510.

Wollast, Robin, Gentiane Boudrenghien, Nicolas Van der Linden, Benoît Galand, Nathalie Roland, Christelle Devos, Mikaël de Clercq, Olivier Klein, Assad Azzi, and Mariane Frenay. 2018. "Who Are the Doctoral Students Who Drop Out? Factors Associated with the Rate of Doctoral Degree Completion in Universities." *International Journal of Higher Education* 7 (4): 143–156.

1 | "I Have to Go Wherever There's an Opportunity"
Graduate Students' Experiences of Placelessness and Writing

Charlotte Kupsh and Zoe McDonald

Graduate students and early-career academics frequently move to pursue the academic's version of the American Dream: a stable academic career (tenure-track or otherwise) with living wages and health insurance. However, as the other writers in this volume describe, the American Dream is disconnected from the realities of the twenty-first-century academic job market. In the past, graduate school marked an entry point into an academic career. Today, transience combines with low living stipends and unstable working conditions to contribute to a larger system of exploitation in which payoff is unlikely. Graduate school is an Odyssean journey of surviving shipwrecks and navigating sirens to return home to Ithaca. However, as a twenty-first-century academic, Dr. Odysseus has less of a chance of landing a permanent position at Ithaca U. and seems more likely to end up adjuncting at several schools while his family goes without health insurance.

Labor migration scholars note moving cuts people off from family ties and social networks, which they depend on for financial stability and a sense of purpose (see Hoey 2014; Kilborn 2009; Pugh 2015). The American Dream frames graduate school and its associated transience as a choice. But choice, exploitation, and place are linked concepts. The more exploited one is, the fewer choices one has. This is not to conflate graduate students as a whole with vulnerable populations (although individual graduate students often are members of other vulnerable groups), but rather to point out the ways contemporary higher education's socioeconomic infrastructure limits graduate students' abilities to make choices. We see exploitation in the implicit requirement that academics move for work, since it has psychological and financial costs that graduate programs do not reimburse, or often even acknowledge. Many of graduate school's most exploitative conditions are framed as choices—but, as Kathryn T. Flannery writes, place always shapes one's choices: "Place alone does not determine lives but represents a set of limits and possibilities. Human actors who people a place are never wholly free to shape the environment or their lives but have to improvise from the possibilities at hand" (2007, 122). How do graduate students survive the Odyssean journey when they are well aware of the low likelihood of landing a stable position or returning to the places they would like to live?

In this article, we use Flannery's notion of limits and possibilities to analyze three graduate students' experiences with academic transience. Ultimately, our goal is to call for mitigating the exploitative effects of this phenomenon.

The need to examine the significance of place, especially as an economically and politically informed concept, is all the more pressing in light of the COVID-19 pandemic and the inequalities it made so visible. The pandemic made the importance of place and the deleterious effects of placelessness much harder to ignore. It drew attention to the difficulties of living and building community in exclusively digital spaces. Elsewhere in this collection, April Cobos and Megan Mize note the immense value of graduate students' interactions outside of formal coursework and professional responsibilities, especially for online students—opportunities that grew sparser still during the pandemic. Further, for graduate students seeking to build community and put down roots in their localities, social distancing and stay-at-home orders made connecting to place difficult, if not impossible. And for the many students who balance graduate school, additional jobs, caregiving responsibilities (see Hanson's and Villanueva's contributions to this collection), and more, the pandemic only exacerbated the existing inequalities that force connection to place to the back burner. While our interviews and initial analyses were conducted before the pandemic began and therefore do not address its effects directly, we know that readers will engage with our text with the pandemic in mind. Thus, we encourage readers to reflect on the ways that place, materiality, and embodiment have become clearer and more pressing in their own lives and to use this text as a reminder that these issues were only exacerbated—not created—by COVID-19.

Why Study Transience? Our Origin Stories

Charlotte

In 2018 I took a sixteen-hour drive from my home in Wisconsin to a prospective PhD program in the east. When I arrived on campus, I learned prospective students rarely visited. "Most accepted students already know they want to come here," the director of graduate studies told me. "They don't need to visit." I was stunned: how could I imagine my life in a place I'd never been? But mentors, advisors, fellow students, and friends told me the geographic location shouldn't matter; a PhD was "only" five years. The implication was clear: a successful academic must be willing to put professional success above personal preference. My scholarship, though, has always been concerned with place. When I ultimately began my PhD at the University of Nebraska-Lincoln (UNL), I wanted to understand how my colleagues had adapted to life in this place. What kinds of scholars made the Great Plains their home? This research is born from the belief that our attachment to places shapes our experiences and successes in graduate school; place and profession are permanently intertwined.

Zoe

I never considered the impact place had on my writing prior to volunteering to participate in a study Charlotte was conducting of graduate students' experiences with transience. After that initial conversation, her study evolved into this article and I joined Charlotte as a cowriter interested in the ways local conditions impact other emerging writers. Although my interview is not included in this article, in it I reflected upon my move to Nebraska from Vermont. In Vermont, taking public transportation, visiting small towns, and attending creative writing classes at the public library provided me with a sense of shared identity with life-long residents. Yet the work of entering into a mutually enriching relationship with the people of Vermont was exhausting. As I moved to Lincoln to start a PhD program, I wondered where I would find the time and energy to get the support I'd need to form social connections and write a dissertation.

Place-conscious writing scholars present an alternative to transience, which in this article we call "groundedness." Central to such a notion is the concept of living well in a specific location. Robert Brooke in *Writing*

Suburban Citizenship: Place-Conscious Education and the Conundrum of Suburbia (2015) describes how suburban environments impact writers. Linda Flower in *Community Literacy and the Rhetoric of Public Engagement* (2008) reflects on the ways Pittsburgh's community literacy project unites African American and white residents over issues of shared concern. Nancy Welch's "Living Room" (2005) investigates the lack of avenues for community members to share their writing with public audiences. From such studies, we develop groundedness as a flexible concept to describe how individuals live well in neighborhoods, participate in their communities, and communicate with their intended audiences. Groundedness is thus about both living conditions and labor conditions. Considering groundedness as an alternative to transience leads us to question the ways graduate students use the possibilities of their new region to positively impact their writing and well-being.

Conducting the Study: Context and Methods

The participants in this study are three graduate students who in 2018 were part of the English Department at UNL, a midwestern public research university. Each was selected from a pool of volunteers based on the distance they traveled from their home state to start their graduate program and their ability to meet for an initial hour-long interview. While these participants and their experiences cannot represent all graduate students, they provide the opportunity for in-depth analysis into three students' values as they describe working within and against the geo-economic systems and practices of contemporary higher education.

Charlotte's initial interviews were semi-structured and open ended, to allow each participant to describe their experience of transience and groundedness in graduate school. These interviews focused on participants' experiences moving, how moving affected their well-being, and the extent to which transience and groundedness impacted their scholarship and writing. In the initial round of interviews, Zoe was a participant in the study. However, after the interview process, we continued to talk about transience and groundedness, and Zoe became a co-investigator. In 2019, six months after the initial interviews, we conducted follow-up interviews with the three participants. This second round of questions allowed us to validate initial findings and investigate how participants' sense of place had evolved. In addition, participants reflected on how graduate students and university administrators could mitigate the negative effects of transience.

The participant interviews focused primarily on Lincoln, which has a population of 287,000 and is the second-largest city in Nebraska (US Census Bureau 2019). At the time of our interviews, UNL, the flagship campus of the Nebraska University system, had twenty-six thousand students, around five thousand of whom were graduate students (Office of Institutional Effectiveness and Analytics 2019, 50). According to Census Bureau data, at the time of our survey, Lincoln was 86% white (US Census Bureau 2019). In 2018 Nebraska voted majority Republican, although voters in Lincoln voted majority Democrat (Briz et al. 2018). As our interviews with participants will show, Lincoln's size, location, demographics, and political leanings influenced our participants' opinions of Lincoln, at times limiting their perceptions of the choices available to them and at times providing possibilities for engagement.

Our participants, whose names have been changed, were Emma, Sean, and Henry:

Emma was a second-year rhetoric and composition MA student originally from a nearby midwestern state who worked in writing centers and food service before starting graduate school. Emma self-identified as queer, chronically ill, and poor. In her initial interview, Emma talked about feeling unappreciated at UNL and disconnected from Lincoln, a place she didn't consider a "real city." However, in her follow-up interview, she expressed more positive views of Lincoln, due in part to a successful semester of teaching and a new romantic relationship.

Sean was a first-year poetry PhD student originally from New England who held a fellowship at a rural Northeastern college prior to starting his doctorate. Sean self-identified as a white, Jewish, queer man who presents as cisgender. Of our participants, Sean was the newest to Lincoln, and while his experience had been mostly positive so far, he wanted to make more connections, especially to the queer and Jewish communities.

Henry was a fourth-year rhetoric and composition PhD student originally from a midwestern state who earned an MA from UNL and taught at a local community college before starting their PhD. Henry self-identified as white, rural, disabled, and nonbinary. Henry had been in the state for almost a decade, the longest of the three participants, and expressed a close emotional attachment to Nebraska. During their initial interview, they were in the middle of working on their dissertation research, which focused on local activist groups.

We analyzed participants' responses using a mix of qualitative coding strategies. We used a combination of in vivo coding, in which we summarized what we saw as salient moments, concepts, and ideas in each interview using short, direct participant quotations, and descriptive coding, where we used several words or phrases to summarize key points that were either emphasized by participants in the moment or that we identified during analysis (see Saldaña 2013). As we analyzed the interviews, we wrote frequent analytic memos summarizing our thoughts and tracking the development of our analysis. Each interview influenced our reading of the others, meaning that, as we noticed prominent ideas in one participant's responses, we read the other responses with those trends in mind. From these coding processes, themes began to emerge. Initially, we read participant experiences as tales of survival and limitations. However, over time we noticed more hopeful themes centered on the possibilities of forming symbiotic relationships, however temporarily, with the places in which participants lived.

In the following sections, we describe the four major themes our participants described as contributing to their sense of groundedness: where they went to school, their social environments, their community engagement, and how place influenced their scholarship and writing. Each of these themes represents choices participants made; however, as we find in our analysis, their choices were made possible and also limited by cultural and economic factors. There are clear overlaps among these themes. We divide them into separate sections for ease of analysis and because our participants framed them as distinct. For the purposes of this article, "where to go to school" refers to the geographic and institutional places where participants held or hoped to hold academic appointments. "Social environments" refers to interpersonal relationships, whereas "community involvement" refers to engagement with established groups outside the university for service work, social engagement, and activism. "Scholarship and writing" refers to participants' creative and academic projects and their writing processes.

Choosing Where to Go to School

The shrinking availability of tenure-track professorships means graduate students often accept the first program or job offer they receive—if they are so fortunate as to receive one at all—regardless of the offer's geographic location. Moving for school or work is often framed as a choice, but our participants presented a more complicated picture. For example, Sean, the poetry PhD student, described frequent moves as part of the academic lifestyle:

> I sort of accepted a long time ago that if I was going to be a poet and try to be a professor and have a career as a writer, I would just have to go wherever there was an opportunity. . . . There is a sense in which I would be lucky to have the

opportunity to live anywhere for a year and write in any capacity and be paid in any capacity, and I would maybe take that if the opportunity came up. But I'm really hoping I can find something that is more permanent.

Henry, the fourth-year PhD student in rhetoric and composition, voiced a feeling of powerlessness when they considered the job market: "There's an end date—I hate that. And it fills me with a great deal of anxiety that I don't know geographically where I'm going to be in a year and a half. It's extremely anxiety inducing, for both [my partner] and me." In her initial interview, Emma, in the second year of her master's, described UNL as her "last choice." In her follow-up interview, she noted, "My choice to come to Lincoln, of course, like many people, was to follow the funding." In these reflections, our participants show that they perceive the academic working conditions for graduate students and early-career academics as unstable. Sean, noting he would be "lucky" to find employment anywhere, echoes the sense of powerlessness and desperation each participant alluded to in our initial and follow-up interviews. These are common feelings among academics, particularly those in humanities fields, as Bousquet (2008) points out:

> Large new sectors of intellectual labor have proved willing to accept not merely the exploitation of wage slavery but the superexploitation of the artist, in part because the characteristics of casual employment (long and irregular hours, debt subsidy, moonlighting, the substitution of reputation for a wage, casual workplace ethos, etc.) can so easily be associated with the popular understanding of normative rewards for "creative" endeavor. (63)

In other words, Sean's feeling "lucky" to work "anywhere" and be paid "in any capacity" seems to reflect a larger trend: academics, particularly in the humanities, and especially in creative fields, choose to accept low-wage positions in part because they feel it's the normal tradeoff for a career that allows them to pursue their passions.

Bousquet (2008) calls attention to the way in which this dominant narrative of a "normal" tradeoff affects what people like Sean accept in terms of working hours, wages, and workload. We see geographic transience as exploitative due to the emotional and scholarly burdens our participants reported. Sean described the impact of this burden: "It feels really disruptive to my life and to my work to think about jumping around the country every few months or year or two years. I think that the kind of work that I want to do would work a lot better in a different way. The kind of person I am would be a lot happier in a different way." We note Sean expressed a close connection between his identity ("the kind of person I am") and his academic work ("the kind of work that I want to do"). A similar tension between work and identity emerged in Emma's responses. "I feel in many ways like someone needs to take [or relieve] my suffering. And I'm really tired," she said as she reflected on the often-overwhelming nature of graduate work. Shortly after, she reflected, "I don't have roots here. I don't have, like, a full life here." When Charlotte, the interviewer, commented aloud that part of the problem might be the short two-year nature of the MA program, Emma agreed. "Yeah, five years [in a PhD program] sounds like a dream to me. Yeah, to be in one place." Her responses connected her academic struggles to her lack of groundedness in Lincoln. This entanglement of personal and professional life is a key feature of transience as exploitation: academia, which asks its professionals to engage deeply with a single area or subject, also seems to expect this intense study to exist in isolation from the scholar's material location. Academics are expected to roll from moving van to departmental office with an unchanged sense of professional purpose. Our participants, however, tell a different story about how realistic this expectation is.

Still, while all our participants expressed a sense of powerlessness in deciding where to go for school and work, they nonetheless stated clear preferences for where they wanted to be. Emma and Henry described wanting to remain close to their families. Emma and Sean were interested in places where they felt they could become part of specific social groups and communities. Henry expressed a longing to return to familiar landscapes. Emma, who considered UNL to have been her "last choice" program, also listed places she would have rather been instead of Lincoln. Our participants were aware that their preferences might be futile, as Sean acknowledged while thinking about the job market: "There are places I do not want to take a job. But so far, it's just been sort of like, 'Where can I go do [my] thing? Okay, I'll go to that place and do [my] thing,' and I have just accepted what comes with that." Henry also acknowledged how the conventional wisdom of going wherever there is a job conflicted with their preferences: "People are like, 'Oh yeah, you just have to go on the market and go wherever you go,' and I'm like 'Yeah, I know, but I want to stay close-ish to home.'" Our participants discussed their strong preferences for geographic places, but in the same breath, acknowledged how few choices they might have.

The dissonance between the places our participants were or might end up and the places they said they would rather be may have significant impacts on their outlooks and, by extension, their well-being. As Jennifer Sinor writes, the stories we tell ourselves about a space influence how we fix the space as a distinct place in our minds (2007, 9). For example,

Emma, who described UNL as "my shoo-in school" and a place she'd chosen out of necessity rather than preference, expressed broadly negative opinions about Lincoln during our initial interview. By contrast, Henry felt attached to Lincoln, but as they considered their inevitable departure, this attachment acted as a limitation as they considered how they'd connect to a new place. Every participant talked about transience as a limitation, affecting both the choices available to them and their ability to feel grounded in place.

Choices about Social Environments

Place scholars such as Nedra Reynolds argue places are constructed socially and physically; people and their social relationships, impressions, memories, and emotions are equally as important to creating a place as the material landscape (2004, 2). In our own experiences as graduate students at UNL, we see one example of the socially constructed nature of place when we meet prospective graduate students. Many of their questions are about people: What are students like in Lincoln? Do graduate students spend time together outside of school? Are there people of my race? Are people in the Midwest really nicer? What's it like to date here? Will I fit in this community? By extension, they ask: what will it mean for me to be a person in this place? As we talked with our participants, we saw how their choices about social engagement in Lincoln impacted their sense of groundedness.

For Henry, conversations about place always returned to social relationships. "When I think of this place, I'm a very people-oriented person, so I think of people," they said. "As a person, I just really like to go meet other humans, so I think that was how, very soon [after moving to Lincoln], I found my people and adapted to the differences in place." Henry chose to create social connections and talk to others about "their encounters with this place." These relationships in turn provided Henry with possibilities for grounding themself and understanding Lincoln. They emphasized the importance of the relationships they formed with the city's homeless population:

> I have made a lot of friends who happen to be homeless. And I've gotten to know kind of how the homeless world of Lincoln operates. . . . My wife would get really upset with me because I would meet people, and then hang out with them, and then sleep with them under bridges. I've loved getting to know the place through them—the way they see and experience it is so different.

Henry's choices about how they engaged with this group illustrates their social conception of place: for them, all people who lived in Lincoln, regardless of socioeconomic standing, were vital to understanding the place. Understanding Lincoln meant understanding the people who lived there. Geographic embodiment, Reynolds writes, is critical to our understanding of place: "Only bodies can make places meaningful, and the bodies that occupy a place give it meaning" (2004, 144). Thus, places are constituted in part by the embodied experiences of people, which we can learn about through social interaction.

However, the close connection between a place and its people can also limit the choices one makes about social involvement, as Emma described in her initial interview. "Nebraskans are very insular people," she said. She explained that, in the MA program, she was not "nearly as close to the native Nebraskans" as with the out-of-state students. She reported feeling out of place and unable to connect with Nebraskans (both students and otherwise), people she perceived as having a completely different culture than people in her home state:

> The Nebraska football thing is crazy. People will look at me and be like "Go Big Red!" [a popular UNL football chant] and I'm like "Uh . . . yeah . . . for sure . . ." . . . In some ways that's because that's all there is out here, right? Omaha is "up-and-coming" but has its own set of problems. I personally do not see the appeal of Omaha. . . . And western Nebraska is, like, straight up Mennonite country. So in some ways, I think you have to cling to what culture you have here.

Emma's experiences with Nebraskans initially narrowed her perceived choices about whom to socialize or build community with. But to our surprise, by the time of her follow-up interview, Emma's perception of Lincoln had changed completely. "I really like Lincoln, and [my roommate] and I like living here. It's a fun town, and there's lots going on," she said. She cited a new romantic relationship as a primary factor in her evolving attitude: "[My relationship] has been wonderfully rewarding, and I think [it] has helped me feel much more at home at Lincoln. . . . I'm happier now because I know [my partner], and we go out more. I have, you know, another community, another member of my network. . . . And I definitely see more of Nebraska." She also talked about the strong relationships she'd chosen to cultivate with the students she taught, which culminated in receiving a university teaching award at the end of that semester. While a host of factors likely influenced Emma's shift in perception, we note she specifically chose to talk about her social relationships in both interviews. Her evolving narrative illustrates how her social experiences initially limited her sense of groundedness but later offered possibilities to connect to the city.

Henry's and Emma's experiences illustrate the ways our participants' choices about their social involvement impacted their groundedness in Lincoln. However, our participants also brought up ways in which their social choices were limited by factors beyond their control. For example, during the two-year fellowship Sean held in the Northeast before moving to Lincoln, he struggled to make social connections in his rural community. He attributed his difficulties to a variety of overlapping social limitations. First, his long-distance romantic partner still lived in the city where he'd gotten his MFA. Maintaining existing relationships in his old home meant making frequent trips away from his new home. For Sean, the effect was a growing sense of conflict between old and new locations: "I felt like I was sort of trying to live in two places at once. A lot of my emotional energy was sapped." In a culture of transience where graduate students must move frequently, making social connections seemed to help Henry and Emma feel grounded in a place. However, transience also limited the opportunities to create these relationships, as we note in Sean's experience.

Sean observed his social choices were further limited by the detached nature of academic work: "I wasn't teaching, so I wasn't interacting a whole lot with students. I had a job where I spent a few hours a week in a basement on campus and I would see the same five professors in the halls." Academic work is often an isolating experience. For Sean, who moved frequently, this isolation was compounded by the experience of living in a new place. In his role as a fellow, he did not have a cohort, and there was no preexisting social structure at the university for graduate students and fellows that he could turn to. "There are things that are happening, even on a small college campus," he admitted. "But when you're thirty-two, going to events on a college campus is not a great way to meet people." While many universities boast a wealth of programs designed to help students form social connections and enjoy college, those resources are often intended exclusively for undergraduates. We see a connection between the lack of social resources for graduate students and the contingent nature of their positions at the university: tuition-paying undergraduates are seen as customers who should be kept happy, but graduate students, who often receive remitted tuition in exchange for teaching classes, are seen as employees who should be grateful—or "lucky," in Sean's words—for the paycheck.

The social choices available to Sean during his earlier two-year fellowship were further limited by the conflict he perceived between his identity and the social values of the rural Northeast. As a queer, Jewish man in a conservative area, after the 2016 presidential election he found himself questioning whether he should make social connections at all: "It definitely made me suddenly look around and be like, 'How much do I want to engage with this community? How much do I want to get to know these people?'" While he'd begun that fellowship with the hope that he could become part of a community, the region's political climate made him hesitant to pursue new relationships.

Though graduate students' social lives are often framed as choices, the racial, sexual, class, and ability infrastructure of places can limit the real choices available to them, and by extension, impact their sense of groundedness in significant ways. Henry took up this point in their follow-up interview, where they talked about how disability has shaped their experience of Lincoln: "The disabled thing has been tough. Lincoln does not have good public transit. The public transit is pretty unreliable and I'm not supposed to drive with my medication. . . . There's a lot of social events I don't go to because I can't get to [them]. It sucks." They also reflected on how their friends and coworkers of color in the department have trouble establishing a sense of groundedness: "I think about the people of color who find themselves living in Lincoln, and people from places where they realize there aren't large communities of people in this space that speak the language or eat the food they're accustomed to . . . I think about the rules they make to acclimate themselves to the space and the negotiations they have to make." We are reminded of David Gruenewald, who writes, "Human communities, or places, are politicized, social constructions that often marginalize individuals, [and] groups, as well as ecosystems" (2003, 7). To suggest that academics can simply be successful anywhere, then, is to ignore the limitations imposed on them by privilege and marginalization.

Choices about Community Involvement

If places are socially constructed, it follows that they are also intricately connected to their communities. Sean and Henry both talked about the choices they'd made to become involved in, or step away from, communities. They spoke of the importance of those connections to their sense of groundedness, and they described how they hoped to continue their community engagement in the following years. Sean planned to search for communities in Lincoln as he continued his PhD, and Henry thought ahead to finding communities wherever they moved to after their job search.

For Sean, communities had offered possibilities in both his academic work and his personal life. During his previous degree program, an MFA, he was heavily involved in a community-based literacy program that ended up having a significant impact on his scholarship and his creative work as a poet. It also changed his expectations for what community engagement could look like, moving him toward more diverse literary communities outside the university. His work in the community grounded him in the place, particularly because it helped him change his focus from the university to the broader community.

In his initial interview, Sean said he wanted to establish similar links to the community in Lincoln. However, he deliberately distinguished between communities within and outside of the graduate program:

> I still feel like I'm definitely looking for a larger sense of community [in Lincoln], which I think is just hard to find any time you move to a new place, and especially if you're extremely busy with a small number of people—which is how all PhD programs work. I feel like I have good friends within [UNL's] program and the program is going pretty well, but I would like to be tapped into larger communities—in particular kinds of communities that I haven't quite found here yet.

Sean spoke explicitly about wanting to make connections in Jewish and queer communities: "I think that I could become more involved in [the] Jewish community here fairly easily," he said, describing his plans to begin attending synagogue more regularly. "I would just have to show up to things and talk to people more often." But engaging with a queer community outside UNL seemed harder. For Sean, the community presented several limitations, chief among them that the more public queer communities—the gay bars and the nightclub—were aimed at younger adults. Sean also described the mental and material limitations he felt: "Part of the problem is I'm not exploring more and not being more outgoing," he said. "But part of that is also that I'm a fucking PhD student—how much time do any of us have?" This sentiment was expressed by all our participants; the time-intensive nature of graduate work often limited their choices about engaging in their communities.

Henry, who was deeply involved with community activism and community-based research in Lincoln, also described feeling limited by the temporary nature of graduate school. At the time of our initial interview, Henry was in their fourth year in the PhD program and knew that after the following year, they would leave Lincoln and the communities they'd worked with there. As a result, they'd made a choice to begin limiting their involvement in the community to avoid hurting community projects and organizations when they left Lincoln: "The anxiety of the endpoint [has] limited and shaped the ways I've been involved in Lincoln activism," they said. They felt a strong ethical responsibility to local organizations, but they also felt guilty about having to limit their participation in organizations they'd worked hard to develop strong relationships with. Similarly, they were anxious about what might happen to existing community relationships and projects after they left UNL. Henry also worried about how they would connect with the community in the next place they lived: "I'm so worried about what my first semester somewhere else is going to be when I don't know the place yet and I don't know the organizations and I don't know the issues that impact that place." While community activism was central to Henry's research and their sense of groundedness, the transient nature of graduate school limited their choices and transformed their community connections into sources of stress.

We found it common for our participants to be unsure about how much to invest in their temporary communities. Knowing that one's time in a place is limited is often a barrier to engagement—what's the point in creating a community that, as Henry reflected, you'll have to abandon in a few short years? Every participant talked about the difficulty of engaging with a temporary community. At the same time, it's clear that when graduate students do invest in their communities, it's beneficial to their sense of groundedness and their well-being. However, as we noted in our analysis of social environments, once again participants found their choices about community involvement limited by the conditions of graduate study.

Choices about Scholarship and Writing

As Sean and Henry mentioned, engaging with the communities in a place can have a significant effect on graduate students' scholarship. Our participants also discussed how they chose to engage with places through histories, natural environments, and politics. These factors often informed their choices about what to study. Our participants saw their academic identities as closely tied to their writing identities. In addition to seeing our participants as scholars whose choices of what to study are informed by their locations, we see them as writers whose very composing habits and processes are influenced by place.

Henry, who was primarily working on their dissertation at the time of their interviews, found place and scholarship to be intrinsically connected. When they moved to Nebraska, they chose to engage with the history, literature, environment, and politics of the place as a means of feeling grounded. They described reading "anything I could get my hands on" by Nebraska writers to understand their new state. "I gobbled all of that up," they said. In addition to helping them feel more comfortable in a new place, their choice to ground themself in Nebraskan literature and history quickly opened up possibilities in their scholarship. They began to research Nebraska's state parks, state history, and local activist movements. Their move toward these subjects wasn't merely because the subjects were convenient. Instead, they described their scholarship as akin to a coping mechanism for the geographic displacement they felt: "I was desperately trying to grapple with, 'What does it mean to write in this place?'" Engaging place opened up possibilities for overcoming the limits of transient academic life. However, as we noted in our discussion of social environments and community engagement, the choices that helped a participant feel more grounded in the face of academic transience were also often limited by the nature of academic work: Henry knew they would soon have to leave the place that had become central to their dissertation research.

Sean, who was both a creative writer and academic researcher, similarly described how the places he had lived provided possibilities for his work: "The community that I'm in affects the work that I do. Part of that is about where I am—and part of that is also about books and the internet and letters and phone calls and traveling—but it's shaped a lot by where I am." For example, even though Sean felt socially disconnected from the rural northeastern community where he spent a two-year fellowship, that place still impacted his scholarship. After finding World War II Nazi paraphernalia at a local antique market there, he began to think and write about the rise of white nationalism and the resurgence of Nazi symbology and discourse, a project he was still working on when he began his PhD at UNL. Sean was also working on another project inspired by a trip to Poland, where he began to interrogate and write about his family's experiences during the Holocaust. Like Henry, Sean saw places as generative tools for his scholarly work; he responded to transience by choosing to focus on places as objects of study. However, Sean also described how places could impact his work without a deliberate choice on his part. As we talked about the variety of places he'd lived, Sean reflected on what he saw as a clear connection between places and the foci of his creative work.

> Basically, I only ever wrote nature poems when I lived in New York City, which is sort of ironic. And it wasn't a thing that I did on purpose. . . . I missed being around trees and fields. And I grew up in the suburbs—I'm not from the woods or anything, but I mean—that just happened. Not that there's no

other place where I would have written nature poems necessarily. Maybe I would have. . . . But I do think that New York shaped what I was doing in that moment.

Sean emphasized that his creative work changed without a conscious choice; places and writing were almost involuntarily associated for him. Places can thereby provide possibilities for writing, as Sean's quotation illustrates. But the reverse must also be true: if places involuntarily "shape" Sean's work, at times they might limit creative work, too. Thus, Sean and Henry's responses implicate the ways in which places can both provide possibilities for and impose limitations on their work.

In addition to shaping the subjects of our participants' work, place and transience also affected their composition processes. Reynolds theorizes about the connection between place and composition, noting that "the kinds of spaces we occupy determine, to some extent, the kinds of work we can do or the types of artifacts we can create" (2004, 157). She argues that writers must be able to "inhabit" and "dwell" in places to learn and work in them (158). Similarly, writers must "inhabit" and "dwell" in their texts, a process Reynolds suggests "begins with *where* the work of writing gets done" (2004, 167, emphasis in the original). In other words, a sense of groundedness in place is associated with a sense of groundedness in the writing process itself.

Henry and Emma described this connection between groundedness and writing. Henry explained that when they felt grounded in a place and comfortable with the people around them, like their advisors and colleagues, they were more willing to take risks in their writing and more emotionally ready to confront failure: "I'm doing this dissertation and I just know it's going to be a process of walking into hurdles, nothing graceful about it. I think the way that I've changed as a writer [at UNL] is just accepting that writing is all about rolling around on the ground, embarrassed. It's not a graceful or pretty process." For Henry, writing always involved displacement and uncertainty, much like their initial experience in Lincoln. Once they felt more comfortable in Lincoln, the place began to help them offset the chaotic writing process; feeling grounded in place helped them feel grounded in their writing. On the other hand, Emma, who was working on her MA thesis at the time of our initial interview, described how her lack of groundedness in Lincoln seemed to translate to a lack of groundedness in her writing: "Here, [my work] feels like just scribblings. . . . It's increasingly rare that I get work done at all now. I feel like the more rooted I am, the more productive I am. It's just been a problem [in Lincoln] because I just don't know if I'm getting work done. It doesn't always feel good or feel like something I'm proud of." By contrast, she described her home state as the place "where I got some of my best work done." Reynolds posits that the way writers dwell in a physical place is connected to their ability to dwell in a pattern of discourse (2004, 165). Emma's struggle to dwell in place had a tangible effect on her ability to dwell in her writing, a phenomenon supported in existing literature.

While we believe all the ways academic transience limits graduate students are significant, the connection between place and scholarship illustrates the most compelling argument for how transience can be an exploitative force. Graduate students are expected to undergo geographic moves for the benefit of their academic work, but their academic work often suffers as a result of that transience. This double bind forces graduate students to make difficult choices between their work and their well-being, choices that reproduce social privileges informing who is most likely to succeed in completing a dissertation and landing the rare tenure-track position.

Recommendations

The previous sections provide insights into how three graduate students perceived the limits and possibilities of where they went to school, their social environments, their community engagement, and how place impacted their scholarship and writing. While Emma, Sean and Henry's perspectives show some limits and possibilities graduate students face, analysis is only an initial step toward remedying patterns of graduate student exploitation. However, our analysis suggests several ways to address these patterns. We want to emphasize that this work must involve more than graduate students alone; those with unequal access to resources cannot be solely responsible for improving their working conditions. Addressing the negative effects of transience requires work on the part of university administrators. As a final theme, we analyze the recommendations our three participants made.

First, graduate students must recognize the possibilities offered by the places they live. As Sean said, "I feel like sometimes in myself and in other graduate students, I see an impulse to try not to live in the place that I moved to." Focusing on the limited nature of one's time in a place and not engaging is a common coping mechanism for graduate students. "But," Sean added, "I don't really think that you can live somewhere for the amount of time that it takes to get a degree and also maintain a parallel life in another place." Trying to live in two places at once is often frustrating and ineffective, as Sean's earlier comments illustrate. While we acknowledge inequality can limit the choices available to graduate students, we find those who attempt to engage with place have more positive experiences. Therefore, we recommend graduate students make deliberate efforts to get to know their place, such as reading local literature, learning about the history of the region, patronizing local businesses, spending time in nature, and traveling in the state.

Second, each participant stressed the importance of work-life balance and choosing to engage with communities outside the university. For example, Henry described the importance of forming friendships outside the university, and Sean described his desire to become involved with queer and Jewish communities. As much as possible, graduate students should try to participate in local events and establish relationships with people outside university walls. In addition to being personally fulfilling, these kinds of connections help graduate students learn more about their communities and help them benefit in their professional lives. Students must also be responsible and respectful as they seek to engage locally, as many scholars of community writing have attested (Shah 2020). Our participants also stressed the importance of finding mentors for both their academic and personal lives: Henry found mentors who also came from working-class backgrounds or were first-generation students. Emma was more comfortable with an advisor who came from the same region she did. As our participants suggested, community connections like these can have positive impacts, including on one's writing and sense of groundedness.

Finally, our participants talked about how living conditions impacted groundedness. In her follow-up interview, Emma attributed her initial discomfort in Lincoln to her decision to live in south Lincoln, which required her to drive or use Lincoln's limited public transportation. By contrast, Sean, who doesn't own a car and lives close to campus and downtown Lincoln, attributed his positive experiences in part to his choice of neighborhood. While the location of one's home might seem like a small consideration, it can have a significant impact. While rent may be cheaper further from campus, there are financial costs of transportation and social costs of missing events. Indeed, many of our participants' recommendations are small in scope and require choosing to see the possibilities in one's neighborhood and surrounding community. Living well among the limitations of a place frequently comes down to small, intentional choices to form relationships with specific landscapes and people.

When asked about what administrators could do to help graduate students establish a sense of groundedness, every participant immediately brought up financial concerns. As other contributors in this volume explore in detail, increased compensation would mitigate many effects of exploitation. We defer to those contributors' expert discussions of financial issues among graduate students. In addition to financial concerns, participants suggested other ways university administrators can improve graduate student working conditions.

Administrators can create a structured orientation to university services and the surrounding community. While such orientations are often given for incoming undergraduates, graduate orientations tend to be limited and informal, a trend all three participants mentioned. As a result, graduate students must either orient themselves, or rely on advice and knowledge from fellow graduate students—options that present clear difficulties and put an additional burden on incoming and experienced students alike. As Henry put it, "It should not be up to our graduate students [to orient themselves], who are already put in this horrible position of 'Welcome to this new place. Here's your teaching assignment. You have one week. Go.'" A formal orientation provided by the graduate program or department ensures accurate knowledge is passed on and conveys to graduate students they are an important part of the program and community. These orientations should include at minimum a tour of campus and an overview of resources available to graduate students, including accessibility offices, counseling services, and health insurance. Orientation to the surrounding community should include an introduction to neighborhoods, transportation options, landlord recommendations, cultural events, and an overview of local history. We recommend this orientation take place two weeks before classes begin, which would allow graduate students time to acclimate. Additionally, graduate programs should openly address the emotional labor involved in graduate study. Discussion of transience's toll on one's well-being should not be confined to hushed hallway conversations but should also take place during department meetings, prospective student visits, and conversations with advisors.

Conclusion

As our interviews and personal experiences teach us, many graduate students struggle to feel grounded. The experience is even harder for those with marginalized identities. This struggle spills into graduate students' academic lives. Graduate students already recognize the limits imposed on their available choices. However, labor migration studies, place-conscious education, and writing studies have yet to examine connections between graduate students and the systemic forces underpinning such struggles. When graduate students feel disconnected from their communities, they see the negative effects in their work. Thus, we see geographic transience as a key element of graduate student exploitation, inextricably connected to issues of low pay, overwork, and uncertainty.

We began this article noting graduate school can feel like a journey in *The Odyssey*, complete with shipwrecks and sirens. Unless administrators and graduate students seriously interrogate the detrimental effects of academic transience and placelessness, the siren call to leave academia will only grow louder. The COVID-19 pandemic has made this reality all the more apparent: place matters, and our physical and social experiences of place impact our mental health, our quality of life, and our intellectual work as academics. The consequences of placelessness can range from high graduate program dropout rates to poor community-university relationships and future generations missing innovations in research and writing. As Tessa Brown writes in the introduction to this collection, when one is "teaching at multiple campuses with no health insurance, a steady job might be worth it, the life of the mind be damned" (21–22). We call on university administrators to acknowledge this crucial reality, and on the academic community at large to acknowledge the importance of place and migration in graduate study and academic life.

Note

We wish to thank Shari Stenberg and Rachel Azima for their generous feedback on drafts of this article. We also thank our study participants—Emma, Sean, and Henry—for allowing us to share their experiences here.

Works Cited

Bousquet, Marc. 2008. *How the University Works: Higher Education and the Low-Wage Nation.* New York: New York University Press.

Briz, Andrew, Tyler Fisher, Beatrice Jin, John McClure, and Lily Mihalik. 2018. "Nebraska Election Results 2018." https://www.politico.com/election-results/2018/nebraska/.

Brooke, Robert E. 2015. "Suburban Life and Place-Conscious Education: The Problem of Local Citizenship." In *Writing Suburban Citizenship: Place-Conscious Education and the Conundrum of Suburbia,* edited by Robert E. Brooke, 1–34. Syracuse, NY: Syracuse University Press.

Flannery, Kathryn T. 2007. "Levittown Breeds Anarchists! Film at 11." In Sinor and Kaufman, *Placing the Academy,* 109–124.

Flower, Linda. 2008. *Community Literacy and the Rhetoric of Public Engagement*. Carbondale: Southern Illinois University Press.
Gruenewald, David A. 2003. "The Best of Both Worlds: A Critical Pedagogy of Place." *Educational Researcher* 32, no. 4 (May): 3–12.
Hoey, Brian. 2014. *Opting for Elsewhere: Lifestyle Migration in the American Middle Class*. Nashville: Vanderbilt University Press.
Kilborn, Peter. 2009. *Next Stop, Reloville: Life inside America's New Rootless Professional Class*. New York: Times Books.
Office of Institutional Effectiveness and Analytics. 2019. *UNL Factbook 2018–2019*. Lincoln: University of Nebraska-Lincoln. Available at https://iea.unl.edu/publications/fb18_19.pdf.
Pugh, Alison J. 2015. *The Tumbleweed Society: Working and Caring in an Age of Insecurity*. New York: Oxford University Press.
Reynolds, Nedra. 2004. *Geographies of Writing: Inhabiting Places and Encountering Difference*. Carbondale: Southern Illinois University Press.
Saldaña, Johnny. 2013. *The Coding Manual for Qualitative Researchers*. 2nd ed. Los Angeles: Sage.
Shah, Rachael W. 2020. *Rewriting Partnerships: Community Perspectives on Community-Based Learning*. Logan: Utah State University Press.
Sinor, Jennifer. 2007. "Writing Place." In Sinor and Kaufman, *Placing the Academy*, 3–24.
Sinor, Jennifer, and Rona Kaufman, eds. 2007. *Placing the Academy: Essays on Landscape, Work, and Identity*. Logan: Utah State University Press.
US Census Bureau. 2019. "Quick Facts Lincoln City, Nebraska." https://www.census.gov/quickfacts/lincolncitynebraska.
Welch, Nancy. 2005. "Living Room: Teaching Public Writing in a Post-Publicity Era." *College Composition and Communication* 56, no. 3 (February): 470–492.

Interlude 2

Invisible Marginalization in Academia
Samah Elbelazi

> "*You just can't bring brown bodies into a white supremacy system and expect [them] to be OK.*"
>
> —Ebony McGee-Watson

As an international Muslim woman, I see oppression and marginalization as two parallel concepts that walk beside me as I pave my way to a professional life in the United States. Both concepts overlap and could mean the same. However, I usually differentiate them to amplify the struggle minorities go through. While oppression is typically visible, marginalization is mostly silent and barely noticed. We see oppression when it visibly limits people's access and recognition; however, marginalization appears as the silent killer when some authorities ignore minorities' existence within their institutions, for example when it comes to featuring them in publications or promoting them in leadership positions. Although my graduate program did its best to address diversity and inclusion, I still felt marginalized. One may not be visibly oppressed but may still be invisibly marginalized. The purpose of this essay is to share incidents where I felt marginalized and helpless as a graduate student.

My PhD journey started out very promising but it became more challenging as I grew intellectually and professionally. I came to the United States with the hope of finding my dreams and creating new ones. I was not aware of how concepts such as race, color, and gender work in higher education. People at home told me that when I traveled to the United States, my qualifications and hard work would bring me recognition. However, they forgot to tell me that some institutions are not fully aware of how to implement the values of equity and diversity and translate them into action. And that it I could expect to be judged based on my skin color, my hijab, and my accent.

In my first year, I was very proud to be the only international student receiving a graduate assistantship. And yet, while I was very pleased to be seen as valued, I was secretly struggling. Sadly, one of my white colleagues expressed concern about giving international students financial aid because they thought these grants were for domestic citizens. Don't international students also have the right to develop professionally? Those candidates have crossed thousands of miles to study and receive appropriate training, the same way as everyone else in the program. Hearing such a comment was alarming because it made me feel unwelcomed. I wanted to tell this person that I had not taken anyone's spot since all the domestic students already had graduate assistantships, and the position I was given had to be filled in any case by a qualified candidate.

When graduate assistant supervisors were assigned by department administrators, my colleagues were matched with their dissertation advisors or professors who shared the same interests. However, I was not given the option to choose mine. Mentally, I was so exhausted—too exhausted to protest; I felt I had to work harder than my colleagues to prove that I deserved the spot. I was worried that my identity and background would be blamed for any inconvenience caused by my asking for a new advisor.

Immediately after I finished my GA assignment, I was offered a teaching associate position. These positions were available for all PhD candidates, but it seemed that they were filled with domestic candidates first; I observed that international, nonwhite candidates had to wait longer to receive an offer. Although I am still grateful for this experience, I cannot ignore the fact that it opened my eyes widely to the unequal distribution of work opportunities. For example, administrative positions were not distributed evenly among TAs. In addition, when it was my turn to get a private office, I was not offered one. This marginalization made me feel that only white candidates receive these promotions and institutional presence despite anyone else's higher qualifications. I felt lonely, tired, and invisible.

These feelings became vivid when my son was diagnosed with a chronic disease. No one emailed to ask about my son or how I was doing, alone in the hospital. Similarly, I did not receive any official support when my country was listed among the seven banned countries whose citizens were restricted from entering the United States. I was scared, insecure, and this whole situation made me feel insignificant.

This invisibility continued even when I attended my university's professional development workshops. Since day one, I did not have a sense of belonging because I was not their primary audience. I was like a trophy, there to decorate the room and fill in the diversity spot. For instance, one of the presentations covered campus visit protocol. It began with the dress code: a white male graduate student was invited to lecture us about expectations for women's outfits, makeup, and hairstyles. I felt alienated as a hijabi Muslim woman, wondering what my dress code would be. One presenter offered to ask and connect me with a Muslim woman professor, but unfortunately, there were no hijabi professors to connect with, at least not in my institution at that time. Even worse, at the same workshop, it was suggested that if a job candidate was offered alcohol, they should drink little sips because it is not appropriate to say no regardless of any religious restrictions. And if the candidate is pregnant, we were told she should hide it and say that she has food allergies that prevent her from drinking and should wear loose clothes to hide her body. These shocking comments show how the lack of diversity and equity awareness can negatively impact women and particularly, Muslim women of color, in academia.

These snapshots from my experience are examples of marginalization that is usually experienced invisibly and in silence. The fact that I am writing these lines should not invalidate the outstanding positions many professors offered me, but my hope here is to verbalize my unheard voice and highlight these unrecognized hurtful moments. After all these years, I feel privileged to speak while others still struggle quietly. If I do not speak up, then I am part of the problem. Whether what I have experienced was intentional or not is not the question. The question is, how should US institutions of higher education recognize and support diversity so that everyone is treated with equity and dignity?

Works Cited

Watson, Jamila, and Ebony O. McGee. 2021. "Endless Exodus: Faculty of Color Leave the Academy in Search for Fulfillment." *Diverse Issues in Higher Education*, July 30, 2021. https://www.diverseeducation.com/stem/article/15105136/endless-exodus-faculty-of-color-leave-the-academy-in-search-of-fulfillment.

Interlude 3

Invisible Labors and Entangled Emergence

Andrew Hollinger

How do grad students live? Like *physically* live. We imagine cramped apartments or houses with roommates, cluttered desk spaces, cartons of leftover takeout. There's laundry waiting to be done, I'm sure. And books! Many, many books—all over the place, books. It's like a scene from a film: perhaps graduate school helps the protagonist find themselves, or their purpose, or true love, or even a rewarding career as a professor. There is something romantic about this scene. Maybe it's the books. Learning, struggling, becoming ourselves. Bohemian.

Here's another version of that story, my version. I'm married and have a nine-year-old son. I am the writing program administrator (WPA) at a large Research-1 institution where I also teach as a full-time lecturer with a 4/4 teaching load—four courses each for two semesters a year. I am earning my PhD (coursework done!) at *another* institution. And yes, there *is* always laundry to be done. The dishes pile up. But it's not romantic. It's work.

I'm not sure what people imagine when they think of "grad school" or "grad students." Somehow even my own life and that of my peers are not what *we* even imagined when we dreamed of being graduate students. Discussions of grad school labor, especially that which is invisible, might begin here, with the material realities behind the dream (or myth): what's the cost of living? The cost of making a life? Which costs are financial, which are emotional, which are physical? And what of that ever-attending urgency? An urgency that pervades and disturbs all moments, particularly those moments when I'm not *doing* grad school. Whether having fun or meeting an obligation, those moments when I'm not *doing grad school,* yet am still managing the feeling of urgency to be on task, productive, working toward an end, are also part of the labor of grad school. Family time and chores may not seem like typical graduate school labor, but the nature of my everyday tasks is different *because* I'm a student. Even mundane obligations take on a more urgent tenor when there is school work waiting to be done. And I felt that way before a global pandemic. The labor of being a student, teacher, parent, spouse has become increasingly precarious.

What's funny (although it's not actually, not at all) is how I'm careful of others' labor in ways that I am not in relation to my own. Because I'm also a WPA, I am responsible for coordinating, supervising, facilitating, and mentoring other full-time and part-time lecturers (some of whom are also in graduate school), as well as my institution's graduate part-time instructors (who are definitely in graduate school). I want those working in and for the writing program to do meaningful and manageable work. I also want the writing program to be successful and innovative, something that requires a lot of labor. I know these things don't have to be mutually exclusive, but it feels that way sometimes: *here's an initiative to help us better reach our students; one more meeting; who wants to help with assessment* . . . all while worrying whether I'm asking for too much.

What is too much? Can I generalize from my own personal threshold? But I don't guard my own labor in the ways I worry others should. Even now, there are papers that need feedback and shirts that need to be moved to the dryer and a birthday party my son has been invited to this evening (a school night!)—the urgency to be everything to everyone presses in, a container that is just too tight. I have my own ways of managing these conditions, but I don't want to push them onto my colleagues and peers. All this is further complicated by my own positionality as a cis, white, male in a situation where I possess a modicum of authority. Where is the line between being a responsible leader, watchful of the labor and effort of those I manage, and imposing my own work ethic on someone else?

Who I was, am, and will be continues to emerge from these entangled moments. The philosopher-physicist Karen Barad explains, "The point is that these *entangled practices* are productive, and who and what are excluded through these entangled practices matter: different intra-actions produce different phenomena" (2007, 58). There are "forces—including ones that get labeled 'social,' 'cultural,' 'psychic,' 'economic,' 'natural,' 'physical,' 'biological,' 'geopolitical,' and 'geological'" (66)—that become so tangled it is difficult to know where one force stops acting on us and another begins. It is *from* the uniquely tangled nature of these forces, some within our control and others beyond us, that who and what we are emerges. The trouble is that we do not always recognize these forces and the way they inform our decisions and practices.

Perhaps the most insidious characteristic of exploitation isn't that it exploits us (bad enough) but that it's so ingrained in our beliefs about how things should work that we don't even recognize it when it's right in front of us—around us, everywhere. I'm trying to break the script just as I recognize and understand the ways that script has affected my own life, decisions, and labor. For example: growing up, I can't remember a time when my dad wasn't working at least three jobs. My mom worked as well, one or two jobs depending on family need. I know that any bootstrap mentality I have comes from watching their labor, *even as—as Victor Villanueva taught us—I also know that pulling yourself up by the bootstraps is one of the great American myths* (1993). I know that my threshold for "busy" can be higher than other people's because there is a part of me that translates "busy" as "love," or "taking care." I know there are times that I work too much. I also know that watching my parents work taught me how to lean into problems and get things done. I know that there is "good" work and that it's pleasurable to do. I know that my labor and my ability to labor have been factors in where and who I am. I don't know if any of that is fair, or ethical, or healthy. It seems that the labor that is most hidden, precious, and invisible is that which emerges from the most tangled forces of all: family, and history, and the desire to thrive.

At the end, for me, only more questions, more labor, remain: *What am I supposed to do now? Where do I go from here?*

Works Cited

Barad, Karen. 2007. *Meeting the Universe Halfway: Quantum Mechanics and the Entanglement of Matter and Meaning*. Durham, NC: Duke University Press.

Villanueva, Victor. 1993. *Bootstraps: From an American Academic of Color*. Urbana, IL: National Council of Teachers of English.

2 | "Like I'm 'The Man'"
Graduate Student Administrators' Experiences

Talinn Phillips, Paul Shovlin, and Megan Titus

In one of the earliest mentions of graduate students engaging in writing program administration, Michael Pemberton (1993) suggested that coursework and apprenticeships could help graduate students learn what it meant to be a writing program administrator. Pemberton argued that composition's "tale too terrible to tell" is that almost every composition specialist is, at some point (and more likely at multiple points) in her career, expected to be a writing program administrator (WPA) (1993, 156), responsible for scheduling and supervising teaching associates and adjunct instructors; developing curriculum; assessing a curriculum's effectiveness; assessing teaching; representing the writing program to university leadership and among faculty (including defending the program during budget cuts, etc.); mentoring teaching associates; and much more. It is now commonplace for writing programs (often housed in English departments or in writing studies departments) to follow Pemberton's suggestion and offer apprenticeships to graduate students in rhetoric and composition (or writing studies) in order for students to gain valuable experience with writing program administration and to alleviate some of the workload on faculty WPAs.

To appropriate Pemberton's metaphor, our tale—providing a data-driven description of the work that graduate student writing program administrators (gWPAs, hereafter) do—is a cautionary one that suggests the field and our programs need to engage in more careful consideration of the work we assign and expect from gWPAs, and of the support we provide for them. For despite the high numbers of gWPA positions available (which are often highly coveted and competitive), we have little replicable, aggregable, data-driven research on the successes and limitations of graduate students' WPA experiences. As we also describe in "Thinking Liminally: Exploring the (com)Promising Positions of the Liminal WPA" (2014), we three coauthors found our own experiences as gWPAs highly rewarding and excellent preparation for future faculty and administrative positions; however, we also found them to be much more demanding and fraught than the literature, which we review below, suggests. This disconnect led us to conduct the study reported here, as we believe it is important to understand the realities of gWPA experiences and consider how they compare to the field's dominant narratives and understandings of gWPAs. For as Elder, Schoen, and Skinnell's survey demonstrates (2014), the number of graduate students pursuing these positions is on the rise. The qualitative findings we share here add to this existing literature to demonstrate the extensive, undercompensated, and confusingly classified labor performed by gWPAs.

Research on the Workload and Experiences of gWPAs

There is little replicable, aggregable, data-driven research on gWPA experiences, although there are several articles and book chapters written by current and former gWPAs that reflect on their personal experiences (see, for example, Helmbrecht and Kendall [2008]; Jukuri and Williamson [1999]; Inman [2011]; and Mattison [2008]). The roles that the gWPAs in our study describe, the workloads they undertake, and the fraught nature of their work are a fairly stark comparison to Pemberton's initial suggestion of a rather benign job description, namely that students could "obtain some hands-on experience with the details of program management" (1993, 160). The work of the participants in this study takes a more complicated shape than the roles identified in Latterell's research, which range from gWPA as "liaison," to "administrative assistant," to "co-policymaker" (2003, 29). Indeed, some of our interviewees described their role as *the* policymaker for the program, which they carry out while also acting as a liaison not only between "the WPA and the teaching staff" (2003, 27) as Latterell suggests, but between their programs and the university at large.

Beyond this anecdotal comparison, however, the question of whether gWPAs' positions are always liminal or not—existing within clearly defined boundaries designed appropriately with graduate students in mind or more closely approaching the type of work senior WPAs engage in—is an empirical one. We were particularly concerned with the lack of detail about workloads within the existing research. Ebest's study, which is now over two decades old, showed that some teaching assistants (TAs) "serve as assistants whose primary responsibilities are to help conduct TA training and counsel other TAs" (1999, 75). But Ebest's study does not look at the intersection of that work with graduate students' attention to teaching and research, nor the administrative position's impact on a student's ability to perform any given task successfully, for example, given the difficult nature of graduate students exhibiting power or authority over other graduate students. Two more recent studies do examine gWPAs' experiences from the gWPA perspective, offering advice to the field on how to better prepare gWPAs for both their immediate and future WPA work. Elder, Schoen, and Skinnell (2014) argue for the importance of recognizing graduate students' shifting perspectives on writing program administration, from a position to be avoided to one that should be embraced. Their analysis suggests that the field needs to better prepare gWPAs and that gWPAs need better access to mentoring and support services. However, this study is focused more on "development of professionalization programs" than on workloads (16).

Edgington and Taylor's (2007) study aimed to begin gathering data in addition to gWPAs' personal narratives. Their survey respondents placed a high value on the experience and perceived marketability their WPA experiences provided, but they also surfaced problems with these positions. The authors further note that these students didn't necessarily recognize that the nature of their jobs positioned them for exploitation. Multiple respondents also reported that their WPA positions sometimes generated conflict with other graduate students. We found Edgington and Taylor's work valuable but their survey instrument left us with many unanswered questions about gWPAs' experiences. Their survey was fairly brief and the article did not allow readers to see relationships between participants' responses. And while participants were asked about job duties and training, these were described in broad terms without any context for those duties. Were participants providing supervisors with minimal help and learning about administrative processes, or were they completing high-stakes tasks on their own? What kind of mentorship was available? How did the number of hours in students' contracts compare with the hours actually worked?

The literature above tends to emphasize delegating responsibility to apprentices for the sake of their development, echoing an apprenticeship framework of graduate education (see Brown's introduction to this volume). Yet Stolley would add that these narratives "are more restrictive and disciplining than we might imagine" (2015, 19) and Jukuri and Williamson point out that the ways gWPA positions involve delegating of responsibility should be interrogated more closely, especially with regards to graduate students' "long-term development" as teachers and scholars (1999, 106). Jukuri and Williamson's is one of multiple narratives (see also Helmbrecht and Kendall 2008; Inman 2011; Mattison 2008) that problematize the benefits of gWPA positions; unfortunately, these narratives do not yet seem to have had a wide influence on the field's discussion of gWPA positions or, as our findings suggest, on the nature of the positions themselves.

In our 2014 essay, "Thinking Liminally," we offer a more in-depth analysis of the concept of liminal writing program administration than space allows us to provide here. We developed the liminal WPA concept to reflect the dissonance between the working conditions of WPAs, their rank or status, and how the field of rhetoric and composition discusses that work. Liminality describes those who live on the thresholds of WPA work—the graduate students, permanent ABDs, non-tenure-track (NTT) faculty, and the people from "the wrong field" who do substantial administrative work but whom, for a variety of reasons, the institution doesn't provide with long-term positions. Liminal WPAs have workloads comparable to faculty WPAs (e.g., management and supervision of others, curriculum development, assessment) but lack the kind of power, resources, and compensation that help senior WPAs do that work. Liminal WPAs' lack of institutional permanence makes their work easy to dismiss or overlook and helps to rationalize their frequently poor compensation. Moreover, upper administration may actually favor liminal positions in order to attempt to control or limit a program since, in essence, a liminal WPA will find it difficult to "fight back." Though liminal WPAs' jobs are not impossible or *necessarily* exploitative—some, like us, prefer it to traditional gWPA work—it is extremely challenging and, as we argue elsewhere (2014), not yet supported by the literature and other structures of the field.

Methods

In an effort to provide a replicable, data-driven understanding of the work that gWPAs do, we designed a survey (Phillips, Shovlin, and Titus 2016) to investigate that work and to flesh out that data through follow-up interviews. Our research questions were:

1. What work do gWPAs do?
2. How does that actual work compare to their job descriptions?
3. Are the job duties and workloads appropriately aligned for graduate students (rather than full WPAs)?
4. If not, how often do graduate students have incommensurate duties and/or workloads? How often are they actually functioning as more senior, faculty WPAs?

We conducted a survey of fifty-eight respondents who identified themselves as part of the field of rhetoric and composition at a range of US institutions. Nine respondents, all current or recent graduate students, then volunteered to participate in forty-five to sixty-minute semi-structured interviews, which Megan conducted using questions drafted jointly based on our initial analysis of the survey results (see appendix A). Of those nine, six were female and three were male. Seven were current graduate students, of whom three were currently gWPAs while the other four had been gWPAs within the last five years. Interview questions asked about material conditions of interviewees' work and workload, relationships with others (graduate students, supervisors, faculty), and satisfaction with their positions; they additionally sought recommendations for the field's treatment of graduate student administrators.

After transcribing the interviews, we segmented and coded them in order to rigorously surface recurring themes and phenomena. The codes were developed by the researchers from the interview data and informed by the experiences described in relevant published gWPA narratives (e.g., Helmbrecht and Kendall 2008). Using Geisler's method for Verbal Data Analysis, Talinn segmented the interviews into topical chains, typically identified by referentials or oral discourse markers (Geisler 2004, 35). The topical chains allowed us to systematically examine different facets of gWPAs' lives and work. Megan and Talinn then developed a nested coding scheme, or one coding scheme situated within another, for the segmented interviews (see appendix B). Segments were first coded into Dimension 1, "gWPA Life," which included six categories based on the content of the interviews and the literature on the subject: **Mentoring** in the position, material **Resources** available to help complete the work, impact on **Academic/Professional Life**, impact on **Personal** life, **Workload**, and **not applicable**. Megan and Talinn refined the coding scheme with Paul as second coder. We achieved a simple reliability of 94% on Dimension 1 and a Cohen's Kappa of .907. This strength of agreement is considered to be very good (Geisler 2004, 81). Talinn then coded the remaining interviews along Dimension 1.

Next, the topical chains were recoded along Dimension 2, "Affect." Talinn and Paul recoded the topical chains to assess participants' affect regarding each chain. We used three categories: **negative affect**, **positive affect**, and **null/not applicable**. We achieved a simple reliability of 88% and a Cohen's Kappa of .866 for Dimension 2. Again, the strength of agreement is considered very good. Talinn then coded remaining data along Dimension 2. Our coding scheme was nested, as we wanted to not only determine the most common topics of discussion but also understand participants' attitudes toward their work. Thus, each topical chain was re-coded depending on the assessment of the participant's overall affect toward that chain as "positive," "negative," or "neutral." Any topical chain coded as "null" in Dimension 1 was coded as "null" for Dimension 2.

In the following sections, we overview our coding results before discussing the interview findings. While our earlier article "Re-Identifying the gWPA Experience" (Phillips, Shovlin, and Titus, 2016) focused on the quantitative results of the study, here we use qualitative analysis to provide voices in context and to gain a deeper understanding of students' experiences. Although our sample size is not large, these interviews help illuminate the conditions under which gWPAs actually work, as well as their attitudes toward that work.

Results

As described above, the semi-structured interview transcripts were coded according to whether **Workload**, **Mentoring**, **Resources**, **Personal**, or **Academic** best described the topic of discussion (see appendix B). While the coding process allowed us to analyze the interviews more systematically from multiple angles, the findings of the coding process for Dimension 1, "gWPA life," were limited. The only surprising finding was that the **Personal** code was never used. The **Personal** code was designed for instances where WPA work had impacted the interviewee's personal life in some way and was based on reports in the literature (Helmbrecht and Kendall 2008); however, neither coder ever identified it as the *primary* topic of discussion (though it was sometimes secondary). The **Resources** code, used when participants talked about material conditions of their work and compensation (e.g., office space, access to copiers, summer salary), was the next least common, identifying 20 topical chains out of 273. The interview included a question about material conditions, but participants rarely discussed **Resources** outside of that question. The remaining codes, **Workload**, **Mentoring**, and **Academic**, were all used fairly evenly, identifying 64, 71, and 59 of 273 topical chains, respectively. When we identified the highest frequency chain for each participant (marked by a highlighted cell in table 2.1 below), these chains were again represented equally; one-third of participants used each of these codes most often. Our Dimension 1 findings are summarized in table 2.1 (all participant names are pseudonymous).

Dimension 2 results were clearer, with six of nine participants describing their work in predominantly positive terms (table 2.2). One partici-

Table 2.1

	Topical Chains	Dimension 1 Code				
Interviewee		Workload	Resources	Mentoring	Academic	Null
Abigail	26	6	3	5	6	6
April	42	10	2	**20**	4	6
Christine	27	8	1	**9**	4	5
Emma	28	3	1	8	**11**	5
Laurie	23	4	1	4	**8**	6
Lily	23	4	2	**6**	4	7
Micah	25	9	0	5	**8**	4
Molly	23	6	3	3	**8**	3
Pat	32	8	4	6	3	9
Sam	24	6	3	5	3	6
Totals	*273*	*64*	*20*	*71*	*59*	*57*

Note. Aggregated coding for Dimension 1, "gWPA life," with most common code by participant set in bold.

pant was almost evenly split between **positive** and **negative** topics, and two participants, Emma and Pat, described their work in predominantly negative terms. Overall, 101 topical chains were coded as **positive**, 73 as **negative**, and 40 as **neutral**, with **Workload** and **Mentoring** most likely to

Table 2.2

	Dimension 2 Code			
Interviewee	Positive	Negative	Neutral	Null
Abigail	11	4	5	6
April	20	13	3	6
Christine	9	6	7	5
Emma	4	18	1	5
Laurie	10	3	4	6
Lily	14	1	1	7
Micah	11	4	7	4
Molly	8	7	4	3
Pat	3	14	5	9
Sam	11	3	3	6
Totals	*101*	*73*	*40*	*57*

Note. Aggregated coding for Dimension 2, "Affect."

Table 2.3

	Workload			Resources			Mentoring			Academic		
	Positive	Negative	Neutral	Positive	Negative	Neutral	Positive	Negative	Neutral	Positive	Negative	Neutral
Abigail	3	2	1	1	2	0	4	0	1	3	0	3
April	2	6	2	2	0	0	12	7	1	4	0	0
Christine	1	3	4	1	0	0	5	2	2	2	1	1
Emma	1	2	0	1	0	0	0	7	0	2	8	1
Laurie	2	0	2	1	0	0	2	3	0	4	2	2
Lily	3	0	1	2	0	0	6	0	0	3	1	0
Micah	5	1	3	0	0	0	3	2	0	3	1	4
Molly	3	1	2	1	1	1	1	2	0	4	3	1
Pat	0	6	3	2	2	0	0	3	2	2	1	1
Sam	6	0	0	1	2	0	1	1	3	4	0	0
Totals	26	21	18	12	7	1	34	27	9	31	17	13

Note: Disaggregated coding for Dimension 2, "Affect."

be coded as **negative**. Table 2.3 shows the frequency of **positive**, **negative**, and **neutral** affect codes per "gWPA Life" codes. In this table, we show a more specific breakdown of table 2.2's **positive**, **negative**, and **neutral** coding. It reveals that the highest numbers of topical chains were seen in **positive** for **Mentoring** (34); **positive** for **Academic** (31); and **negative** for **Mentoring** (27). It also shows that participants discussed **Mentoring** the most (70 topical chains) and **Resources** the least (20 topical chains).

Discussion

Workload

The **Workload** code was particularly useful in helping us to identify participants whose duties and workloads were incommensurate with their status as graduate students. When asked, "How was this position described to you? What was your job description?," participants described a range of job descriptions that were often inaccurate and, in a number of cases, also involved work that was incommensurate with the field's understanding of gWPA work. Some of them offered that the job as they experienced it was time-consuming, complex, politically dangerous, and/or lacked supervision. Several interviewees had nebulous job descriptions and ultimately found themselves completing a wide variety of duties. For instance, Pat recalled "a short job description, a few bullet point items. Typical duties entailed maybe three or four items. I think it had to do with planning meetings." He observed, however, that his job included far more "logistical" details than he was prepared for, such as extensive scheduling and event planning, and those were the duties that took the most time (and also led him to discuss his workload in negative terms). In Pat's case, those logistical details that he was unprepared for, which were *not* in his job description, overwhelmed him and he eventually left the position.

Christine, who learned after she was hired that she would be acting director of the writing program during her first summer on the job, also reported engaging in substantial and politically fraught duties: "I'm organizing the fall orientation workshops and then I'm also responsible right now for taking care of undergraduate grade petitions, waivers, . . . any plagiarism case that arises over the summer, . . . as well as any teacher concerns." Christine's work—particularly given that she was serving as acting director—clearly took up many tasks that faculty WPAs would be expected to complete; however, the extent to which Christine noticed this (or cared) seemed to be mitigated by her strong positive relationship with her faculty WPA, which also led to her more neutral discussion of her workload. Thus, despite encountering tasks that were outside her job description (and seemed, to us, quite inappropriate), Christine felt well-supported and well-advised by her mentor and perhaps was then more likely to perceive those additional duties positively.

Finally, when asked about a job description, Emma simply stated, "There was no job description." However, she gave a long list of duties that she and her co-gWPA were expected to fulfill, such as:

- plan and implement a weeklong orientation for new TAs
- co-teach the TA practicum course
- facilitate small group meetings with TAs
- observe new TAs
- hold workshops for TAs several times a semester
- tabulate assessment numbers for the faculty member's report

These duties were far more time-consuming than had been represented to Emma when she accepted the position. The fact that so much of it involved supervising peers marked Emma's position as clearly problematic to us. Emma couched much of her discussion of workload in negative terms, noting that "it was almost like [she and her colleague were] a faculty member" and although they "were respected by the new WPA . . . that was not always the perception within the department." Emma revealed that when the new WPA tried to secure more funding for Emma and her colleague, this "ended up creating a lot more friction in the department." To Emma, this was ultimately at times "a thankless job" that subjected them to "a lot of disparaging language from people outside of the rhetoric and writing programs in terms of what our goals were and the party line we had to toe." Without a concrete description of Emma's duties, then, there was conflict among department members with regards to compensation, workload, and the like.

Further, Emma's department, mentors, and supervisors seemed to underestimate the time and complexity involved in her work. Thus, in Emma's case, a clear job description might have protected Emma from taking on duties that would be more appropriately completed by a faculty member but would also have given her department and colleagues a clearer sense of Emma's role. Perhaps an accurate job description wouldn't have actually changed Emma's situation, but it would have at least made it more clear to all concerned when boundaries were being crossed, thus making more accountability possible.

Resources

We also asked interviewees about the material conditions of their work (e.g., office space, office location, copier access, compensation, travel support). All interviewees received release time from their usual teaching duties as compensation (although the value of this varied widely depending on the standard load) and, in some cases, additional funding for professional development (e.g., travel funding for conferences). Those who worked for large portions of the summer reported receiving additional stipends for that work, and several noted that their WPA positions gave them opportunities to earn extra money, for example, by teaching the classes of instructors who became ill. Yet no participants reported earning additional pay during the nine-month academic year for the administrative work they were doing, even though multiple interviewees said that their actual workload substantially exceeded their contracted hours, and many had workloads that were more appropriate for tenure-track faculty. These findings were consistent with Edgington and Taylor's findings (2007, 154) and with our own survey results (Phillips, Shovlin, and Titus, 2016).

Our respondents' comments on the **Material** resources available to them as gWPAs revealed some gWPAs who shared the same conditions as other graduate students and others for whom their gWPA status afforded them more private space in better locations. Abigail reported, "Our offices are kind of sad. We have two offices, total, for all of the graduate students. And they're just broken up into cubes and the [gWPAs] are in those offices just like all of the other graduate students." Sam's discussion of resources was also slightly more negative; he commented that his office "was shared with ten other people. It was really small. Some people felt claustrophobic." But he clarified (in more positive terms) that he actually found that the camaraderie generated by the close quarters outweighed the negative effects of the space.

Unfortunately, when interviewees had better material conditions, this seemed to become a site of tension and jealousy. Emma described "an amazing office" in a prime location. However, she also notes that this nicer office was "actually a source of contention" with other graduate students and department members. Similarly, Pat's office was initially shared with one other gWPA in a renovated space; his discussion of his experience was equally positive and negative. Pat stated that "the university was very proud of this collection of offices. . . . It was a showpiece for them and that also hurt us because this part of the [campus] became very attractive to a lot of people and it took very little time before people were interested in our space." Within a few months, Pat and his office mate had been demoted to sharing a windowless storage area with a pillar in the middle of the room with two other graduate students. Unfortunately, providing gWPAs with additional resources sometimes created friction within the department and/or among other graduate students, a problem we discuss in more detail below.

Academic/Professional Life

Within topical chains coded as **Academic/Professional Life**, we were interested in how graduate students' coursework and degree completion were impacted by their WPA work. For instance, did the gWPA position slow their progress toward a degree? Did it make life with other graduate students more difficult? Much of the "academic" discussion focused on gWPAs' relationships with other graduate students. Unfortunately, becoming a gWPA typically meant a negative shift in interviewees' relationships with their peers, a finding shared with Edgington and Taylor (2007) and with multiple narrative accounts of gWPA work (Mattison 2008; Jukuri and Williamson, 1999). The transition to administration forced all participants into a somewhat liminal space in that they were not faculty, but no longer quite graduate students either. Nearly all interviewees said that, at a minimum, other graduate students became more guarded around them after they became gWPAs, demonstrating some fear of the interviewees' new institutional authority. Christine encapsulated this shift best:

> I think people are more closed-mouthed about their teaching when we're kind of out socially than they might be otherwise. I think people who want advice about their teaching will bring it up. But I think people who are maybe a little bit concerned about it or . . . some people who . . . have had negative attitudes towards their students or towards their teaching, they don't really talk to me in the same way anymore.

Christine had only been a gWPA for a few weeks when she gave this interview, but already cited this tension as a drawback of her new job, which she was otherwise enthusiastic about. And although Laurie's comments about academic and professional life were ultimately more positive than negative, she also mentioned "lots of uncomfortable jokes about like, 'Oh, I better not say anything about this thing that I'm not excited about, or the program or the curriculum.'"

Emma seemed to have had the worst experience, describing blatant misogynistic behavior directed toward her and other gWPAs. She reported that an incoming TA referred to Emma and other gWPAs as the faculty

WPA's "concubines." Emma also poignantly articulated the state of being "caught between" her peers and her superiors that others described.

> There were a couple of times where I said [to other graduate students], "Listen, even if you disagree with what was happening, we had to do what we were told." . . . So there was definitely that conflation between role and academic and who I was as a person. A couple of times I had to put the [TAs] in their place by saying, "Don't judge me for what I was told I had to do, for the roles and responsibilities, for who I was."

Although Emma's experience with her peers was the most negative, others also described the awkwardness of supervising or disciplining their peers. For example, Lily, who had mostly positive things to say about her academic and professional experience, also reflected on whether and how to discipline a fellow graduate student who hadn't attended mandatory, not-for-credit pedagogy workshops: "What can we really do? It's not a formal class, it's not something that we've technically . . . we've said it's required, but we don't have anything to back that up. . . . There was a little struggle there because I didn't really, I guess, have the authority to require them to be anywhere."

Micah's experience had lower stakes than Emma's, but was still fraught:

> [T]he year that I was a TA practicum leader, there was a member of my [cohort] and she ended up being placed in the small group that I led. . . . We got along fine, but the other member and I have radically different working styles, radically different pedagogical outlooks, and so being in a semi-supervisory capacity . . . created an awkward sort of situation, fraught with all kinds of potential for perceptions of misuse of power or silencing the other member when that wasn't the intention.

Overall, the segments coded **Academic/Professional Life** suggest that writing programs should be much more conscious of the ways that becoming a gWPA may damage that student's relationship with peers and seek ways to mitigate that effect. One option is creating spaces to actively reflect on and scrutinize such experiences as developmental tools for what students may face as future faculty (although faculty members are much better paid for enduring the attendant unpleasantness). We might construct these problems as important experiences with interpersonal conflict that, coupled with reflection and transparency, could encourage administrative development. Of course, another method is to simply not ask gWPAs to supervise peers. Doing so will always put those supervisors in a problematic position because, as Lily put it, "I didn't really . . . have the authority to require them to be anywhere." Graduate students don't actually have the authority to supervise other graduate students (much less adjunct faculty) and all involved know it; asking them to do so anyway creates situations that are uncomfortable at best and untenable at worst. At the very least, faculty and staff can support gWPAs in these roles by creating clear requirements for all student workers.

Mentoring

Mentoring was the most challenging code that we worked with. We acknowledge that "mentoring" is a complicated, sometimes contested term that we use in rather uncomplicated ways, but a coding scheme asks researchers to create a handful of boxes that categorize a wide range of experiences. Extending beyond what the code's name implies (i.e., relationships with supervisors), these topical chains often included what interviewees loved most about their work, as well as the source of their greatest problems. We focus here on interviewees' relationships with their primary supervisors (the faculty WPAs in these writing programs) because they seemed most critical to any gWPA having successful experiences and because the field seems to share an intrinsic value that graduate students should receive substantial levels of mentoring. However, many interviewees felt their gWPA positions also benefited them by providing access to a wider group of faculty and administrators who also provided mentorship, which we do not discuss extensively here. Finally, several interviewees also described receiving support from other gWPAs.

When mentorship went well it seemed to be the highlight of these gWPAs' experiences. Abigail, for instance, reflected on the value of being able to observe her mentor: "Just observing the director manage a committee meeting where, she's really just incredibly flexible and pragmatic—to see how she responds to things that you have to learn how not to have a knee-jerk affective response sometimes to things—I think that's been incredibly helpful for me in terms of being a future faculty person. I want to be her one day [laughing]. She's really amazing."

Micah expressed similar sentiments: "I would say there were two prongs to the advising; one, the way they did the work in front of me and in the conversations that happened. They were remarkable models. . . . The other thing was being open to having conversations about questions that I was having." April went even further, noting, "Probably my favorite part of the job, honestly, was being able to work with Professor [Y] and really getting to know her and learning from her. I've learned so much from her." April described the many things she had learned from Professor Y that hadn't been part of her WPA coursework, adding, "I felt like I was always in a safe space. And Professor [Y] always protected me in ways that she didn't have to, honestly." This protection was especially important because of April's faculty-like workload. Her high-profile position came with a workload that took much more time than the job description suggested, required her to negotiate directly with a number of university professionals, and required expertise and specialized knowledge that her supervisor didn't have. In many respects, April seemed to be managing a high-stakes position while fairly isolated in her day-to-day tasks; yet the strong mentorship and support from Professor Y helped April to thrive in her position, and she discussed her experience in predominantly positive terms.

For others, relationships with supervisors were more problematic. Although Pat had a good relationship with his faculty WPA, he observed that she was very busy and that her mentorship was in high demand, which ultimately made his experience more negative. He noted, "I could see that her time was very full so she would make time for me, but at the same time, I almost felt guilty about going to her with my questions. I found myself trying to juggle people to consult with if I had a problem." Laurie, who also had a positive relationship with her faculty WPA, still commented that the way the faculty member positioned himself seemed to shift some of his authority onto her, resulting in strained relationships with her peers. "Our director of composition positions himself as very not 'the one in charge,'" she said. "I think it's pretty easy for people to think that I am the one controlling everything about what happens in [the program] . . . like I'm 'The Man.'" Among the interviewees, the nature of mentoring relationships seemed tightly connected with whether graduate students had positive experiences, and we can see a problematic slippage between mentorship and management.

Conclusion: Graduate WPAs or Liminal WPAs?

In sum, these interviews suggested that the field may not be doing enough to mentor, prepare, and compensate gWPAs, significant numbers of whom we argue are better described as liminal WPAs (see also Phillips, Shovlin, and Titus, 2014). Moreover, the multiple pressures wrought on departments and institutions as a result of the COVID-19 pandemic have created more fraught conditions for more liminal WPAs, not fewer. As faculty and staff are cut, it's likely that graduate students are being asked to take on some of the excess workload, making their situations even more challenging. For example, in 2021 at one of our institutions, a TA who left the program early in the semester was replaced by a gWPA who was provided with less than base compensation for teaching the remainder of the course. The chair simply expected the gWPA to do it because "nobody else [could]" and because the student's role as gWPA put her in the middle of the department's response to the staffing shortage. As such, gWPA workloads are complex, politically charged, and at times comparable to those of tenured faculty (and perhaps more problematic, given their status as graduate students), yet they are "compensated" in most cases with a course release and tasked with managing these workloads while completing their own coursework and dissertations.

Understanding the situations of liminal graduate student WPAs is vital in re-envisioning what it means to support them, whether on the job or in the graduate curriculum. Support can (and should) entail many different things. Although unions are no panacea, like Brown (this volume), we do think that graduate student unionization could play a powerful role in forcing balance between status, roles, and compensation. It's the *imbalance* between these things that opens the door wide for exploitation, not the roles or status themselves. Many graduate students are perfectly qualified for the more sophisticated roles they fill as liminal WPAs; a union could prevent them from being compensated at poverty wages. Additionally, a union might define certain workloads or activities as beyond the scope of a graduate student position and force an institution to contract with the student as a staff member instead. At a minimum, unionization forces institutions to define worker roles, which could help make the disparities more apparent between what is expected of most graduate students and the extraordinary workloads that a few graduate students take on, thereby providing those students with additional leverage in pursuing adequate compensation, appropriate contracts, etc.

It is clear that gWPAs' work and their feelings about that work are sometimes much more complicated than the previous literature suggests. Ultimately, we identified at least five of our interviewees as liminal WPAs. Pat and Sam were essentially "turned loose" to create the job they wanted or, at the very least, found their job duties dictated by the ends they were supposed to achieve, rather than the description they were given. Sam was asked to develop his own small program across multiple campus units and did so with little supervision. April seemed to have a tremendous amount of responsibility—more than any other participant except Emma—yet also had great support and mentorship from her faculty WPA. Christine and Emma both ran their programs on an interim basis; Laurie's position was much more substantial than those of gWPAs at her institution, involving partial oversight of one hundred course sections per semester and significant TA mentoring. She notes that "I think it's pretty easy for people to think that I am the one controlling everything" despite the presence of a faculty WPA. April, Laurie, Christine, Sam, and Emma were doing most of the work of a faculty WPA but with the institutional status and pay grade of graduate students.

The distinction of being a liminal WPA is important in considering how typical concerns about administrative work—compensation, workload, working conditions, power and authority necessary to do the job, others' perceptions of the WPA—are all exacerbated for graduate students and impact their ability to be successful in their jobs and in their academic and professional lives. Again, this distinction is even more important now, two years into a global pandemic with all its attendant pressures, than it was when we collected data. Graduate students are more exhausted and vulnerable than ever, and those who are also parents have been trying to juggle childcare for months upon months without necessarily receiving any kind of extension of funding to make their work more manageable. It is more important than ever before that they have achievable workloads and are compensated fairly.

April, Laurie, Christine, Sam, and Emma all reported being viewed as having the power of faculty WPAs even though faculty were sometimes present. These study participants did much of the work of faculty but that work was masked and minimized behind the label of "gWPA," which suggests that they were serving as office assistants or, at most, working closely with a faculty WPA and receiving careful mentorship. Yet Emma was actually the one *providing* mentorship to a faculty member while doing much of his work as he learned the new job. And they certainly weren't being compensated commensurately to the skills they were being asked to execute. Graduate WPAs are already in a risky position because they must negotiate the realities of their status and how an administrative position seems to affect the perceptions of others. While the position may entail goals and objectives more in line with the expectations of faculty WPAs, other faculty may view liminal gWPAs as little more than office assistants (e.g., descriptions in Latterell 2003, Pemberton 1993). Their fellow graduate students may see them and respond to them as superiors or department employees, while they are in fact navigating being just another graduate student in the program. While some of these issues may be present in traditional gWPA positions, they are strongly exacerbated within liminal positions.

The labels we use shape our understanding of the work, its resources, and its consequences. Thus, distinguishing between liminal WPAs and traditional gWPA positions is important for supporting liminal WPAs like

April, Laurie, Christine, Sam, and Emma in their work. Although the conventional wisdom has been to argue that graduate students, untenured, and NTT faculty should not be assigned to liminal positions to begin with, Charlton et al. (2011) and Elder, Schoen, and Skinnell (2014) show that the number of gWPAs in programs continues to increase, as does the number of graduate students interested in WPA work. Accordingly, the field's understanding of the distinctions between being a graduate or faculty WPA matters. When the work of liminal WPAs is hidden behind labels like "graduate student" or "staff," it enables the field to pretend that liminality doesn't exist—that people in those positions are something other than their realities and experiences dictate, leaving them out of the literature and professional discussions. Ignoring or masking liminal work hampers graduate students and all of us from developing a body of scholarship and professional support that will help them achieve success.

Because gWPAs like April, Laurie, Christine, Sam, and Emma lack the institutional status and power of faculty WPAs, the field needs to recognize the actual work they do in order to help them identify structures and develop strategies to succeed in that work. For example, the three of us coauthors found in our own gWPA experiences that it was important to think about power differently than faculty WPAs might. Though as graduate students the three of us lacked the kinds of formal power that faculty WPAs have, we recognized that we had valuable informal power that stemmed from doing a job that no one else wanted to do and grew through forging relationships with allies—support staff, librarians, other liminal university workers, and even members of upper administration. We also came to recognize that we could benefit ourselves and our programs by choosing different problems to tackle. For instance, instead of wide-scale curricular reform, Paul and Megan led efforts on a writing textbook project, something that the university wanted done but not badly enough for faculty members to show up and complete it. Talinn, who was interim director of the writing center, avoided trying to change institutional culture or initiate new projects like tutor observations or a new workshop series because she recognized that the returning director might see them as producing undesired additional work. Instead, she focused on completing short-term projects that had lasting effects like codifying policies, improving the scheduling system, and designing new marketing materials (see also Phillips, Shovlin, and Titus 2014; 2018). As a field, we need to help liminal university workers develop strategies to do their jobs successfully instead of assuming that strategies and scholarship developed for senior faculty will work for liminal workers or for all graduate student administrators.

In "An Exercise in Cognitive Dissonance: Liminal WPAs in Transition" (Phillips, Shovlin, and Titus, 2018), we suggest program-level responses to liminal positions, specifically liminal graduate students, in our midst. To highlight a few, we argue that programs must analyze their positions carefully, write accurate job descriptions that are widely understood and that are coupled with concrete mentoring, and envision gWPAs as invested in their programs for the long haul while also respecting their rights to leave a position. Although some of these shortcomings surrounding gWPAs' working conditions have been cited before, our research indicates that the field has not yet acted sufficiently on the results of its scholarship. We resist detailed suggestions here in order to emphasize the implications of our results for understanding graduate students in liminal positions; however, we would like to elaborate on the issue of compensation.

We need to compensate people based on their actual work, not on a job description of gWPA-as-office-assistant. We don't dispute that some graduate students primarily engage in low-stakes and lower skilled work; yet our findings demonstrate that others clearly do not. Difficult circumstances like faculty members' medical leaves and sabbaticals often lead to the creation of liminal positions that ask graduate students to step into roles initially designed for faculty. There are sometimes good reasons to create liminal positions and, in some cases, we believe that graduate students truly are the best people for those jobs. But there is no excuse for the wholly inadequate compensation that some of our participants described. It is not acceptable to ask graduate students to do the kind of supervisory and programmatic development work that Emma was doing and compensate them with a course release. It is not acceptable to create jobs like April's that regularly required thirty hours a week or more and compensate her with a course release. Offering graduate students liminal positions may be unavoidable; offering them inadequate compensation is a choice to exploit.

It is easy to dismiss liminal WPAs (and especially those who are graduate students) as aberrations—present only in bad programs that should be censured. This attitude misses the point: liminal gWPAs do exist. Our survey suggested that 20 to 30% of the graduate students who responded are most likely liminal WPAs. The interviews, which we conducted with participants from a wide range of graduate programs, confirmed that liminal WPAs are a real presence across a variety of graduate programs. Given the prevalence and continued expansion of gWPA positions, it is imperative that the field do more to understand the work that graduate students *actually* do and the impacts of that work. Our study clearly shows that gWPA positions vary tremendously, and it is thus important that both graduate students and faculty are honest about what a given position entails. Note that we are not (and explicitly reject) arguing that all gWPA positions should be simply office assistant work in a highly structured, mentored environment. Nor are we arguing that no gWPA position should fit that model. A graduate student like Pat had the opportunity to be a liminal WPA but seems to have preferred a more traditional gWPA position. Students like Sam (and the three of us) reveled in doing liminal WPA work and having such freedom and responsibility to chart our own courses. Emma, perhaps, would have been happy as a liminal WPA if she had felt that her work was really valued.

We are less concerned with the details of gWPAs' duties than about ensuring that we are all honest about what that work is, treat it with due respect, and provide *all* WPAs with tools to do that work successfully. Thus, it is vital that graduate students and all WPAs have access to adequate training and support to do their work and that they are compensated appropriately for it. Finally, the most vital takeaway from this study is that we must listen to the tales that gWPAs tell in order to adequately revise our own narratives, which influence how we supervise, teach, collaborate with, and facilitate graduate students' development.

Works Cited

Brown, Tessa. 2023. "Introduction." In *Graduate Students at Work: Exploited Scholars of Neoliberal Higher Ed*, 1–25. Lawrence: University Press of Kansas.

Charlton, Colin, Jonikka Charlton, Tarez Samra Graban, Kathleen J. Ryan, and Amy Ferdinandt Stolley. 2011. *GenAdmin: Theorizing WPA Identities in the Twenty-First Century*. Anderson, SC: Parlor Press.

Ebest, Sally Barr. 1999. "The Next Generation of WPAs: A Study of Graduate Students in Composition/Rhetoric." *WPA: Writing Program Administration* 22, no. 3 (Spring): 65–84.

Edgington, Anthony, and Stacy Hartlage Taylor. 2007. "Invisible Administrators: The Possibilities and Perils of Graduate Student Administration." *WPA: Writing Program Administration* 31, nos. 1–2 (Fall/Winter): 150–170.

Elder, Cristyn L., Megan Schoen, and Ryan Skinnell. 2014. "Strengthening Graduate Student Preparation for WPA Work." *WPA: Writing Program Administration* 37, no. 2 (Spring): 13–35.

Geisler, Cheryl. 2004. *Analyzing Streams of Language: Twelve Steps to the Systematic Coding of Text, Talk, and Other Verbal Data*. New York: Pearson Longman.

Helmbrecht, Brenda M., and Connie Kendall. 2008. "Graduate Students Hearing Voices: (Mis)Recognition and (Re)Definition of the jWPA Identity." In *Untenured Faculty as Writing Program Administrators*, edited by Debra Frank Dew and Alice Horning, 172–190. West Lafayette, IN: Parlor Press.

Inman, Joyce Olewski. 2011. "Reflections on Year One as an Almost-WPA." *WPA: Writing Program Administration* 35, no. 1 (Fall/Winter): 149–152.

Jukuri, Stephen Davenport, and W. J. Williamson. 1999. "How to Be a Wishy-Washy Graduate Student WPA, or Undefined but Overdetermined." In *Kitchen Cooks, Plate Twirlers and Troubadours: Writing Program Administrators Tell Their Stories*, edited by Diana George, 105–119. Portsmouth, NH: Boynton/Cook.

Latterell, Catherine. 2003. "Defining Roles for Graduate Students in Writing Program Administration: Balancing Pragmatic Needs with a Postmodern Ethics of Action." *WPA: Writing Program Administration* 27, nos. 1–2 (Fall/Winter): 23–39.

Mattison, Michael. 2008. "Just between Me and Me: A Letter to Myself about Being a Graduate Student Tutor and Administrator." In *(E)merging Identities: Graduate Students in the Writing Center*, edited by Melissa Nicolas, 11–23. Southlake, TX: Fountainhead.

Pemberton, Michael. 1993. "Tales Too Terrible to Tell: Unstated Truths and Underpreparation in Graduate Composition Programs." In *Writing Ourselves into the Story: Unheard Voices from Composition Studies*, edited by Sheryl Fontaine and Susan Hunter, 154–173. Carbondale: Southern Illinois University Press.

Phillips, Talinn, Paul Shovlin, and Megan L. Titus. 2014. "Thinking Liminally: Exploring the (Com)Promising Positions of the Liminal WPA." *WPA: Writing Program Administration* 38, no. 1 (Fall): 42–63.

———. 2016. "(Re)Identifying the gWPA Experience." *WPA: Writing Program Administration* 40, no. 1 (Fall): 67–89.

———. 2018. "An Exercise in Cognitive Dissonance: Liminal WPAs in Transition." In *WPAs in Transition*, edited by Courtney Adams Wooten, Jacob Babb, and Brian Ray, 70–83. Logan, CO: Utah State University Press.

Stolley, Amy Ferdinandt. 2015. "Narratives, Administrative Identity, and the Early Career WPA." *WPA: Writing Program Administration* 39, no. 1 (Fall): 18–31.

White, Edward M. 2002. "Teaching a Graduate Course in Writing Program Administration." In *The Writing Program Administrator's Resource: A Guide to Reflective Institutional Practice*, edited by Stuart C. Brown and Theresa Enos, 101–112. Mahwah, NJ: Erlbaum.

Appendix A: Representative Topic List for Interviews

Background

- Would you define yourself as a WPA? Why or why not?
- How would you define and describe that WPA position?
- Why did you choose to take this position?
- How was this position described to you? What was your job description? And, would you recommend this position to a friend? Or, how did you explain it to the person following you?
- If you hold a WPA position at your institution, what kind of position

is it? Through what process did you apply for the position? What compensation was provided?

Details of the WPA Experience

Material Perspective

- How are your position, job duties, benefits, etc. different than those of non-graduate student administrators? Describe work environment in comparison with other administrative staff (e.g., own office, shared with fewer people, computer access, printer access, location of office relative to where the work has to be done, travel funding).
- How visible is/was your WPA identity, and how visible are/were the job requirements for that position?

Relationships

- Describe your relationships with other grad students and/or faculty. Did they change when you became a WPA and, if so, how?
- To what extent do/did you feel protected in your position?
- What mentoring did you receive in your WPA position?
- Who or what was your support system in this WPA position?

Effect of Experience

- How satisfied are you in your WPA position?
- What were the benefits and drawbacks of current (and any past) WPA position?
- How has the current (and/or past) WPA position impacted your work?
- How has the position impacted your WPA self-identity?
- How has the position impacted others' perceptions of the senior writing program administrator and of the discipline in general?
- To what extent do you feel that your WPA identity is represented in the existing scholarship?
- If you are on, or recently have been on, the job market, how do you frame your WPA experience?
- How likely are you to accept another WPA position as a graduate

student, as a faculty member (before or after tenure), or as non-TT faculty/staff?

Preparing Future WPAs

- What preparation did you have before taking on your WPA role?
- What other aspects of WPA work were you exposed to but didn't necessarily have to do?
- What does the field need to do in order to better prepare future WPAs?
- Which of the following definitions of a WPA position most resonate with your graduate student WPA experience?
    - a WPA position that is going through a shift, phasing in or out a position or center at an institution, and thus often GSA or non-credentialed, non-diploma'ed individuals are hired. The institution or hiring committee might not have a background in composition and rhetoric or knowledge of what a specialist might bring to the position.
    - a position taken by GSA or non-credentialed, non-diploma'ed individual for a temporary period of time.
    - a position in which a GSA or non-credentialed, non-diploma'ed individual is expected to engage in WPA-like (full blown WPA) work.
    - a GSA or non-credentialed, non-diploma'ed individual's state as they learn real WPA work by engaging it from their disempowered point of view, rather than through curriculum that directly related to WPA work.

Appendix B: Coding Scheme

Dimension 1: gWPA Life

List of Categories

Note: Megan is the interviewer; her text should not be considered part of the coding. If you strongly feel that more than one code applies, then we prefer that you apply the codes "mentoring" or "workload" over the other codes.

Mentoring: Code as **Mentoring** any topical chain in which the participant . . .

- Refers to a direct relationship with a senior faculty member in which the senior faculty member provides direction and guidance or a lack thereof (e.g., senior WPA, boss, etc.)
- Refers to aspects of the graduate program that did/didn't prepare the participant for the job
- Refers to aspects of the field at large that did/didn't prepare the participants for the job

Resources: Code as **Resources** any topical chain in which the speaker . . .

- Refers to specific material conditions of the job, e.g., technology, office space, support staff (secretaries and/or underlings), travel funding

Workload: Code as **Workload** any topical chain in which the speaker . . .

- Refers to the volume of work he/she must complete
- Describes the type of work he/she completes
- Discusses how he/she feels about that work

Personal Life: Code as **Personal Life** any topical chain in which the speaker . . .

- Refers to any impact on personal well-being (e.g., illness, sleep, diet/exercise, etc.)
- Refers to any impact on personal relationships (e.g., family, significant other, friendships, etc.)

Academic/Professional Life: Code as **Academic/Professional Life** any topical chain in which the speaker . . .

- Refers to any impact on schoolwork (e.g., dissertation progress)
- Refers to any impact on relationships with colleagues (e.g., visibility of position to other graduate students)
- Refers to any impact on career (e.g., job market, current job, etc.)

Null: Code as **Null** any topical chain to which none of the above categories apply.

- The interviewer (Megan) is the only speaker in the topical chain.
- The topical chain refers to some condition of the interview (e.g.,

sneezing, needing to close a window, needing to answer a phone call).
- The topical chain serves as the introduction or conclusion to the interview or provides instructions about how the interview will be conducted.
- The topical chain is otherwise "off topic" for the interview.
- The topical chain is "on topic" but still doesn't fit any of these categories (e.g., responses to how one applied for the position and respondents' recognition of WPA scholarship sometimes qualify as "null").

Dimension 2: Affect

1. *After coding for gWPA experience, please re-code each category according to the participant's affect/feelings/emotional response to that aspect of experience.*
2. *If the code for gWPA Experience was "null" then that cell must also be coded "null" for affect.*
3. *If the speaker describes both positive and negative aspects of the experience, then choose the predominant affect (i.e. choose either positive or negative).*

List of Categories

Negative Affect: Code as negative affect any topical chain in which the speaker . . .

- Refers to their gWPA experience as being overwhelming, more than anticipated
- Refers to their gWPA experience as negatively impacting other aspects of academic life (e.g., schoolwork, academic relationships, future job prospects)
- Refers to their gWPA experience as negatively impacting other aspects of personal life (e.g., family time)
- Refers to their gWPA experience using adjectives that infer a negative affect, such as "resentful," "stressful," "frantic," "crazy," etc.

Positive Affect: Code as positive affect any topical chain in which the speaker . . .

- Refers to their gWPA experience as manageable, as meeting expectations

- Refers to their gWPA experience as positively impacting other aspects of academic life (e.g., schoolwork, academic relationships, future job prospects)
- Refers to their gWPA experience as positively impacting other aspects of personal life (e.g., family time)
- Refers to their gWPA experience using adjectives that infer a positive affect, such as "passionate," "exciting," "satisfying," etc.

Neutral Affect: Code as neutral affect any topical chain in which the speaker refers to his/her gWPA experience but there is no indication of positive or negative feelings about that experience.

Interlude 4

The Ethics of Progressive Internships

Meagan Gacke-Reed

In the fall of 2017, I received an email from the associate dean of the Liberal Arts College at Texas Christian University (TCU) where I was a doctoral student, asking for feedback regarding graduate student interest in cross-departmental, paid internships for the following summer. Prior to this email, I was not aware of any coordinated effort, departmental or otherwise, to place liberal arts graduate students in internships. I responded positively, stating that I would apply for such an internship if given the opportunity. My positive reaction was grounded in my interconnected professional and personal realities and aspirations. As a PhD student in English literature, I was on a nine-month stipend, with limited opportunities for livable-wage university funding through the summer months. In addition, after arriving in Fort Worth to pursue my PhD in 2014, I had gained a partner and a stepdaughter, tying me to the region. Given my new unwillingness to relocate after graduation, I was poignantly aware that I needed to be open to alternative careers. Tenure-track jobs are limited in our area and adjuncting after graduation was not an option: my partner makes a working-class wage, which is increasingly unlivable for a family in the growing DFW metroplex. I considered this internship, then, a jumping-off point for cultivating wider professional experience and making connections outside the university as I explored "alt-ac," alternatives to academia, careers.

In the spring of 2018, Associate Dean Peter Worthing sent a follow-up email to the students who had expressed interest. The email we received read as follows:

> [The Liberal Arts] College is collaborating with [our school of business], which has developed an undergraduate Entrepreneurial Intern Program (EIP). This program places undergraduate business students as summer interns at local businesses in order to gain valuable experience with up-and-coming businesses. This is a unique opportunity for [Liberal Arts College] graduate stu-

dents to expand their skill set and explore employment opportunities beyond academia.

I submitted an application to EIP, noting my expert written communication skills. The program matched me with a local startup, a life-science supplier search engine I'll call SciSearch. The startup's owner needed an intern to manage her digital presence and social media accounts while she chased new leads as part of the launch phase of her business. At our first meeting, my new boss explained to me her career experience in the life sciences marketing industry, and how her experience led her to see a gap in the marketing process, which her present entrepreneurial journey sought to fill. Admittedly, after my first meeting with her, I felt overwhelmed and underprepared; I had to google the term *life sciences* before I fully understood how SciSearch fit into the larger pharmaceutical industry. However, my countless experiences encountering and mastering new and difficult subject matter in the graduate classroom suddenly became a transferable skill as I committed to reading and comprehending as much publicly available information as I could about this industry.

Over the course of the summer internship, my job duties included the following:

- Researching and practicing business-to-business (B2B) social media content development, dissemination, and engagement for SciSearch's Twitter account and my boss's personal LinkedIn account;
- Performing keyword searches to discover new business leads on LinkedIn's Business Service search engine, revising keyword search procedures as necessary to produce the best lead-generating results;
- Giving guidance to my boss on how to apply General Data Protection Regulation (GDPR) provisions to SciSearch's Terms and Conditions of Use;
- Creating and editing professional blog content for the SciSearch website.

When the summer internship was over, I returned to TCU to work as a graduate student for a stipend, accepting an administrative aid role instead of returning to the writing classroom. I soon discovered how my internship skills transferred back to this new role. As the graduate assistant in the Office of Research and Graduate Studies, I managed the separate social media pages for the Office of Research and the Office of Graduate Studies. While working for SciSearch, I had learned how to use tagging trends to attract followers, so I used this methodology to increase the number of followers on the offices' social media pages. I also had discovered the significance of using LinkedIn to make meaningful, professional connections in today's job market. Given this point, I convinced our dean to include an interactive presentation on LinkedIn during our Graduate Student Career Boot Camp. As for my work with the GDPR, I didn't suspect that reading the language of the GDPR over the summer would be the first of many moments that I read and applied federal law to practice; as an aid in the Office of Research, I applied federal law and guidance to practice every day when I reviewed research protocol. Finally, when the director of research compliance at TCU asked if I would review and edit the research compliance policy documents she was getting ready to publish, I said yes, and I felt confident in my ability to be an editor.

I have two strong reactions to my experience participating in what was viewed as a progressive internship opportunity for liberal arts PhD students at TCU. First, holistically, the internship fit well into the larger narrative I was writing about my professional identity while I was a graduate student. In this narrative, I am trained to adapt quickly, multitask, manage and organize large projects, and manage/write administrative business communication. Perhaps, then, cross-departmental internships can be a way for liberal arts graduate students seeking alt-ac careers to strengthen their marketability after graduation. My second reaction is to view my internship at SciSearch as lacking in its ability to propel me toward full-time employment after graduation. Ultimately, my summer dip into the world of private-sector employment left me with no real connections to future professional work. SciSearch was a fresh start-up, so the owner was not hiring for full-time positions. Even if she was, while I performed well, her first hire was not going to be an English PhD graduate student who had no idea how to create/build/manage a business start-up. Truth be told, undergraduate students from TCU's school of business were exponentially more knowledgeable regarding entrepreneurial journeys than I was as a doctoral student in English.

So, how can universities effectively implement alt-ac professionalization for PhD students, especially those in the liberal arts? I suggest a progressive but purposeful vision. Do these students have accessible mentors who are actively building professional networks for alt-ac students to join? How is the department advertising graduate students as ideal candidates for industry jobs in the local community? Graduate students pursuing alt-ac futures need tangible support from within the department to gain experience and make connections. Given this point, liberal arts departments may have to consider *purposefully* hiring nontraditional, or *progressive*, professors and mentors.

I left TCU in August 2020. My status at the time of my departure was ABD—"all but dissertation" to degree completion. I did not have a single mentor from my department who could help me navigate what turned out to be a long five months until I accepted an entry-level position in a clinical research compliance role. I currently work for another clinical research organization as a study start-up specialist. I did not mention my internship with SciSearch during interviews for these roles because the internship simply did not provide clear evidence of alt-ac professionalization.

3 | "It's Dangerous to Go Alone"
Explorations of Unbalanced Labor and Mentorship in a Blended Learning Doctoral Program

April Cobos and Megan Mize

Introduction

When doctoral programs expand their offerings to include remote learning options, on-campus and distance students inevitably experience labor and community differently. Ethical issues can arise as a result of institutional reliance on the unpaid labor of graduate students, particularly those completing their degrees on campus, as they negotiate issues with hybrid educational formats. While recent research has typically explored experiences and obstacles particular to distance students, as well as the impact on community within blended learning environments at the undergraduate and graduate levels (Philipsen et al. 2019; Vanslambrouck et al. 2019; Kyei-Blankson, Ntuli, and Donnelly 2016), it has only begun to consider the implications for on-campus student labor in hybrid graduate programs.

While the data collected in this chapter reflects pre-pandemic working conditions, the urgency of this work has only increased due to the changes in the educational landscape as a result of COVID-19's impact. During the spring 2021 semester, graduate enrollment increased sharply, up by 4.3% compared to the previous spring; many graduate programs adopted online elements, offering either fully remote or hybrid options (Wood 2021). More people were able to take advantage of the flexibility offered by a hybrid graduate experience. Additionally, the president of the Council of Graduate Schools, Suzanne Ortega, acknowledges "the importance of increased flexibility in delivery methods" in fostering diversity and inclusion in graduate programs as well, stating, "We've long believed that improved access would further diversify the graduate student body, and these data provide supporting evidence" (Hazelrigg 2021). The pivot to online instruction during the pandemic has broadly normalized and illustrated the opportunities hybrid and online graduate programs offer to increase the applicant pool and generate revenue. This recognition has led to an increase in the creation of permanently hybrid or fully online programs (Wood 2021).

With such high stakes amid rapidly changing teaching and learning environments, now more than ever it is necessary to recognize how such alterations rely on, yet often obscure, the work of on-campus students. Digital hybridization efforts may include designing courses for universal access, establishing professional opportunities, and generating informal social events necessary for building community beyond coursework. In many instances, this essential work will fall to graduate students, who take on tasks such as transcribing audio, sharing materials, or repeating comments made in the room so remote students might better follow the conversation. This work has an additional element of personal risk during an on-going pandemic, as on-campus students now run the danger of exposure to a virus that may have long-term consequences for them. While this labor is increasingly necessary and a vital component to helping programs, faculty, and peers navigate the online learning environment, budget restrictions and entrenched notions of what counts as "labor" have largely prevented an increase in financial support for graduate students engaged in both the formally recognized and informal—and thus typically unacknowledged—labor of facilitating hybrid learning experiences, community, and access.

By considering a specific example, this chapter details the ways in which local and distance students' experiences diverge, particularly in regard to mentorship opportunities, resulting in undue expectations on residential students to address programmatic and social gaps for their peers. Examining these concerns in a relatively young program can help other graduate programs acknowledge and address the realities of graduate student labor within increasingly digital and blended learning environments.

Study Background: Program Context

Established in 2006, the English doctoral program at Old Dominion University (ODU) was one of the first to offer a distance-learning option to students seeking a terminal degree in English studies. On its official website, the PhD program describes itself as offering "innovative," "creative reinterpretations" of fields within the English discipline (ODU English Department 2019). Originally conceived as a professional writing PhD for individuals already working in related fields, the online option emerged, in part, as an effort to appeal to potential students connected to regional military bases. As the program proposal was prepared for the State Council of Higher Education for Virginia, the program evolved into a more extensive English studies degree. In 2019 the program claimed to appeal to "those who are pursuing an academic career as well as to professionals with careers outside the classroom or at another educational institution" (ODU English Department 2019). At that time, the doctoral program offered multiple tracks such as literary and cultural studies; rhetoric, writing, and discourse; and technology and media. Students could choose between full- or part-time status, as well as on-campus or distance options. For those who opted to participate at a distance, residency requirements could be met through a two-week Summer Doctoral Institute (SDI), which consists of hybrid and fully on-site courses. According to ODU's Institutional Research Department, between the inception of the program in 2006 and the spring 2018 graduation, one hundred forty-six students had been enrolled in the program, with ninety classified as "off-campus students," fifty-one classified as "on-campus students," and five having both on- and off- campus status. During this same period, thirty-six English PhD degrees were conferred, twenty to off-campus students and sixteen to on-campus students.

There are two options for coursework in the program: synchronous and asynchronous. The majority of classes meet synchronously, meaning that both campus and distance students must be available at a particular block of time once or twice a week for a live class. Campus students will typically attend class in the physical buildings of the campus with the assigned course professor, who is local and campus-based, while distance students attend online via software like Zoom. Typically, the distance students can see the campus classroom with the camera focused on the instructor; the cameras pan to a student in the classroom if they touch the button to speak. Those in the physical classroom can see all of the distance students on a large projection screen. These details on ODU's English doctoral program are vital to understanding the unique situation experienced by this particular set of graduate students. The graduate program pioneered a new way of offering advanced learning opportunities, prioritizing technologies and pedagogies for distance learning.

However, the technical delivery of distance courses has unintentionally led to a lack of focus on the more traditional and exceedingly important component of the graduate experience: mentorship. Faculty mentorship is more readily accessible on campus, leading to a void that must be filled for distance learners. More specifically, the dichotomy between "on-campus" and "distance" students can lead to bifurcated experiences in regard to labor expectations and community formation. Our findings confirm that on-campus graduate students are often implicitly expected to support the learning experience of distance colleagues within courses and beyond. Such uncompensated, and often unacknowledged, obligations include maintaining peer mentorship systems, disseminating program information informally, and creating social and professional events.

As these residential students foster a productive doctoral community outside official program parameters, they also take part in course work, research, and assistantships. Tensions arise when distance students, graduate faculty, and program administrators assume that residential students are capable of managing these extra responsibilities and tasks without considering how such labor might impact performance and mental health within a rigorous academic program. Residential students, who are notably in the minority, are inadvertently responsible for supporting the majority's (distance students') learning experience and altruistically strive to use their perceived agency through voluntary peer mentorship to address systemic gaps in the technical and emotional structure of a relatively new program.

This chapter is inspired by the authors' pre-pandemic experiences as graduates of ODU's English doctoral program. We began our graduate experience as on-campus students; Megan Mize completed both her coursework and dissertation as a residential student, while April Cobos completed her coursework at ODU and then her dissertation while living abroad due to her partner's career. Thus, we acknowledge that our experiences color our perceptions of peer mentorship and programmatic gaps. During our tenure as on-campus students, we were actively involved in generating opportunities for community-building and professional development for our colleagues. Fortunately, we were spared the experience of completing our graduate work and supporting our peers during a pandemic. However, we witnessed and responded to entrenched institutional patterns and barriers that we expect have continued with expanded hybrid and remote instruction at ODU and beyond.

Sometimes, our efforts to support our peers were part of our roles as officers for the English Graduate Organization (EGO), a graduate student organization recognized and supported by the university. The organization's goal was to help foster professional and personal connections between all English graduate students (both master's and doctoral level) at ODU. As voluntary officers, we and others organized panels on professionalizing topics, such as conference preparation, job searches, preparing a CV, and publication. In the absence of departmental or university opportunities, the organization also secured additional means of travel funding for conferences, a necessary part of professionalizing and networking in academia, and hosted socializing opportunities for both campus and distance students, as a way to help develop camaraderie among the graduate students and with the faculty.

However, much of this labor occurred far outside the parameters of EGO. For instance, during one of the first SDIs, distance students would arrive on campus to find no one there to greet them, guide them to the dorms, or share campus information (such as a map, housing guidelines, food services, or parking information). Distance students spent two weeks going to classes, returning to the dorms, working on classwork, and then heading home, rarely interacting with non-institute faculty or on-campus peers as the latter did not take part in summer courses. In subsequent summer semesters, both the authors and other residential students strove to redress this lack by creating a series of events, both social and professional, to foster a sense of belonging. This work was entirely voluntary on the campus students' part, as the graduate organization was only active and funded during the regular academic year (August through May).

As a result, confusion abounded regarding the department's responsibility for this oversight. Distance students often assumed the department facilitated these events and thus should receive credit or even rebuke (if students were not satisfied with the efforts made). Of course, the confusion arose because the department's website describes SDI's events as follows: "The SDI facilitates programmatic needs such as community building, research development, and faculty-student interaction ... Local students are also encouraged to register and participate, as the English Graduate Organization has extracurricular planning as part of the SDI's program" (ODU English Department 2019). Yet, the graduate organization extracurricular planning is not officially overseen by the department, despite being mentioned on the department website. As such, during our tenure as officers at least, much of residential students' efforts on behalf of distance students was unpaid, yet often taken for granted as part of the SDI program. There was never a formal or sustained collaboration between the organization and the department, nor a strong faculty presence in this planning to engage distance students during their stay in the local area.

Campus students also established and ran Dissertation Bootcamp, which Megan created, and others facilitated over the years, to address the void following coursework. Initially designed as a three-day, writing-intensive retreat with invited speakers such as the university style editor, the bootcamp continued for years with English department participants at all stages of the process, from pre-prospectus students to alumni. Each year, the on-campus, multiday bootcamp was designed and facilitated by students for students during the summer. Throughout the year, individual participants continued to voluntarily facilitate bootcamp days, often communicating entirely via social media and distance conferencing software like Zoom. Notably, the bootcamp operated without any formal departmental support; it was, at its core, a writing group. Yet at one point, a faculty graduate program director wanted to include the Dissertation Bootcamp on the official program website as an example of a unique resource the *program* offered, highlighting the ways the department capitalized on and coopted unpaid student labor.

Not all peer efforts to generate opportunities and decrease the disparities in learning experiences are complex in nature. The students within this particular hybrid program often work in small ways to support each other, from collaborative Google Docs for real-time shared notes, to backchannels so that students in the physical classroom can report immediately when there are technical issues with audio or visual elements, to the creation and maintenance of social media spaces to share and discuss the expectations of a program whose representatives may seem unreachable. Campus students often serve as intermediaries by establishing an online connection during class time, typically through platforms like Facebook's Messenger, Slack, or Discord, because doing so allows distance students to receive a timely response to a question or even a technical difficulty while the instructor is focused on delivering the course content. Still other instances of efforts to address gaps exist, with both campus and distance students striving to manage technological, programmatic, and emotional concerns for one another. Such emotional and, sometimes, physical labor is exceedingly important, yet often occurs without overt acknowledgment, becoming a sort of invisible thread within the tapestry of the program, without which much of it would unravel.

We offer this localized example of a hybrid graduate program as a means of illustrating the often invisible and unacknowledged work graduate students perform for one another. Through our study, it is possible to witness the way peer mentorship is strategically used as a means of attempting to create and share agency and access. In the survey we discuss below, on-campus students report a stronger sense of individual agency, which in this context roughly translates to their ability to influence their learning experience. Residential students also acknowledge their ability to approach faculty and administrators to solicit information and results, which likely leads to this sense of agency. When their distance colleagues report a disconnectedness and a lack of access from such opportunities, they sometimes remark that their peers are the ones addressing that void. Some distance students even assume it is the residential students' obligation to do so.

Our findings suggest that some distance graduate students view their campus peers as actants for facilitating their learning experience, responsible for creating opportunities for access to the program and enabling their agency. We also found that residential students appear to accept that their access is a privilege their distance colleagues do not have and, in some cases, explicitly work to use their proximity to others' advantage. This sort of exchange, often rooted in a sense of cohort and collegiality, can also be understood as invisible or emotional labor that residential students feel obligated to fulfill because of their positionality and agency (Payne 2019). As such, the work of residential students can be likened to the nineteenth-century concept of the "angel in the household," in which domestic and emotional labor was feminized and erased (Woolf 1979 [1904]). (Indeed, one survey respondent even referred to Megan as "a saint.") Likewise, in the absence of programmatic structures dedicated to addressing the communication and professional development gaps in a hybrid program, residential students' seemingly "voluntary" labor is, in fact, necessary in order to foster the well-being of peers during the learning process, prepare students for professional life beyond the program, and ensure the reputation of their doctoral program. Yet due to the voluntary nature of this work and students' subordinate position within the hierarchy of academia, this work is easily appropriated and often unacknowledged. If this work is not rendered visible and its value recognized, such exploitation will only intensify as more institutions establish permanently hybrid graduate programs in the wake of COVID-19.

Research Questions and Methodology

Our own experiences in the program shaped the following research questions related to the graduate labor required to address systemic gaps in support within a hybrid program: (1) How does the hybrid approach to programmatic delivery impact both the residential and distance populations, in terms of labor and agency? (2) While students can access the classroom regardless of their location, what opportunities for learning and mentoring are available to students in a hybrid graduate program outside of class time? (3) What consequences does it have on all student populations when peers, moving through the graduate process themselves, take on the work of generating and sharing program information, professional development, support mechanisms (both technical and emotional), and so on, that have traditionally been the purview of faculty and administrators? (4) How do students come to view their roles within a system that privileges courses as the only learning experience students need without mechanisms to encourage the more peripheral learning opportunities of the traditional graduate experience? (5) Most importantly, what strategies could address such issues as universities increasingly lean into the hybrid/distance models at all levels?

Since the authors both graduated from the program identifying as campus students and served in roles associated with a residential doctoral student identity, we developed a survey for both campus and distance students who are currently in the program or recently graduated in an attempt to create a more comprehensive picture of student perceptions of the program, peer mentorship, and student labor and, hopefully, to establish clearer answers to the questions above. Thus, the survey questions focus on students' experiences participating in events established by the department and those established by peers, their perceptions of opportunities for mentorship with faculty and peers, the perceived challenges of working with faculty or peers, and the reasons why they did or did not participate in such activities.

Ultimately, we used the survey to illuminate alternate strategies for increasing distance student engagement and perceived agency without perpetuating the need to rely on campus colleagues' volunteerism. As graduate programs increasingly move into digital spaces, it is vital to identify ethical strategies for addressing barriers to successful learning and professional development for doctoral students within blended learning environments.

Survey Results

In May 2019 we deployed a survey with seventeen total questions, ten multiple-choice and seven open-ended, through Google Forms. We recruited participants via social media groups of current and former ODU English program doctoral students. In total, the survey received thirty-three responses from students identifying themselves at various stages of the program or as having completed the program, as can be seen in figure 3.1.

Of the thirty-three respondents, nine (27%) had completed the dissertation program, eight (24%) were students currently in coursework, seven (21%) were working on their dissertation projects, six (18%) were currently working on their prospectus, two (6%) were currently studying

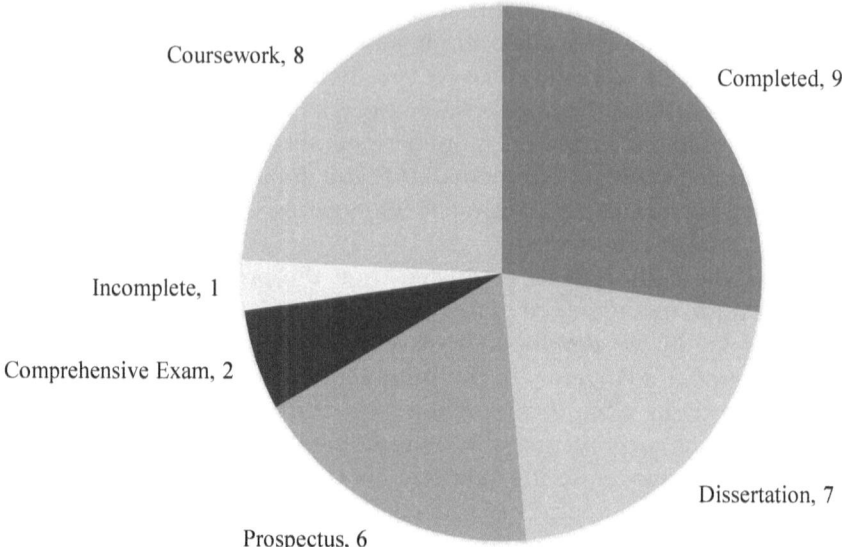

Figure 3.1, Current program status of survey respondents.

for comprehensive examinations, and one (3%) responded they did not complete the program, identified in figure 3.1 as "incomplete," although this student did not specify if they dropped the program by choice or maxed out in time per university regulations. Of the thirty-three respondents, only thirty-two answered the question regarding their status as a campus or distance student, by which twenty-three indicated they were distance students, defined as students who do not live in the immediate or surrounding area of the university or who do not attend classes during the school year on campus; while five respondents identified as campus students, or those regularly attending classes on the physical campus in Norfolk, Virginia. The remaining four respondents indicated that they had been both a campus and a distance student at some phase of the program. Although our survey does not account for variables such as race, gender, disability, and family status, we recognize these are also important factors in regard to students' opportunities for success. As such we offer our conclusions with the acknowledgment that other variables may have significantly influenced the respondents' experiences.

The respondents were asked about their employment status during the course of the program. Eighteen of the thirty-three (55%) indicated they were full-time employed in teaching or academia beyond a graduate student appointment. Of those eighteen, sixteen (89%) were distance

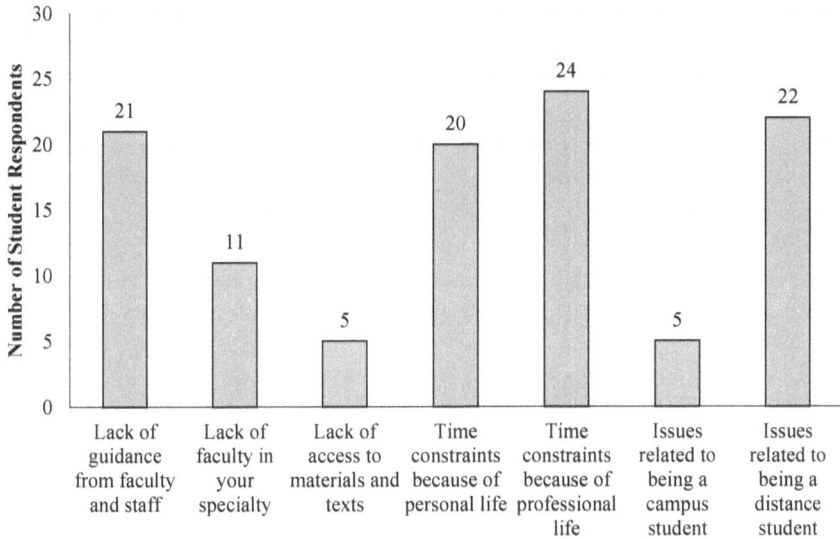

Figure 3.2, Challenges faced by doctoral student participants throughout their programs.

students. Another two distance students indicated they were employed full-time outside of the university setting, in software development and marketing jobs. Only one campus student indicated only being employed as a teaching assistant, while the remaining twelve students indicated some kind of mixture of academic employment or a change of employment status throughout the course of the program. Nine students indicated they had been officers of the graduate student organization and/or had organized events and workshops. Six of those nine were residential students during at least part of their tenure in the program. Five of the thirty-three indicated they "Facilitated Events for Writing Accountability" and nineteen of the thirty-three replied they participated in these writing accountability activities. Thirty students indicated they "Attended Workshops and Events" while thirty-one acknowledged they "Attended the Summer Doctoral Institute." The SDI is mandatory for all distance students, and for campus students who are taking a summer course.

The researchers also included a multiple-choice question inquiring into what has been the most challenging for students during the course of the program. Respondents could select as many answers as needed. Figure 3.2 depicts the results.

The top four challenges reported by all respondents were: time constraints because of professional life (73%), issues related to being a distance student (67%), lack of guidance from faculty and staff (64%), and time constraints because of personal life (61%). In conjunction with this question, the participants were asked if they felt their role as a distance or campus student impacted their ability to successfully navigate the program. In response, twenty-two of twenty-three (96%) distance students said yes, and of nine identified campus students, five (56%) said they were impacted, as well.

In a follow-on, open-ended question asking for additional information about how they felt their role as a distance or campus student impacted their experience, which received thirty-one responses, there was a clear disparity. Two distance students gave positive replies: "Best possible situation for myself and financial situation and family" and "Being able to take classes as a distance student is making this PhD possible. There are very few universities offering a Comp/Rhet PhD within driving distance of my home/work." Three distance students offered more neutral or equivocal statements, but the twenty remaining distance respondents had lengthy replies that indicated four major themes in regard to their additional constraints or challenges as distance students:

- Lack of access and personal connection to faculty
- Lack of communication between faculty through the available technological tools (email, Skype, etc.)
- Difficulty in obtaining programmatic resources and information
- Feeling disconnected from the program as a whole

In contrast, only one campus student noted additional challenges related to being a campus student, which was expressed as "expectations placed on campus students to participate in campus activities and support distance students," while the other responses indicated an overall positive experience related to being on campus, such as "I think being a campus student has given me more access to faculty and more opportunities to network with them, to get opportunities to collaborate or get more out of a course."

One of the final sets of questions focused on peer mentorship. In response to the question "Have you received support or mentorship from peers within the program," thirty-one students indicated yes (94%) while one student indicated no, and one student indicated maybe. In a follow-on, multiple-choice question, which asked about both official and unofficial peer mentorship, respondents replied they received the kinds of support indicated in figure 3.3. (Again, they could select as many answers as they wanted.)

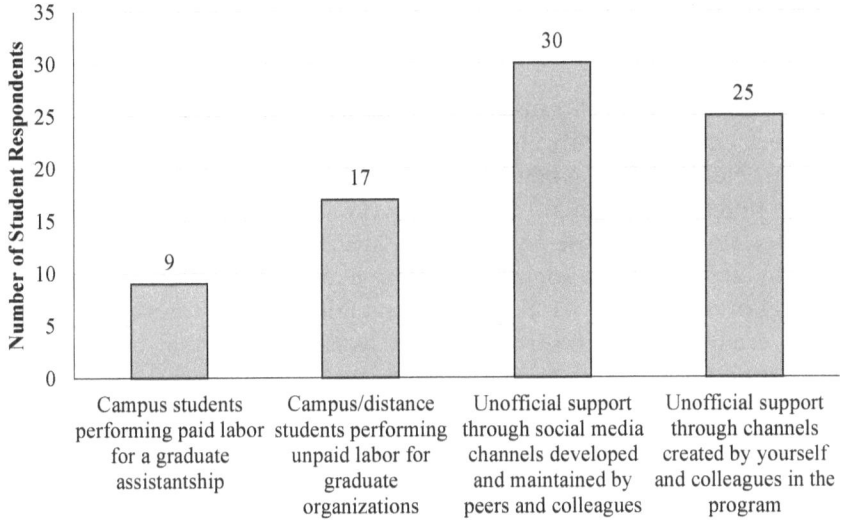

Figure 3.3, Types of peer support and mentorship received by participants.

For this question, the intention was to determine the kind of peer support students felt they had received throughout the program. We wanted to see if distance students assumed the campus students did have a paid role, such as through a graduate assistantship that covered these peer mentorship opportunities, and to determine the kinds of peer support both distance and campus students found to be the most beneficial. The numbers indicate that the majority of students found the most productive support through unofficial channels, with thirty of thirty-two respondents checking "Unofficial Support through Social Media Developed and Maintained by Peers and Colleagues." This trend toward valuing informal peer support is further emphasized as twenty-five respondents (76%) marked "Unofficial Support through Channels Created by Yourself and Colleagues in the Program." Only nine (27%) felt like they received paid support from peers through official channels like graduate assistantships, in positions like the assistant to the graduate program director. Seventeen (52%) believed they received assistance or support by campus or distance students performing unpaid labor. This highlights the often-invisible nature of voluntary peer mentorship as labor, as many distance students did not recognize either paid or unpaid labor as being as imperative as social media or self-created channels.

Respondents were also asked in a closed-ended question to rate their satisfaction with mentorship opportunities formally offered by the department or faculty. Strikingly, a majority of respondents indicated some level of dissatisfaction or neutrality. Eleven (33%) respondents reported feeling neutral, eight (24%) dissatisfied, and six (18%) were extremely dissatisfied. Only eight (24%) indicated they were satisfied; none claimed to be extremely satisfied. Notably, for this query, there was no clear division in the perception of mentorship opportunities between residential and distance students, whose levels of dis/satisfaction were relatively consistent. In fact, distance students were more likely to respond that they were neutral or satisfied. In a follow-up, open-ended question, several respondents credited their dissertation chair as offering formal mentorship, while others cited a lack of consistent, formal engagement. A respondent who answered the above question regarding satisfaction with mentorship as "neutral" stated, "I think the department intends to be supportive, but there aren't many (any) intentional opportunities for listening sessions, open forums, etc. with administration that work for distance students." Several responses highlighted the complications posed by being a distance student in particular. One distance student answered, "I feel left out in terms of mentoring by experienced faculty as a distance student ... I feel lost in terms of making meaningful connections with faculty who have a degree of expertise in my fields of interest." Many respondents again gestured towards peer mentorship and student-created support. For instance, one participant claimed, "Mentorship in the program is generally initiated by unpaid student leaders in English organizations or by the student administration support during SDI." Another distance participant stated:

> Aside from working with my dissertation chair, there were no formal departmental mentorship opportunities. There were precious few informal mentorship opportunities, either. Mentorship, both formal and informal, was entirely student-body driven, and those students who didn't recognize or realize this felt utterly separated. . . . I worked hard to develop mentoring relationships during SDI sessions that I maintained after coursework. I found these mentoring opportunities deeply satisfying, but entirely separated from any official departmental practice, policy, or program.

By and large, respondents indicated that they felt responsible for finding and maintaining mentorship relationships, and, in the absence of willing faculty, that they turned towards each other for support. At the same time, of those reporting higher levels of participation, many foregrounded their own efforts in establishing mentorship connections. For instance, one individual answered: "I think I've been highly proactive in seeking out mentorship. If I had not been, it wouldn't have found me. You have to be assertive in this program and ask for what you need."

Finally, survey participants were given the opportunity to share additional commentary regarding their experience within the doctoral program. Once again, several participants commented on the desire for a more formal mentoring structure with doctoral faculty, pointing to a desire for consistent oversight, training, and communication. One participant suggested: "ODU should make a concerted effort to ensure that faculty advisors for PhD students truly advise those students . . . There should be regular intervals when advising/mentoring occurs, especially for distance students who have no opportunities to see professors on campus." Another individual highlighted the value of being a residential student, even prior to the doctoral experience:

> I was often late in finding out information about the program (everything from forms and required programmatic aspects to being late to be added to an unofficial dissertation group). It was a largely alienating experience for me . . . If I had not been an on-campus graduate student prior to enrolling in the distance PhD program, I don't know that I would have made it through (I had prior connections to students and professors that helped).

Once again, distance respondents emphasized their connection to their peers, crediting them with improving their experience significantly. One distance participant acknowledged the pre-existing academic and professional background of their peers, stating, "So many of my fellow students have been kind, supportive, encouraging—probably in part because so many of us are already teachers and want to help others. I see that spirit of wanting to teach and help other people in my fellow students."

It is worth noting that little was explicitly said about on-campus activities or community; even for residential students much of these interactions appeared to occur online. However, due to their proximity and access, responses generally indicated that campus students are often seen as useful conduits or even privileged. This perception was shared by at least one campus student, who stated, "As a campus student, I often felt responsible to support my distance peers who did not have the access I did."

Discussion of Survey Results

The survey data highlight several areas of concern for students: (1) the way physical learning space can impact a student's feeling of belonging and connectedness to the program; (2) the impacts of mentorship in graduate student programs; and (3) the need for more institutionalized practices across the department or university facilitating the hybrid program. From these responses, we found that the program relies on the unpaid labor of its residential students in order to facilitate the learning of its distance students, a situation further complicated by the expectations of distance colleagues and the sense of obligation suggested by residential respondents. In particular, residential students perform free labor that should be performed by administrative staff and faculty, working to situate distant colleagues within the program and professionalize all colleagues for a career beyond the program. In some cases, like formally recognized professionalizing events such as the Dissertation Bootcamp and SDI support, residential students could be compensated. Other labor, like increased opportunities for faculty mentorship, both formal and informal, is not quite so easy for students to perform or replace.

Physical Learning Space and Students' Sense of Belonging

The lens of agency and authority is fruitful for discussions of the complex dynamics that occur in a hybrid doctoral program such as this, given academia's hierarchical structure in terms of relationships between professors and doctoral students. Students seek agency in order to be perceived as viable candidates for graduation while simultaneously establishing themselves as authorities within their own specialties. Virtual and physical spaces impact these dynamics, both within faculty-to-student relationships and among peer-to-peer relationships. According to the survey results above, in an open-ended question, only the distance students spoke of the limitations of technology and being physically distant. In contrast, some residential students indicated they felt able to establish agency and authority more easily than their distance peers. For example, one campus student stated, "Being on campus allowed me to forge closer relationships with faculty in the program as well as around campus. This meant that I had access to information or to someone who had the information much easier than those in the distance program."

However, the limitations imposed on the distance students because of the restrictions of physical space also end up imposing additional demands on the campus students. When identifying elements that negatively impacted their learning experience, in an open-ended question, one campus student highlighted "expectations placed on campus students to participate in campus activities and support distance students."

Statements such as this indicate that campus students feel they are seen as available or willing to contribute to this unpaid emotional labor.

While professors, dissertation committee members, and program administrators are framed by respondents as authoritative, they often lack the easy and consistent access to the distance students and the institutional and programmatic support needed to sufficiently aid these distance students in feeling connected to the physical campus. This often leaves faculty reliant on the campus students to aid in making those connections, as they can more easily infiltrate and support the distance population of learners. This grants contextual agency to the campus students but also establishes an expectation for their labor because of the situated knowledge and experiences they have in regard to their distance colleagues.

This particular program's unique context leads to additional concerns regarding agency, specifically who is assigned the labor of addressing space-related concerns, whose labor is underrecognized or undervalued, and who receives credit for the labor. Often, there is a level of invisibility involved in such efforts, a lack of acknowledgement by others in authoritative, or peer, positions for how this labor was achieved. Notably, the labor is most visible when it is absent. If such tasks do not occur, then critique ensues. The individuals most likely to navigate these needs are the residential students, who must also be prepared to handle the emotional impact of critique when their voluntary support efforts are not delivered in ways that address the needs of all involved. For instance, while still students serving as volunteers, both authors experienced backlash when their efforts to support and include distance students did not align with individual preferences or needs, an experience worth noting as the program did not formally train individuals in effective or inclusive practices or provide resources (in the form of hardware or programs) that would accommodate such needs. In hindsight, the authors also acknowledge an underdeveloped awareness of accessibility strategies for online experiences (for instance, failing to provide closed captioning or transcripts of events). Such failure could have excluded students who sought information and community. Yet it is the institution's responsibility to train emerging practitioners in such vital practices, instead of assuming in-person students will intuit or arrive already knowing how to include all peers in hybrid activities.

Recent scholarship has also studied the impacts of the physical learning space on teaching behaviors and students' abilities to actively engage and learn (Beery et al. 2013). Being geographically displaced from the physical classroom can lead distance students to feel isolated and removed from the course community (Moore and Kearsley 1996). The survey confirms this with twenty-two out of twenty-three (96%) distance students stating they felt negatively impacted by their distance from campus. However, scholarship has yet to analyze the experience of those who remain in a central classroom in hybrid programs, failing to consider how their learning process and sense of community is impacted when the classroom exists in dual spaces. In our own survey, five out of nine (56%) on-campus students stated they were impacted by their closeness to campus, feeling the pressure to accommodate distance students, as indicated in the response above. If Web 2.0 tools are the answer to the problems of isolation and the lack of community distance students face, then how do we understand the additional labor taken up by residential students who must learn to effectively use and often troubleshoot those tools to ensure their peers are included? Ironically, as Kupsch and McDonald highlight in chapter 1 of this book, many residential students have in fact relocated to take part in such programs, in some instances leaving stable, full-time employment, established support systems (such as family), and familiar spaces. Also, as marked by Billingsley in this volume, on-campus students may find themselves in precarious straits, depending on the level of financial support offered by the institution and constraints such support imposes on the student, adding to the difficulty of their experience. In hybrid programs, these individuals who move, and in some instances rely upon campus employment, may be rewarded by taking on the support of peers who have not relocated and have not foregone those elements that often contribute to one's well-being within a stressful environment.

All of this is further complicated by being in close proximity to authority figures (instructors, advisors, supervisors) witnessing the performance of their learning process, (supposed) technological prowess, and willingness to collaborate. Within courses, such students are often relied upon to resolve course delivery issues that would not exist in a traditional classroom and for a mode of course delivery they did not opt to participate in as residential students, calling into question how much agency they really exercise within the choice to perform these actions.

In the survey, the few residential respondents did not complain about their additional labor, framing it as a duty to help others. We surmise that this silence may be due in part to the fact that the scholarly conversation regarding distance learning has, rightfully, largely focused on distance learners' experience, yet has neglected to paint a comprehensive picture of hybrid programs and those students still located in physical classrooms. To say anything negative about helping distance colleagues suggests a lack of empathy and willingness to collaborate; even in the course of writing this article, we have struggled with this concern. However, the residential experience is legitimately affected by the shift to hybrid and online learning. The time, effort, and emotional cost is real. The space in which to acknowledge and value such work has not yet been created, thereby making it challenging for residential students to articulate the experience without seeming critical of the experience they strive to support.

The Impacts of Mentorship in Graduate Student Programs

Another major point of concern noted through the survey data is mentorship, particularly distance students' struggle to feel strongly connected or to have clear access to mentors. In the case of ODU's PhD program, the majority of faculty members hail from traditional doctoral programs or have formerly taught in graduate programs with the traditional course delivery format, which requires students to be physically present in the same room as the instructor. Notably, the program has mandated that all doctoral courses be made available to distance learners, removing instructor choice entirely in terms of course delivery. Nevertheless, the program does not provide formal, sustained technological and pedagogical training for adapting to new digital spaces or altering teaching strategies in order to effectively connect with students in hybrid class spaces. The lack of formal training in regard to faculty mentorship is felt by both campus and distance students. A campus student replied to an open-ended question about faculty mentorship by identifying "very little faculty support—what we had I felt like we as students created out of necessity." Similar concerns were echoed by a distance student responding to the same question:

> Not knowing the faculty is a big issue, not having access to them during office hours, etc. (I've tried Skyping in during office hours but no one has ever answered—I guess you have to have an appt.) There are things people on campus have a way better understanding of—like the comps process, for example—than I do. Distance students are also often locked out of the conversation through the technology—having to keep ourselves muted prohibits legit discussion. I've had some classes with classmates whose faces I've never seen bc they sit outside the cameras range. There is also an expectation that we have outside faculty on our diss committee, but what a hassle that will be—how does a distance student get to know faculty from outside the department? We barely get to know the ones in the department. I learn so much by logging into class early and listening to on-campus students and professors come in chatting.

These students echo common concerns identified in scholarship about mentorship in hybrid spaces, such as the inability to establish relationships and communicate with faculty and students, unequal access to resources and information, and unintentional privileging of certain students over others. These issues are likely to have a ripple effect of consequences in terms of instructors' ability, or even willingness, to lead the traditional peripheral learning experiences of a graduate program for distance students. As a result, faculty may unintentionally lean on their local students to help address some of these issues. In some cases, faculty may not even realize their in-person students are quietly doing such support work in the background.

However, as students enter into and progress through graduate programs, many report increased anxiety and concerns around workload, insecurity, and feelings of inadequacy, regardless of their proximity to the school (Gerdes and Malinckrodt 1994; Bowman, Bowman, and Delucia 1990). Mentorship from both faculty and peers is often referenced as a vital strategy in overcoming such concerns, with Kelly and Shweitzer (1999) claiming that "mentoring is considered to be the heart of graduate education." In an overview of mentoring scholarship, Budge (2006) states, "Mentoring is an important career training and development tool that socializes employees into the organization, lowers work stress, and increases mentors' and mentees' self-efficacy and self-esteem" (72). Indeed, research indicates a correlation between mentorship, completion rates, and professional success (Scandura and Williams 2001; Lovitts 2001; Fagenson-Eland, Marks, and Amendola 1997). In this volume, Wang, Xiong, and Ye echo this sentiment in regard to the perceptions of employability by Chinese doctoral students after graduation. They argue that "interactions with advisors and other professors also affected interviewees' career expectations. Some interviewees indicated that their advisors had given them significant guidance for future career development" (222).

Naturally, no one individual faculty member or administrator can fully address the gamut of needs for every student. Thus, as peer mentorship is both desirable and likely to occur, the ideal peer mentorship experience should be mutually beneficial to all participants, avoiding a one-way flow of information and effort. Grant-Vallone and Ensher (2000) analyze the impact of a formal graduate student peer-mentoring program, considering the following factors: psychosocial and instrumental support provided by mentors, the relationships between support and satisfaction with the peer-mentoring program, and graduate student stress levels. They found that peer mentors provided more social and emotional support than instrumental support. Likewise, Chesler and Chesler (2002) found that peer mentoring establishes emotional and professional support networks of individuals with similar experiences and status within the academic hierarchy. As such, peer mentorship can add to the variety of mentor roles students encounter during their time in the program, often with a focus on shared psychosocial concerns and experiences. Yet, such emotional labor and time dedication should be explicitly acknowledged, rather than tacitly expected. Furthermore, a formal peer-mentoring program should be designed in such a way that it avoids replicating the issues the graduate writing program assistants (gWPAs) face, as Phillips, Shovlin, and Titus highlight in this volume. Formalized graduate mentoring positions benefit from clear parameters to prevent them becoming new opportunities for exploitation; roles such as these should serve students' needs more than the program's needs.

Effective Practices for Ethically Supporting Hybrid Programs

Cook et al. (2009) outline the following disincentives for faculty to participate in distance education: lack of institutional technical support, increased workload, lack of release time, the lack of financing for related costs, and concerns about the impact on the quality of the course. These faculty concerns may unintentionally lead to exploitation of in-person graduate assistants when they are viewed as the solution to addressing these programmatic problems. Given the lack of interactivity between parties due to the constraints and issues related to agency and authority, and the reliance on residential students as unacknowledged conduits for addressing various programmatic needs, we argue for practical strategies to implement institutionalized practices into the program rather than relying on socialized or volunteer practices.

Kuk and Banning's (2014) research on a primarily distance education doctoral program makes some suggestions about the institutionalized components that need to be in place in order to effectively deliver a doctoral program, including communication, advising, instruction, technology, cohort model, and face-to-face interaction. Our survey results point toward similar needs, leading us to suggest some practical applications for creating mentorship, communication, and agency within a hybrid program. These suggestions focus on more institutionalized, structured mentorship opportunities, more explicit communication practices to aid in the connectivity to campus, and more aid (and reward) towards helping faculty succeed in implementation. While these suggestions come from the survey results and our experiences connected to this specific university, the similarities with Kuk and Banning's research suggest these kinds of initiatives are important considerations in university programs nationwide, particularly as more institutions move toward implementing partial or full distance graduate student programs.

Our suggestions for implementation in related distance or hybrid doctoral programs include the following:

- Make mentorship an explicit outcome of the program in multiple forms, as modeled by the University of Michigan's Rackham Graduate School (2006).
    - Clearly outline what it means to be a faculty mentor: time, expectation, oversight, and articulation of the supervision.
    - Clearly outline what it means to be a peer mentor (as part of program assistantships): time, expectation, oversight, and articulation of the supervision.
    - Develop mentorship contracts for mentors and mentees, both faculty and peer-to-peer, to discuss and set expectations for one another.
    - Provide administrative oversight to ensure consistency of communication, benchmarks, so on.

- Ensure mentorship is mutually beneficial to faculty and students alike, thereby increasing all participants' sense of agency and choice.
    - Acknowledge faculty for taking students to conferences, publishing with them, or working on grants.
    - Acknowledge peer mentorship in appropriate ways, such as including mentoring hours in the students' assistantship, funding for summer professional development and social events, etc.

- Provide training for faculty members and students in regard to creating mentorships and communicating with students in a nontraditional PhD program.
    - Ensure that all involved in mentoring have frequent opportunities to learn the technologies related to a distance education, with a particular focus on new faculty members who might not have prior experience with such technologies (Kuk and Banning 2014).
    - Train faculty on strategies regarding how to help distance students connect to the campus community more readily.

- Train both faculty and students in accessibility guidelines, strategies, and resources, so that all efforts to engage with students are universally accessible.

• Establish various types of mentoring opportunities available to all students, such as listening sessions, open forums, monthly video conferences, work groups, and so on.

- Build this into faculty members' responsibilities so compensation and acknowledgement are received, and faculty with a diversity of research interests are available as mentors.

• Create a campus point of contact and establish periods of time to connect with this resource (Sumner 2000).

- For instance, a graduate assistant could serve as a named liaison between the distance students, program administrators, and faculty with regularly scheduled meetings to assess needs and concerns.
- A graduate assistant role might also be appointed to attend to similar needs for on-campus students, ensuring their unique concerns are represented.
- Pair small groups with on-campus students who serve as peer mentors as part of their assistantships.

• Implement a yearly or biannual survey of all campus, distance students, and faculty to more clearly and regularly address the concerns of all parties involved (Kuk and Banning 2014).

The above list is not exhaustive; rather, it is a starting point for ensuring equity of labor for all stakeholders invested in the success of both residential and distance students within a program. We acknowledge that budget and other responsibilities may limit a program's ability to take up such suggestions. However, even incorporating a few strategies is likely to have a large impact. Future implementation of these suggestions into a graduate hybrid or distance program should also be intentionally designed with an intersectional lens informing effective practices. This way the program acknowledges and addresses the diverse needs of a student body from varied backgrounds and should in particular work to overcome the biases women, disabled individuals, and people of color and other minorities face in traditional environments, avoiding replicating marginalization in hybrid spaces (Pruitt and Isaac 1985; Wright and Wright 1987).

Concluding Implications

Our research shows that when doctoral programs make the move to include online education, residential students remain critical to a program's success, negotiating the privileges afforded by ease of access to the physical institution and their primary relationships with distance peers. But "ease of access" should not be confused for equity of labor or even ease of action. Performing the material and emotional labor that should be done by faculty and administrators does not actually grant residential students more agency or opportunity, particularly when a program publicly appropriates that voluntary work as a unique and marketable programmatic feature. Rather, residential students serve as tools in a system that is risky for them to challenge because of their precarity as early career academics. In the department in this study, the system uses resident students' volunteerism to bolster the deficiencies of hybrid or online programs not designed to provide learning experiences beyond coursework, often without acknowledgement. By failing to make that work visible, the system does not assign value to the labor provided by these individuals and thus does not have to compensate for it.

While our survey did not include the perspectives of faculty, the relative recentness of distance learning programs suggests that the large majority of current faculty members matriculated from traditional doctoral programs and were not distance students. Many of the issues graduate students face likely emerge from the reality that faculty may not have the necessary background or training to support courses consisting of both distance and in-person students. As expanding modes of course delivery emerge, such as the "hy-flex" model used to facilitate students' fluctuating needs during a pandemic, faculty should be continually trained in both the technologies and pedagogies that allow them to support the success of their distance students in a way that is not detrimental to residential learners. Programs should also consider providing assistantships designed specifically to facilitate distance learning issues within and without the classroom, so that faculty are not tasked with addressing a second learning sphere without additional support.

Furthermore, this initial anonymous survey does not account for the way individuals from different populations and backgrounds might experience this expectation of labor differently. Future work might delve specifically into the experiences of women, disabled individuals, and people of color and other minorities as they provide support in hybrid graduate programs. For instance, *Peitho*'s Spring 2019 Special Cluster on Gendered Service defines emotional and gendered academic labor specifically as tasks often implicitly assigned to, or taken up by, women because of the association with feminine qualities (Payne 2019). Undoubtedly the explicit and implicit expectations of labor and the obstacles those expectations present for graduate students are impacted by the identities of those involved and deserve further examination.

At the time of this chapter's original composition, there were only a few hybrid English PhD programs similar to ODU's. Now, as the pandemic stretches on, more such programs are in development. Without comprehensive training and clear expectations and funding built into the design of hybrid graduate programs, many students and faculty will be left to carve a new and unique path through the doctoral process, creating learning strategies and pedagogies within this emerging graduate framework. The struggle and labor inequities are further compounded by the pandemic's fluctuating nature, as instructors and students are forced to contend with and support changing course modalities, sometimes within the same semester. For students with disabilities, this fluctuation is even more frustrating as some modalities might be more accommodating than others. Further, the pandemic's ability to segregate students with and without disabilities is significant. Faculty and staff designing hybrid and remote problems must anticipate and mitigate these systemic differences.

While we argue that such trailblazing is better done in tandem between the stakeholders involved, the traditionally isolating nature of academia and the power dynamics between faculty and students, as well as the lack of extended and extemporaneous interactivity created by constrained online spaces, can lead to these efforts occurring without much interaction or transparency between involved parties. In other words, due to their perceived roles as the learned and the learners, and the lack of social space to challenge these boundaries and identities, faculty may not adapt their established teaching strategies at all or with little input from those they seek to mentor. Meanwhile students may not share the mentorship infrastructure they construct or other adaptive strategies to the obstacles created when the learning space is decentralized. When given an open-ended opportunity to discuss their experiences as doctoral students in English, our respondents spoke almost exclusively about mentorship and community, referencing individual interactions as vital to the learning process; no one referenced coursework. Yet online programs, such as ODU's, often only formally offer coursework; courses are situated as the be-all and end-all of learning. This situation leaves the development and delivery of the other learning experiences students value, such as communal engagement, mentorship, and professional development, to the students themselves. As hybrid and remote graduate programs continue to expand, faculty and administrators must more deliberately formalize methods for engaging distance students outside of coursework without exploiting on-campus students or neglecting opportunities for mentorship.

Works Cited

Beery, Theresa A., Dustin Shell, Gordon Gillespie, and Eileen Werdman. 2013. "The Impact of Learning Space on Teaching Behaviors." *Nurse Education in Practice* 13, no. 5 (September): 382–387.

Bowman, Robert L., Vicki E. Bowman, and Janice L. DeLucia. 1990. "Mentoring in a Graduate Counseling Program: Students Helping Students." *Counselor Education and Supervision* 30, no. 1 (September): 58–65.

Budge, Stephanie. 2006. "Peer Mentoring in Postsecondary Education: Implications for Research and Practice." *Journal of College Reading and Learning* 37 (1): 71–85.

Chesler, Naomi C., and Mark A. Chesler. 2002. "Gender-Informed Mentoring Strategies for Women and Engineering: On Establishing a Caring Community." *Journal of Engineering Education* 91, no. 1 (January): 49–56.

Cook, Ruth Gannon, Kathryn Ley, Caroline Crawford, and Allen Warner. 2009. "Motivators and Inhibitors for University Faculty in Distance and E-learning." *British Journal of Educational Technology* 40, no. 1 (July): 149–163.

Fagenson-Eland, Ellen A., Michelle A. Marks, and Karen L. Amendola. 1997. "Perceptions of Mentoring Relationships." *Journal of Vocational Behavior* 51, no. 1 (August): 29–42.

Gerdes, Hilary, and Brent Mallinckrodt. 1994. "Emotional, Social, and Academic Adjustment of College Students: A Longitudinal Study of Retention." *Journal of Counseling and Development* 72, no. 3 (January–February): 281–288.

Grant-Vallone, Elisa J., and Ellen A. Ensher. 2000. "Effects of Peer Mentoring on Types of Mentor Support, Program Satisfaction and Graduate Student Stress." *Journal of College Student Development* 41, no. 6 (January): 637–642.

Hazelrigg, Katherine. 2021. "Graduate First-Time Enrollment Increases, despite Substantial Decline of International Graduate Students." Press release, Council of Graduate Schools, October 14, 2021. https://cgsnet.org/press-releases/graduate-first-time-enrollment-increases-despite-substantial-decline-of-international-graduate-students/.

Kelly, Shalonda, and John H. Schweitzer. 1999. "Mentoring within a Graduate School Setting." College *Student Journal* 33 (1): 130–148.

Kuk, Linda, and James H. Banning. 2014. "A Higher Education Leadership Distance Ph.D. Program: An Assessment Using Blocher's Ecological Learning Theory." *Creative Education* 5, no. 9 (May): 701–712.

Kyei-Blankson, Lydia, Esther Ntuli, and Heather Donnelly. 2016. "Establishing the Importance of Interaction and Presence to Student Learning in Online Environments." *World Journal of Educational Research* 3 (1): 48–65.

Lovitts, Barbara E. 2002. *Leaving the Ivory Tower: The Causes and Consequences of Departure from Doctoral Study*. Lanham, MD: Rowman and Littlefield.

Moore, Michael G., and Greg Kearsley. 1996. *Distance Education: A Systems Review*. Belmont, CA: Wadsworth.

Old Dominion University (ODU) English Department. 2019. "Program." Retrieved from https://www.odu.edu/englishdept/graduate/phd-english.html.

———. 2021. "Summer Doctoral Institute." Retrieved from https://www.odu.edu/englishdept/news/2019/8/summer_doctoral_inst.

Philipsen, Brent, Jo Tondeur, Bram Pynoo, Silke Vanslambrouck, and Chang Zhu. 2019. "Examining Lived Experiences in a Professional Development Program for Online Teaching: A Hermeneutic Phenomenological Approach." *Australasian Journal of Educational Technology* 35 (5): 46–59.

Pruitt, Anne S., and Paul D. Isaac. 1985. "Discrimination in Recruitment, Admission, and Retention of Minority Graduate Students." *Journal of Negro Education* 54, no. 4 (Autumn): 526–536.

Scandura, Terri A., and Ethlyn A. Williams. 2001. "An Investigation of the Moderating Effects of Gender on the Relationships between Mentorship Initiation and Protege Perceptions of Mentoring Functions." *Journal of Vocational Behavior* 59, no. 3 (December): 342–363.

Sumner, Jennifer. 2000. "Serving the System: A Critical History of Distance Education." *Open Learning* 15, no. 3 (November): 267–285.

University of Michigan. 2006. *How to Mentor Graduate Students: A Guide for Faculty at a Diverse University*.

Vanslambrouck, Silke, Chang Zhu, Bram Pynoo, Valérie Thomas, Koen Lombaerts, and Jo Tondeur. 2019. "An In-Depth Analysis of Adult Students in Blended Environments: Do They Regulate Their Learning in an 'Old School' Way?" *Computers and Education* 128 (January): 75–87.

Wood, Colin. 2021. March 23. "As Enrollment Crashes, Universities Are Reinventing Themselves." *Edscoop*, March 23, 2021. https://edscoop.com/university-enrollment-crashes-pandemic/.

Woolf, Virginia. 1979 [1904]. *Women and Writing*. Orlando: Harcourt.

Wright, Cheryl A., and Scott D. Wright. 1987. "The Role of Mentors in the Career Development of Young Professionals." *Family Relations* 36, no. 2 (April): 204–208.

PART II

THE LABOR OF TEACHING AND RESEARCH

4 | Will This Take Me Anywhere?
Investing Time in Graduate Student Teaching

Elliot Shapiro

> *"Teaching properly takes up a lot of time, and teaching excellence is not valued in a way that compensates for that time."*
> —Cornell graduate student (2018)

Introduction: The Ends of Graduate Study

This hybrid essay—part personal essay, part research reflection—examines how graduate students in one local setting perceive teaching as part of their professional training. The epigraph above is drawn from surveys of graduate students reflecting on teaching and teacher training. In discussing this survey data, I focus on the time graduate students invest in teaching and the potential costs and benefits of those investments. Time is every graduate student's most valuable and least renewable resource. How they spend their time in graduate school will shape their future careers. This seemingly obvious fact, and this essay's seemingly narrow focus, should not obscure the larger point. This volume helps make visible a mismatch between the alleged purpose of doctoral education—tenured employment—and the range of possible outcomes, which may include academic appointments with varying terms and responsibilities. This essay argues that, when investing their time, graduate students should devise a balanced portfolio rather than following a strategy that overloads on research and skimps on everything else.

Few academic careers can be navigated with treasure hunt maps—follow footprints; X marks the spot—that begin with admission to graduate school and end with tenure. Here, I try to chart a path between two uncomfortable truths. On the one hand, there is the undeniable fact that, for academics, no credential has greater value than the publication of top-notch, groundbreaking research. Teaching, service, administrative work—none of these come close. For faculty at Research-1 (R1) universities, when it comes to tenure and promotion, other aspects of the job may not count at all. On the other hand, there is the equally (and increasingly) undeniable fact that most PhDs will not end up as professors in R1 universities. Most will end up in jobs where things other than research *also* matter. These other kinds of work may include administration, service and, of course, teaching. Those who end up in these jobs may discover that the messages they received about priorities do not always line up with market forces.

In academic circles, tenured employment is often seen as the apex of achievement: a marker of success, a source of prestige, unusually secure employment. At well-endowed institutions, the compensation for tenured faculty can be generous (relative to other nonprofit fields, at any rate). Graduate programs are increasingly diverse, with preprofessional degree programs expanding, yet many academics still fixate on the graduate school-to-professoriate pipeline. Cassuto and Weisbuch (2021) explore in detail the negative consequences of this fixation for almost everyone involved (and argue for rethinking the PhD). If a tenure-track position at a research university is seen as the singular goal of graduate study, the primary focus of one's time in graduate school should be research—indeed, some argue that research should be the exclusive focus. Under this scenario, other kinds of work, other kinds of training, can be seen as distractions from this goal. Graduate faculty—who are overwhelmingly employed at research institutions—may convey this message more or less explicitly to their graduate students. The graduate student quoted above seems to have gotten this message.

Even in the most prestigious graduate programs, however, one cannot predict who will end up with tenure-stream appointments and who will seek some other form of academic employment, or some other form of employment altogether. Layers of academic employment exist between tenured professordom and the potentially exploitative hell of precarious adjunct labor. These in-between layers include many tenured professors at two- and four-year colleges whose research agendas may be limited by the conditions of employment. The in-between layers also include a (surprisingly) large pool of people who do academic work at academic institutions but do not have tenure. I say surprising because I have been one of these people for more than twenty years *and* (here's the surprising bit) I've spent much of my career feeling professionally invisible.

I pause to acknowledge a filter that shapes everything I've written so far. My twenty-plus year career as a non-tenure-track faculty member—whose primary job is teaching—has been spent primarily at a prestigious R1 university (see also Shapiro 2008 for a fuller discussion of my experience). I am surrounded by people who were lucky enough to secure tenure-track employment at the kind of place their graduate advisors thought of as the apex. I am also surrounded by other people with careers like mine: academics with long-term jobs but no tenure. To an important degree, people like me didn't realize how many of us there were, in part because, until recently, the institution didn't really acknowledge we existed in significant numbers. By one count, my home institution employs more than two thousand such people.

More than one thousand people on Cornell's Ithaca campus hold "continuing academic" positions: they include teachers, researchers, extension associates, librarians, and archivists. People at my institution with academic job titles who do this kind of work were recently reclassified as research, teaching, and extension faculty (RTE for short). In 2018 a committee was charged by the dean of the faculty and the faculty senate to consider representation of non-tenure-track faculty within the senate. This committee conducted a census of academic titleholders, including continuing lecturers, research scientists, research associates, and extension associates (all of these ranks can also be designated as "senior"), as well librarians and archivists. The census also accounted for a handful of non-tenured professorial titles, including clinical professor, research professor, and professor-of-the-practice (Cornell University Committee 2018). The committee's findings revealed a notable gender gap between the university faculty (tenure stream) and RTE faculty. In 2001 the university faculty (UF) was 22.8% female, while the RTE faculty was 44.8% female. In 2017 the UF was 31.7% female, while the RTE faculty was 48.5% female.

For many of us on the RTE track, teaching and other forms of graduate labor have shaped our postgraduate careers, sometimes as much as, or more than, our research has. Certainly this holds true for my immediate colleagues: lecturers and senior lecturers in a free-standing writing program. Some of us joined the staff right after graduate school (myself included); some showed up at Cornell several jobs into a career. In my case, the credentials that led to a career as a long-term, non-tenure-track faculty member are rooted in the academic labor I did as a graduate student—teaching, tutoring, and study skills counseling. I see these examples of graduate student labor as an unofficial curriculum that ran parallel to my official PhD training. (Jean Anyon [1980] originally described "the hidden curriculum" evident in elementary school settings; Anyon's terminology has been widely dispersed across studies of education, as in the *Glossary of Education Reform*, which defines "hidden curriculum," as "the unwritten, unofficial, and often unintended lessons, values, and perspectives that students learn in school" [Glossary of Education Reform 2015].)

While graduate faculty may consider tenure-track employment the desired outcome of a graduate career, graduate students should probably consider nontenured academic appointments a possible outcome. If they haven't already, PhD students should certainly consider tenure-track employment at institutions where teaching is highly valued. These positions likely won't include the prestige and compensation associated with R1 employment. Seth Kahn (2020) notes that faculty pay is often *inversely* related to teaching loads—the more you teach, the less you earn—even as he insists that this value system obscures the ways that teaching is valued. When seeking (and holding) teaching-oriented positions, credentials not directly related to research take on increased importance. When career plans prioritize teaching, teaching experience—the primary focus of this article—ceases to be a distraction from the acquisition of professional credentials. Teaching can become the credential that defines a career.

Especially in the humanities, graduate students would be wise to consider the range of things they can learn—the range of contributions they can make—while they are graduate students. For some, this might be considered hedging their bets. Even graduate students with excellent research credentials may discover that other professional experiences make the difference between academic career plan B and no academic career at all. These other experiences may also open unexpected doors and reveal unexpected sources of satisfaction.

I hope my reflections can be read in conversation with this volume's short essays, which explore the visceral dissonance graduate students experience when they try to sort out the relationship between graduate training and professional pathways. I'm thinking particularly about Andrew Hollinger's essay about the tripled-life of a professional writing program administrator who is also a PhD student and a parent; and Sarah Welsh's essay about the failure of PhD faculty to imagine the possibility that a graduate degree might lead somewhere other than tenure.

In the next section I turn to survey data on graduate student teaching that addresses questions of how time is invested. Time represents a fairly narrow focus within the study of graduate teaching I have initiated. As the survey section indicates, most of the data cited is drawn from graduate student responses to just three questions of more than forty asked on an end-of-semester survey. In the discussion section the follows, and the epilogue focused on pandemic-era developments, I move between the detached language of labor economics and something more affective. For the bulk of the essay, I talk about investment, returns, and dividends. But I end up, surprisingly, with love.

Survey: Studying Graduate Teaching

Cornell offers first-year writing seminars (FWS) in some thirty departments. More than three hundred FWSs are offered annually. Approximately 65% are taught by graduate student instructors. During fall 2018—in consultation with colleagues and stakeholders—I designed and distributed three surveys focused on FWS teaching. I distributed these same three surveys following spring 2019. One surveyed graduate student instructors the semester after they taught writing seminars. A second surveyed faculty the semester after they taught FWSs. The third survey was addressed to course leaders—faculty who serve as mentors and supervisors of graduate instructors. Faculty who teach writing seminars *and* serve as course leaders were invited to respond to both the faculty and the course leader surveys. No one was invited to respond both semesters, even if they taught and/or served as a course leader both semesters.

In 2018–2019, the graduate instructor survey was distributed to 173 graduate students from thirty-one departments. Seventy-eight complete responses were recorded (fifty-two after the fall semester; twenty-six after the spring semester). Graduate instructors who taught both semesters were polled following the fall semester only. Parallel surveys for faculty were distributed fall and spring, with faculty who taught both semesters polled only in the fall. The sample size for every question is smaller in the spring data set. This reflects the smaller number of courses offered during the spring semester, and the fact that anyone who taught writing seminars both semesters was invited to respond to the fall survey only.

In this review, I focus on quantitative and qualitative responses to the last three questions from the graduate student survey. Two questions ask respondents about time spent on teaching and the professional value of that investment. In addition to sorting responses to the first two questions, I quote extensively from graduate student responses to the final, open-ended question. The three questions read as follows:

1. I believe that teaching a FWS will be useful for my academic career. [Respond using 5 point scale: 1 = strongly agree; 2 = somewhat agree; 3 = neither agree nor disagree; 4 = somewhat disagree; 5 = strongly disagree.]
2. How does your weekly time commitment for your First-Year Writing

Seminar compare to the time spent on other teaching positions or teaching assistantships you have had at Cornell? [Respond using 5 point scale: 1 = much less; 2 = less; 3 = about the same; 4 = more; 5 = much more.]

3. Please comment on any aspect of your teaching experience [open-ended].

Survey Results

The responses to the first and second questions resemble slightly distorted mirror images (figures 4.1 and 4.2). An overwhelming majority of respondents—95%—checked "agree" or "strongly agree" when asked if they see FWS teaching as professionally useful, with the overwhelming majority of that 95% checking "strongly agree." Only two out of seventy-four respondents checked the neutral box. One graduate student teacher checked "somewhat disagree"; no one checked "strongly disagree" (see figure 4.1). The chart flips when graduate instructors are asked to compare the time commitment of FWS teaching to other teaching positions they have held at Cornell. Thirteen of seventy-four respondents (18%) found that teaching an FWS and other TA work required comparable time commitments.

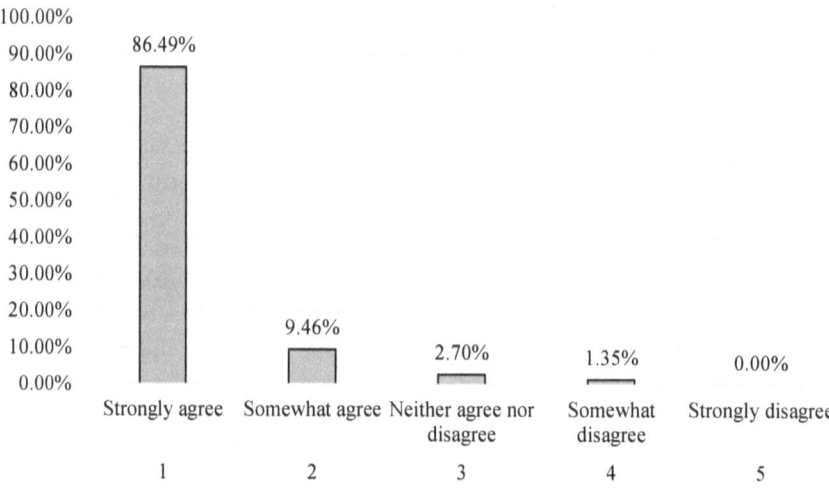

Figure 4.1, Responses to GSI Question 69: I believe that teaching a FWS will be useful for my academic career. (Seventy-four responses: fifty fall; twenty-four spring).

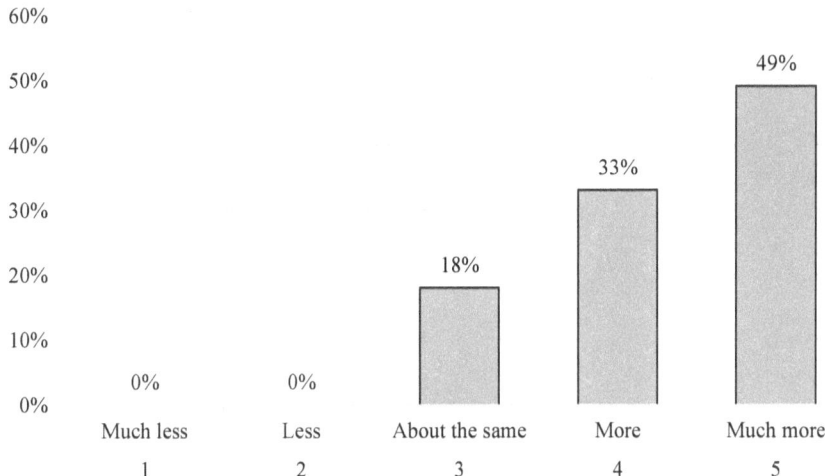

Figure 4.2, Responses to GSI Question 70: How does your weekly time commitment for your First Year Writing Seminar compare to the time spent on other teaching positions or teaching assistantships you've had at Cornell? (Seventy-two responses: forty-eight fall; twenty-four spring).

The other sixty-one believed that teaching a FWS took "more" or "much more" time than other teaching commitments they had at Cornell. Not a single person said FWS teaching was *less* time-consuming than other TA-ships (see figure 4.2).

Faculty who taught FWSs also responded to a question asking them to compare FWS teaching to their other undergraduate teaching. Most faculty saw FWS teaching as more time-consuming than their other undergraduate courses. However, the distribution was not as stark as it was for graduate teachers. The faculty question reads, "How does your weekly time commitment for your First-Year Writing Seminar compare to time spent on other undergraduate courses you have taught during the past two years?" 69% of faculty respondents reported that the time commitment was "more" or "much more"; 31% said it was "about the same." Not a single faculty member considered the time commitment to be "less" or "much less" (see figure 4.3).

As noted above, the final open-ended question in the graduate survey follows questions about professional development and time, which presumably shaped the open-ended answers. The impact of survey design does not negate these graduate students' evident concern with time: how it is valued, and how time spent teaching serves their academic careers. The data set includes twenty-nine responses (nineteen fall and ten spring)

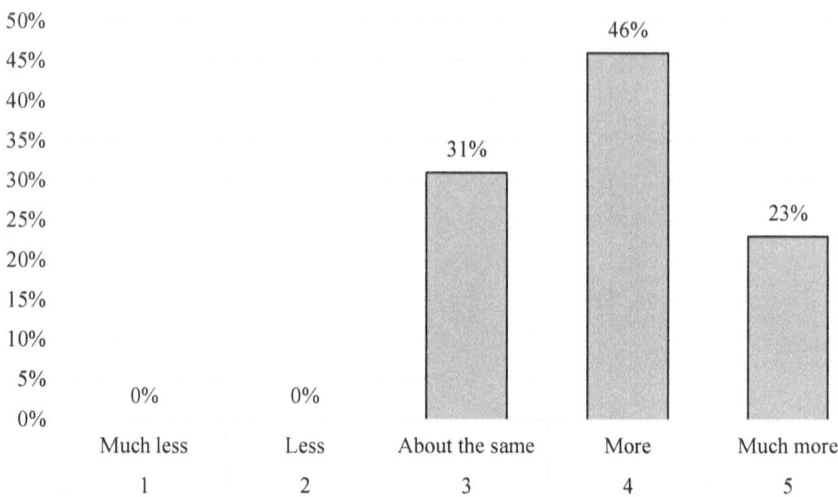

Figure 4.3, Responses to Faculty Q34: How does your weekly time commitment for your First Year Writing Seminar compare to time spent on other undergraduate courses you have taught during the past two years? (Twenty-six responses: eighteen fall; eight spring).

to the final, open-ended question: "Comment on any aspect of your teaching experience." The qualitative responses were overwhelmingly positive. Two examples quoted below address the pleasures of teaching, and of teaching this particular audience:

> I love teaching in this program and would teach freshmen forever if I could! I spend a lot of time on it, but enjoy it and always end up loving my students . . . (Fa18)

> It's my favorite part of graduate studies at Cornell! (Sp19)

Several wrote about the hands-on value of the teaching experience, and the opportunity to design a course of one's own.

> It was a FANTASTIC experience. With that in mind, starting from "scratch" creating a course as well as running the course takes much longer than I expected. This, in itself, is a good learning experience. (Fa18)

> I love the FWS program! I wish grading didn't take so much time, but I find it to be better than a normal TAship because you have autonomy over the schedule and material, and can tailor the class to your students' needs. (Fa18)

> I love teaching FWSs. The work load is at times difficult but being the instructor of my own class and engaging students in a topic I am passionate about is immensely rewarding. (Sp19)

> You can take 100 swimming classes, but the only way you're really going to learn is by getting in the water. (Fa18)

A few comments criticized the training program for FWS instructors, or the mentoring FWS instructors receive. But here I focus on students' experience as teachers, not their preparation for that work. (See Austin and Moreland in this volume for a fuller discussion of graduate teacher preparation for first-year composition. For specifics about Cornell's training program, see Shapiro 2015.)

> I love teaching here! In this survey I have been critical of the formal preparatory process, but overall I find the job rewarding, meaningful, and enjoyable. I think we all know that the only way to really learn how to teach is to just get out there and do it. (Fa18)

Critical comments, almost without exception, focused on time. Some respondents asserted that, because the time commitment was greater than standard TA-ships, the stipend should also be greater.

> Teaching an FWS requires much, much more time than a normal Teaching Assistant position. Anyone that says otherwise is lying. That we are paid the same is, to be blunt, absurd. (Fa18)

Only one directly questioned the professional value of the experience, in a comment that was otherwise mostly positive.

> I enjoy teaching and I enjoyed my FWS experience, though I'm very wary to say that it will "help" my academic career, and even warier that it should continue to be marketed as such. . . . I'm suspicious that anyone will look at my CV and be struck particularly by this teaching experience. Other than this . . . teaching an FWS has been a great experience: challenging, engaging, and informative in equal measure. (Sp19)

As is already evident, many of the positive comments mentioned the professional value of the experience. A few mentioned their own commitments to teaching. In some cases, these commitments appear to have preceded their teaching experience; in others cases these interests developed through their teaching.

> I am very happy to have taught an FWS because it was a rewarding experience in itself and I think (hope) it will be valuable for my future job applications.

> One thing instructors should understand is that an FWS is significantly more work than a simple TAship. (Fa18)

> I thoroughly enjoyed designing and teaching my own class. While the workload was certainly heavier in comparison to other classes I've been a TA for, the benefits in terms of professional development made this more than worthwhile. (Sp19)

> I love teaching First-Year Writing Seminars. Though I do find them to be a heavy commitment in terms of time, I believe it's worth it (I should note that I am pursuing a teaching-oriented career). (Fa18)

> This experience has fundamentally reoriented my pedagogical investments toward smaller classes that integrate writing in learning, causing me to consider more jobs at small liberal arts colleges. (Fa18)

While a number of respondents spoke about the value of teaching experience and professional experience more broadly, only one—quoted at the head of this essay—directly addressed the industry-wide imbalance between the value placed on research and the value placed on teaching.

> Teaching properly takes up a lot of time, and teaching excellence is not valued in a way that compensates for that time (vs teaching not well and publishing, teaching less well and engaging more in the department, etc etc) (Fa18)

Discussion: Assistantships and Invisible Credentials

Assistantships

I begin this discussion section by considering comments that compare the time commitment required of FWS teachers with positions in which graduate students actually assist someone. In Cornell's First-Year Writing Seminar program, graduate teachers are instructors of record. But, administratively, they are classified as teaching assistants. Cornell graduate students in any field who receive full assistantships enjoy identical benefits. Given this volume's concern with labor and exploitation, the relationship between time spent and money earned should be explored further.

Cornell PhD students receive reliable (and relatively generous) funding, primarily through assistantships. University policy defines an assistantship as "an arrangement in which financial support is given to a graduate student who engages in teaching and/or research in furtherance of the university's academic mission, as well as his or her graduate education."

Cornell supports graduate students through four kinds of assistantships: research (RA), teaching (TA), graduate (GA), and graduate research (GRA). Funding for all four types of assistantships is identical: "Students on full assistantships receive full tuition credit and a stipend" (Cornell University 2013). Health insurance is also included.

The assistantship policy refers to "academic mission" and "the advancement of . . . graduate education." The policy does not use the words "labor" or "compensation." Nevertheless, three out of four categories of assistantships involve payment, work, and a weekly limit to hours worked. Research assistants do research "that is not directly thesis related." Graduate assistants receive a stipend in exchange for work (such as program administration) that *is not* their own PhD research *and* does not fit the description of either research or teaching assistantships. Teaching assistants teach, either in support of a professor, or as instructors of record. While the value of the stipend is not calculated on an hourly basis, RAs, TAs, and GAs are supposed to work "15 to 20 hours a week, averaging no more than 15 hours per week for the base stipend" (Cornell University 2013s, 5, 6). Graduate students supported by a category of assistantship that involves work (TA, RA, or GA) are permitted to work no more than five hours per week at some other job, with total hours worked not to exceed twenty hours per week. Graduate research assistantships function differently. GRA funding supports graduate students as they conduct *their own* research. GRAs *are not* subject to the same fifteen to twenty hour per week limit that characterize the RA, TA, and GA positions. (GRAs are allowed to work up to eight hours per week at some other job, three hours per week more than RAs, TAs, or GAs.)

The difference between what we might call the working assistantships (RA, TA, and GA) and the GRA mark a fundamental difference both in how work is classified in academic institutions and how time is commodified. The RA, TA, and GA job descriptions demarcate the hourly limits of the work graduate students do each week that does not *directly* advance their degree completion. This means that graduate students should not spend more than twenty hours per week teaching, doing research for someone else, or doing some other kind of work that does not directly advance their own scholarship. These three types of assistantships are designed to liberate graduate students from the need to support themselves by working *more*. In this important regard, funded PhD students inhabit a different world than the world of undergraduates, or tuition-paying graduate students. A generous stipend—three or four times more than a graduate student could earn working comparable hours at a campus job—coupled with a weekly limit on hours worked, is intended to ensure

PhD students can survive financially and still advance their own research. (While the cost of living in Ithaca has increased substantially in my time here, Ithaca remains considerably more affordable than regions like California's Bay Area where, as Tessa Brown notes in her introduction, graduate student funding is simply insufficient.)

By contrast, the GRA description translates the infinitely elastic world of PhD study, research, and writing into human resources terminology: "Because considerable time and attention is required for thesis research, the time devoted to the Graduate Research Assistantship (GRA) assignment is expected to be significant; hours spent . . . are not tracked" (Cornell University 2013, 5). In other words, when academics (including graduate students) do their own "work"—their own research and writing—they spend as much time as it takes. (The quotation marks surrounding "work" draw attention to the deep-rooted tendency among academics to conflate "work" with scholarship, a conflation that implicitly erases, or downgrades, other kinds of work—e.g., teaching, administration, mentoring. One goal for this article is to highlight the erasure of other kinds of work.) In considering the rationales—economic and educational—for the assistantship model, I would argue that teaching *does* advance a future professor's education, although its role in advancing scholarship may be less obvious than, say, archival research, field work, or data analysis. The bureaucratic ambiguity built into the assistantship policy—in which a stipend is an arrangement, not a salary; in which the assistantship serves the university's academic mission, and the student's education—has a real basis in how people learn on the job. Research and teaching—even when one assists others—do inform and advance graduate education.

The combination of self-reporting and administrative decentralization creates loopholes that graduate students may exploit or through which graduate students may be exploited. For TAs in particular, there is no mechanism to account for the possibility that a student worked five hours at some other job during a week when they also exceeded the fifteen-hour average limit of their assistantship. (No one but a teacher really knows how much time their own teaching takes; even teachers can't account for their time with absolute accuracy.) In any case, while TA, RA, and GA positions are supposed to average no more than fifteen hours of work per week, graduate students are typically assigned responsibilities, not hours. Graduate students are expected to track their own time. This is, arguably, a marker of respect. (I don't report the hours I spend on teaching or administration, and I wouldn't want to, not least because I wouldn't want to think about how little I am paid per hour.) Supervising faculty are often a graduate student's primary advisor, a committee member, or another faculty member who may be in position to make a career, or damage it. If an assistant's hours exceeded the allowable limit, communicating this information to a supervisor could be extremely uncomfortable and could have significant negative consequences. That this risk exists in any work environment doesn't make it any less toxic in graduate school. Absent a solution to the potential problems inherent in this system, I can do little more than recognize that these problems exist and that the risks can be at least partially mitigated when supervising faculty recognize the importance of tracking hours worked and assigning responsibilities accordingly. (Would that I could ensure that this actually happens.) It also matters that assistants are paid between three and four times what they would earn if they were working by the hour. If graduate students at my institution had to support themselves by working sixty hours per week, there would be little time left to advance their scholarship.

When considering relative time commitments for different TA assignments, one distinction is crucial. Assisting a professor usually does not involve designing a whole course. Teaching a writing seminar does. Designing a whole course represents a substantial time commitment. At my institution, this planning is supported by a six-week training course required of all graduate student teachers of FWSs. The training course focuses on helping students build their courses, while also serving as a laboratory for seminar teaching. The single credit students earn by taking this course may not, in itself, do much to advance their progress toward the degree, but the training course is a tangible credential—a line on their CV—that may help them market themselves as teachers, should they choose to do so. The greatest value of the time invested in course development is likely to reveal itself if students are asked, as job candidates, to present sample courses. A job candidate who can present a sample course they have already taught has a significant advantage over someone who has to invent a hypothetical course for an interview. Moreover, a new hire who can adapt an already planned course will find the transition to a new job easier than if they had to build every course from scratch. In these two substantive ways, the time invested in teaching a course they design may pay dividends when graduate students become job candidates, or salaried academics.

Invisible Credentials

> "The doctoral curriculum is modeled on the work of a professor at a research university—a career goal that the vast majority of doctoral graduates won't (or will not wish to) achieve."
>
> —Cassuto and Weisbuch, *The New PhD* (2021, 15–16)

Graduate faculty in academic programs assume that research—and the promise that research holds—represents the singular, essential credential their students need to be successful on the job market and in academic careers. At some level, this position is unassailable. Strong, publishable (or published) research is the gold standard. Nothing else has the potential to open as many doors. But there are not enough doors. There are not enough tenure-track jobs to ensure a job for every graduate student with strong research credentials. Cassuto and Weisbuch, quoted above, argue that these facts necessitate a full-scale redesign of graduate education.

The professors who train PhD students are mostly employed at research institutions. In addition to training graduate students, these faculty review the credentials of other PhDs. Through job searches, tenure reviews, manuscript reviews, grant and prize committees, and other forms of peer review, tenured professors serve as the gatekeepers for their professions, within their institutions and across the academic world. The view of academic achievement held by tenured faculty at PhD-granting institutions is shaped by the work they do to certify the research qualifications of their own graduate students, colleagues at their home institutions, and colleagues at other institutions. Through professional service and administrative responsibilities, research faculty see—every day—the value of research credentials (values they reinforce through the decisions they make). The credentials that lead to jobs where research may not feature so exclusively are less visible to the faculty who train PhDs.

In academic (versus preprofessional) programs, graduate students are taught to see their future careers through the lens of the research universities that train them. They are taught to value research because that is what research universities value. The student quoted above who noted that teaching well is not rewarded is correct if we consider tenure-track employment at a research institution to be the baseline. But, for most other academic jobs—including tenure-track positions at most public universities, liberal arts colleges, and community colleges, not to mention teaching-oriented positions off the tenure track—teaching well *is* rewarded (especially if we count employment a reward). If we consider the possibility that the future for a PhD might include academic employment in a teaching-oriented position, on or off the tenure track, teaching stops being a distraction from real work and becomes a pathway that might lead to real work. When graduate students recognize that paths exist other than the paths followed by the faculty who train them, the time invested in some kinds of labor—notably teaching—begins to look less like a short-term investment in food and shelter and more like a long-term investment in a career. Getting faculty to recognize this may be another matter.

Indeed, students who are already aiming for teaching-intensive professorial positions may already be more keyed into the teaching credentials they want to develop than their advising faculty are.

I turn from the language of economics to affect as I consider the emotional tensions in the comments quoted above. I see nothing contradictory about comments that say, of FWS teaching: "it's demanding," or "it's time consuming" and "I love it." (Six of twenty-nine qualitative responses to the final, open-ended question used the word "love.") People often choose graduate study because they see it as a pathway to meaningful work, which may or may not include tenured employment at a research university. For many people, teaching *is* meaningful work. Teaching is demanding, challenging, and time-consuming—and people love it.

These comments mirror my own experience. For me, academia has never been a foreign country. My great-grandparents were Eastern European Jews who arrived in New York City in the late nineteenth and early twentieth centuries. Within a generation my ancestors had landed in the middle-class or the bourgeoisie. Education provided pathways for class mobility. One of my grandmothers attended college in the early 1930s; the other would have done the same had she not married at seventeen and moved from Brooklyn to New Jersey. One grandfather commuted by train from Morristown to the New Jersey College of Law in Newark. My other grandfather graduated from Harvard in 1929, then from NYU Medical School. My parents met on the steps of the Rutgers University library.

My father was a professor of history. My older brother and I attended college simultaneously; our years as PhD students overlapped. For me, getting a PhD never felt like a risky path. I spent three years after college doing other things; I didn't want to go back to school just because academia was familiar. Early in my graduate career, my father told me that every graduate student decides to drop out every semester. If I hadn't been teaching, I probably would have dropped out. Teaching kept me in, especially during my worst semesters. During my best semesters, graduate school was my job, not my life. Teaching, tutoring, and study-skills counseling were part of the job; they sustained me, financially and otherwise. I worked as a teacher, tutor, and study-skills counselor because the work was engaging and because I needed the money. I also found, repeatedly, that teaching and tutoring led to other professional opportunities. (That pattern has continued.) At some point I began to suspect that the unofficial curriculum I pursued as a teacher and tutor would shape my career path.

Having grown up around academics, I knew enough about the academic class system to know that, since I was not studying at a top-tier program, I should not count on following my graduate career with a tenure-track job at a top-tier institution. I did not expect to make a career as a non-tenure-track faculty member, mostly at a single institution, but I'm not sorry I have. I've become increasingly aware, as I've built this career, that I am not alone. When graduate students ask about my career path, I'm always hesitant to offer myself as a role model, for two reasons. First, I'm too aware of the accidents that have shaped my path, and the cultural capital that has smoothed the way. Accidents are not easy to replicate or plan for (although learning to take advantage of accidents is a useful skill). Cultural capital is not evenly distributed. Second, I've always thought the pool of people doing what I do was vanishingly small. But, as I have learned how many people follow similar paths—two thousand-plus at my own institution—I have learned to see my career path as something people do (perhaps as a second or third choice), rather than merely the result of a unique series of accidents.

To the graduate student, quoted above, who is skeptical about whether their teaching experience will help their career, and who writes, "I'm suspicious that anyone will look at my CV and be struck particularly by this teaching experience," I would say that, when you craft a CV, you could bury this experience, or you could highlight it. The expectations of the jobs you apply for should shape whether and how you highlight it. But highlighting it may make your career.

Epilogue: Late Pandemic Notes

Among the ways my professional life has changed during the pandemic is the relatively minor fact that I have reduced the data-gathering operations that inform this essay. For the better part of two years, the part of my job that involves training and mentoring graduate instructors and TAs has focused on unexpected challenges: remote teaching; classroom safety; the heightened risk of burnout. Lately, I've advised teachers to do less—to protect their time and energy, because every aspect of daily life requires more effort. Responding to a survey may be a *small* something extra, but I haven't wanted to ask anyone to do *anything* extra.

Most of the graduate teachers with whom I currently work closely are scientists. Given the nature of science funding, the pressure to follow in an advisor's footsteps may be more intense for science students than for their students in the humanities. In some science fields, graduate students are essentially admitted, not just into a department or program, but into a lab. Their advisor is their boss. Some students are funded through grants their advisor has applied for. They begin to publish with their principal investigator (PI) and other collaborators early in their graduate career, while attempting to move their own research to the point when they can become the lead author on papers that will still include their advisor's name on author's list. Because a student's research and their PI's research are often closely linked, the time a student spends on teaching may look like time lost, not just for the student's research, but for the professor's livelihood. In the weeks that I wrote this essay, an interesting thread emerged. Within the (small) sample of graduate students I talk with most regularly, a number of students who were finishing in 2021 had applied to jobs other than (or in addition to) the R1 positions their graduate programs have officially prepared them for.

Many factors shape a decision to pursue less-conventional career paths. In my discussions with graduate students, three principal factors emerge. One is the scarcity of jobs and the associated ramping up of competitive pressure. Some students have gotten the message that they don't just need excellent research credentials—this agenda has been pushed since Day 1—they also need teaching credentials, *and* they should publish *about their teaching*.

A second factor is personal satisfaction. Students are wondering how the expected responsibilities of professional scientists—running a lab, applying for grants, supervising a team of students and postdocs—will align with other professional interests, such as teaching and service. And they are wondering how the expectations of an academic career will affect their family lives.

The third factor—the COVID pandemic—has heightened all forms of pressure, but has also, for some, reinforced the importance of considering personal satisfaction and work/life balance as factors in the decision-making matrix. Forced distance from family members or life partners has pushed some students to consider whether the conventional academic contract—in which you give up geographic choice in favor of the best job (or any job)—is worth the trade-offs. For some graduate students, forced changes in their work habits made them realize they wanted to pursue different modes of working. Despite the trauma associated with the pandemic, for some graduate students the disruptions have helped them focus on personal priorities, have helped remind them that the official curriculum and their personal priorities may not always align, and have provided occasions to consider alternatives.

Note

Thanks to my colleagues at Cornell, in and out of the Knight Institute, for creating an atmosphere where teaching is taken seriously. Thanks to the colleagues—faculty and graduate students—who have contributed to the study of graduate student teaching, and, more than that, for their committed, engaged, passionate teaching. Thanks to Tessa Brown, Laura Brown, and David Faulkner for their incisive comments on drafts of this manuscript.

Working with graduate student teachers is one of the most satisfying parts of my professional life. This work kept me in this job when I wasn't sure I wanted the rest of it. Special thanks to the students who contributed to this essay through their insights. Thanks to Deborah Starr for more than I can enumerate.

Works Cited

Anyon, Jean. 1980. "Social Class and the Hidden Curriculum of Work." *Journal of Education* 162, no. 1 (Winter): 67–92.

Cassuto, Leonard, and Robert Weisbuch. 2021. *The New PhD: How to Build a Better Graduate Education.* Baltimore: Johns Hopkins University Press.

Cornell University. 2013. "Graduate Student Assistantships," Policy 1.3, Cornell University Policy Library. Last updated November 22, 2013. https://www.dfa.cornell.edu/sites/default/files/policy/vol1_3.pdf.

———. 2019. "University Policy 1.3, Graduate Student Assistantships." Cornell University Policy Library. https://policy.cornell.edu/sites/default/files/policy/Volume%201.3%20Graduate%20Student%20Assistantships.pdf.

Cornell University Committee on Academic Titleholder Representation, 2018. "PPT Slide Overview of Preliminary Recommendations." https://cpb-us-e1.wpmucdn.com/blogs.cornell.edu/dist/3/6798/files/2018/09/CATRslidesFINAL-1fxrv7d.pdf.

Glossary of Education Reform. "Hidden Curriculum." 2015. Glossary of Education Reform. https://www.edglossary.org/hidden-curriculum/.

Kahn, Seth. 2020. "We Value Teaching Too Much to Keep Devaluing It." *College English* 82, no. 6 (July): 591–611.

Shapiro, Elliot. 2008. "Survival and Failure, Adaptation and Acceptance." *ADE Bulletin* 146 (Fall): 18–27.

———. 2015. "Towards an Integrated (Graduate Student) Training Program." *Across the Disciplines* 12 (3). https://wac.colostate.edu/docs/atd/graduate/shapiro2015.pdf.

Interlude 5

Establishing *Ethos* for a Translingual GTA—The Unwritten Labor

Anis Rahman

"I didn't really expect you to be an English teacher."
"What do you mean?"
"Never mind, I didn't mean to say it like that. Sorry!"
"It's okay, but did you expect someone else to teach this class?"
This was part of an unexpected conversation I once had with a student during our student-teacher conferences. She did not say it out of contempt or disrespect, I think; it was more her telling me of her surprise to see a person of color as an English writing instructor. Perhaps my somewhat accented English contributed to her shock, too. However, she did tell me that she views English as "white people's language."
"Can you tell me why you think so?"
"I just think so."
This happens pretty much every time I enter a classroom as a teacher of first-year composition: I notice, while setting up my PowerPoint slides, somewhat covertly odd looks from some students, who seem a bit confused. They probably expect a different person to come teach them English writing—maybe a white, middle-aged person.

As an international graduate student and a *brown* person of color, I have always had my insecurities, a sense of a lack of belonging to academia in the United States. The above-mentioned incident happened at my master's institution, where I taught only one section of first-year writing per semester. Here at my new doctoral institution, I am required to teach two sections of first-year writing per semester, a change that seemed a bit challenging at first. However, my training was intensive, and my mentors really helped me out during the orientation period. Conversation with fellow graduate students who have been at the institution for some time was helpful and reassuring. However, in my cohort, I was the only international graduate student, originally hailing from Bangladesh; I was also the only one with somewhat of an accent because of my multilingual background, speaking Bangla, English, a bit of Hindi and Urdu.

The first day of teaching in any first-year writing class has always been interesting to me. Perhaps the context contributes to this factor: as a person of color and with a multilingual background, I enter the classroom with different baggage than other teaching instructors like me. I do not intend to say I am the only one who might struggle with the first-day-of-teaching worries. However, I do want to underline the worries I have to go through because of my identity—it always seems to me that I have to take an extra step to establish my ethos as an English instructor. The extra steps are usually more psychological, and they definitely trigger some physical and/or tangible ones. For example, I always try to be ready to answer my students without any delay since a delay in response might trigger a doubt in their mind that I may not have the language/word to respond to their queries. They might think this brown person's English is not good enough and hence, he is incompetent to teach English. So, my tangible extra steps include always rehearsing class lectures more with these thoughts in mind. I'd contemplate possible student queries on class content, write them out on a sheet of paper, and prepare for possible responses.

My first day of teaching at my new institution as a doctoral student was uneventful. However, I did experience the "same old" look from some of my students. I stayed calm and went through the plan I usually have for the first day of classes—the usual stuff—the introduction, rundown of the syllabus, and a diagnostic write-up toward the end of the class. The look of disbelief, if I may call it so, that some of the students have at the beginning usually tapers off at one point of the semester. However, at the beginning of the semester, it feels like the same battle I just fought last semester—a battle to prove myself as an English instructor.

Mine is an experience I wanted to share. I am not sure whether other writing instructors of color like me (or GTAs, as we are officially called) go through the same experience. But I do feel this is an added challenge, added labor for us, for me personally. In addition to engaging in extra preparation regarding the questions I might face, I also try to notice how I sound so I can reduce the sound of my other languages while I speak English. This reduction of accent sometimes requires conscious and active effort. Repressing parts of my other "selves" like this sometimes feels like reducing part of me for my students, which is laborious. I still do this for the sake of ethos as a person of color teaching English in predominantly white spaces in midwestern universities. I feel that I have to walk the walk and talk the talk a bit more than other teachers of writing. For example, a monolingual English-speaker may never have to worry about having his/her accent being a mixed one, like I sometimes do. My accent is influenced by all the languages I speak—English, Bangla, Hindi, and Urdu. Not that my English is unintelligible or anything, but for many it seems a bit "weird," maybe a bit "off" from the mainstream.

This added pressure sometimes even triggered thoughts of leaving US academia and going back to Bangladesh, but I persevered. Part of the reason I stayed is because I think I need to be here to change the scenario—the mental one in the students' minds. The notion that English is the "white-people's language"—whereas it surely isn't. Millions of people learn and use this language in Bangladesh, where I learned it first. People there often learn English the day they learn the dominant language, Bangla. This simultaneous language learning happens because both English and Bangla are mandatory subjects in the curriculum, from primary to high school level. Thinking about my linguistic background this way, which is more fittingly described as "translingual," gave me inner strength to persist in academia in the United States.

A little bit of theory may help to understand my linguistic background. I lean toward identifying myself more as a "translingual" since, in the words of Suresh Canagarajah, I often "shuttle between" the languages that I speak (2006, 591). When pronouncing an English phrase that I have come across for the first time, I am often thinking what the Bangla phrase would be for that and vice versa. This closely aligns with Horner et al.'s interpretation of a "translingual" approach: "By contrast, a translingual approach takes the variety, fluidity, intermingling, and changeability of languages as statistically demonstrable norms around the globe" (2011, 305). As in Horner et al.'s description, my languaging often includes more than one language—it is fluid and intermingles with other languages from my "linguistic resources and repertoires" (Leonard 2014, 232). García's definition of translanguaging also grasps the core of my languaging practices nicely: "In conceptualization, translanguaging differs from code-switching in that it refers not simply to a shift between two languages, but to the use of complex discursive practices that cannot be assigned to one or another code" (2014, 112). Deeper reflection on my linguistic background and also conversations with my supervisors and their continuous support of my professional and scholastic growth have helped me persevere in academia in the United States.

The tactics that I use to persist in academia include reflecting critically about my linguistic situation and teaching practices, being resilient, counseling with supervisors, and also prepping more and harder to earn the ethos that I may lack in some students' eyes. Being in academia, teaching English in predominantly white spaces, I can make a positive impact—a change we desire—a notion that English is indeed a colorless language like Bangla, Hindi, Urdu, and Arabic, my other languages. I wanted to recount this story especially to incoming international graduate students in my field because I want to assure them it is possible and becomes easier as you persevere. I have been asked numerous times by my batchmates and junior scholars in Bangladesh how I teach American students and if they are respectful of me. Though these questions do not directly manifest the tensions and worries that these prospective graduate students feel, they do underline their worries/insecurities. I hear them—sounds like they are asking a series of questions, "Is it possible for us to teach American students?" "Will they accept us?" "Can we establish ethos as instructors?" And I understand because I have been there and come this far . . . And that's why I tell them, "Ethos is possible, but hard-earned."

Works Cited

Canagarajah, Suresh. 2006. "Toward a Writing Pedagogy of Shuttling between Languages: Learning from Multilingual Writers." *College English*, 68, no. 6 (July): 589–604.

García, Ofelia. 2014. "Countering the Dual: Transglossia, Dynamic Bilingualism and Translanguaging in Education." In *The Global-Local Interface and Hybridity: Exploring Language and Identity*, edited by Rani Rubdy and Lubna Alsagoff, 100–120. Bristol: Multilingual Matters.

Horner, Bruce, Min-Zhan Lu, Jacqueline Jones Royster, and John Trimbur. 2011. "Opinion: Language Difference in Writing: Toward a Translingual Approach." *College English* 73, no. 3 (January): 303–321.

Leonard, R. Lorimer. 2014. "Multilingual Writing as Rhetorical Attunement." *College English*, 76, no. 3 (January): 227–247.

5 | Learning to Teach, Teaching to Learn
Sara Austin and Kelly Moreland

Adding to this volume's review of graduate student workers' experiences, this chapter focuses on graduate students' content expertise as they teach first year writing courses. Specifically, we (re)imagine who can and should teach "writing about writing" (WAW)–style first-year writing courses, with attention to graduate students who may or may not identify as compositionists. Writing about writing is a content-specific approach to first-year writing (FYW) that places learning (and writing) about the discipline of writing studies at its center, so that students are not only practicing the activity of writing but are studying how writing works—i.e., the discipline of writing studies—as the course content. Several writing-studies scholars have contributed to the movement advocating for a writing-studies focus in first year writing, including Deborah Dew (2003), Wendy Bishop (2003), and Douglas Downs and Elizabeth Wardle (2007), as well as the "WPA Outcomes Statement" (2014). Importantly, we see a distinction between "writing about writing" as course content and *Writing about Writing*, Downs and Wardle's textbook, now in its fifth edition. Our focus here is on writing about writing as a content-specific approach to FYW, and specifically how graduate teaching assistants (GTAs) experience teaching FYW within that approach.

Following a case study of thirteen GTAs at our institution, we argue that in order to teach WAW in FYW courses, GTAs need sufficient preparation, including time, to expose them to the content they will be responsible for teaching. In this chapter we share findings from the study and share our recommendations for ways GTAs might be adequately prepared to teach writing about writing content in their own classrooms. More broadly, our study asks to what extent graduate students might learn a discipline by teaching it. Elsewhere in this volume, Shapiro argues that graduate students ought to be prepared through teaching opportunities. If this is the case, how might educators prepare and support graduate students for that learning? Though rooted in our discipline of writing studies, the implication that graduate students acquire disciplinary knowledge through teaching, and therefore should be supported in that learning-by-teaching, transcends disciplines. Our own findings suggest that students from a range of English subfields can "claim the field [of writing studies] as their own" (Wardle and Downs 2013) if given sufficient opportunity to do so.

In writing programs—often housed in English departments—graduate students who are teaching FYW for the first time at that institution (and maybe for the first time at all) are often required to enroll in a composition pedagogy course. Sometimes called a composition practicum, this course is where they learn about the discipline of writing and writing pedagogy. There is now a plethora of research on graduate teaching assistant[1] (GTA) preparation and development in writing studies, focusing most heartily on the graduate composition pedagogy course and what it ought (or not) do for its students (see, for example, Dobrin 2005; Estrem and Reid 2012; Reid, Estrem, and Belcheir 2012; Restaino 2012; and Yancey 2002.) In some cases, GTAs are expected to teach FYW during their first semester as a graduate student, leaving them little to no time to prepare. In others, GTAs are required to take a writing theory or pedagogy course, or so many graduate credits in English, before they are permitted to teach. Thus, pedagogy courses look quite different among institutions—a universal set of expectations for GTAs' prior learning or preparation for teaching FYW does not exist. So, while the pedagogy course is undoubtedly integral to the preparation and development of GTAs teaching first-year writing, we see scholarship that primarily focuses on these pedagogy courses as an invitation to expand upon research about GTAs in writing studies. We do so by considering how GTAs experience the FYW curricula they're expected to teach—what they themselves learn about writing from teaching writing about writing—as opposed to what GTAs learn about writing from their studies elsewhere, which may or may not include such a pedagogy course.

In part due to this focus on the composition pedagogy course, Jessica Restaino suggests that much of the work on GTA education "does not theorize the early experience of graduate students as writing teachers and its potential shaping of graduate students' understanding of composition as a discipline, nor the relationship between how writing instruction has been theorized and how it is practiced in the classroom" (2012, 2). Here, Restaino emphasizes a distinction between what GTAs learn in their classrooms, where they are the teachers, and what they learn as students of writing theory and pedagogy. She suggests a need for scholarship that focuses more on the disciplinary learning that results from practical classroom teaching. In this chapter, we take up Restaino's call as we theorize

GTAs' "understanding of composition as a discipline" (2012, 2) through their experience as writing teachers.

In a study of the effects of professional development on the teaching of writing, Zoch et al. found that "when given the opportunity to write with specific kinds of support and instruction, teachers changed their beliefs about writing instruction" (2016, 1), namely by adopting new or revised writerly identities themselves or by newly recognizing the importance of writing instruction. In other words, learning *about* writing through professional development had an effect on how the teachers approached both their own writing and their writing instruction. While Zoch et al. didn't study WAW pedagogy in its own right, their findings provide an opening to consider the ways in which graduate students learn a discipline by teaching it. Shelley Reid investigates the question of what GTAs learn about writing in "Teaching Writing Teachers Writing," where she claims that "current composition pedagogy is based on the premise that writing well is difficult; people who do not believe that premise themselves may only go through the motions as writing teachers" (2009, 202). Here, Reid speaks to the importance of introducing GTAs to the difficulty of writing—a concept that, as new GTAs often come from undergraduate careers as English majors and may view themselves as "naturally" good writers, they may not have encountered previously (Reid 2009, 201). These works by Zoch et al. and Reid suggest, however, that GTAs can learn to both practice and teach writing in new ways by experiencing writing studies content through professional development and learning to recognize that content in their own writing practices.

Furthermore, research suggests that some GTAs take away just as much if not more knowledge from the practice of teaching FYW as from their pedagogy course. Reid, Estrem, and Belcheir conducted a study of GTAs at their institutions, looking to find the effects writing pedagogy education had on the GTAs' teaching performance. The authors reported that the GTAs at their institutions "were influenced more strongly by prior personal experiences and beliefs and their experiences in the classroom than by their formal pedagogy education" (Reid, Estrem, and Belcheir 2012, 33–34). This study and its findings provide an additional opening for our work here, where we're focused less on what GTAs learn about *teaching* and more on what they learn about (the study of) *writing*, specifically from teaching a WAW approached FYW course. Moreover, in "On Learning to Teach," Reid suggests that GTAs take on three modes of learning—declarative knowledge (knowing what), procedural knowledge (knowing how), and metacognitive knowledge (reflective knowing)—as they (prepare to) teach FYW, especially for the first time (2017, 133). Though these three modes of knowledge are important for learning to teach—that is, GTAs must learn declarative, procedural, and metacognitive knowledge about *teaching*—Reid notes that it is equally important that GTAs learn about *writing* in these ways.

Proponents of WAW assume that, in order to be effective teachers of writing, GTAs must learn *about* the discipline of writing studies. Since GTAs at our institution use a WAW framework in their FYW courses, we had an opportunity to study GTAs from three subfields of English studies as they did this work. Wardle and Downs's work on WAW sets up some distinctions about writing and the teaching of writing that are important in the context of our study. First, as they suggest above, WAW makes explicit the difference between *pedagogy* and *content* in FYW courses. In the context of WAW and this study, pedagogy refers to the *how* of teaching—the sometimes-philosophical and sometimes-practical approaches that individual instructors take up in their teaching. Content, on the other hand, refers to the *what* of learning—the material that students are being asked to learn in their FYW classes, from what they're reading to what they're writing about. WAW is interested in the *content* of FYW. It asks that students learn—i.e., read and write about—the discipline of writing studies. Therefore, WAW interrupts more traditional approaches to teaching FYW in which students would write what Wardle calls "mutt genres"—writing assigned in FYW that might mimic the contexts of other academic writing situations but "their purposes and audiences are vague or even contradictory" (2009, 774). Wardle's argument, then, is that these "mutt genres" don't present authentic writing experiences for students and so they aren't doing much of anything in the way of teaching students about writing. But studying writing studies content, through approaches like WAW where students read and write about the discipline, *does* teach students about writing—not just how to do it, but what the discipline knows about writing and how it works.

As a content-specific approach, writing about writing "seeks . . . to improve students' understanding of writing, rhetoric, language, and literacy in a course that is topically oriented to reading and writing as scholarly inquiry and encouraging more realistic understandings of writing" (Downs and Wardle 2007, 553). Downs and Wardle suggest that teaching such content could be a substantial adjustment for its instructors, and most notably, they claimed early on that WAW "cannot be taught by someone not trained in writing studies" (2007, 574). Though Downs and Wardle clarify their argument in more recent work, advocating for the "need to build instructor expertise in order to make writing about writing work," their point remains that "writing studies . . . is a field with content; faculty members in any and every English-studies-related field don't know (can't be expected to know) that content, and can't be expected to step into a writing class and teach *about writing* without knowing that content" (Wardle and Downs 2013). So, given the limited amount of time many GTAs have to prepare for their (often brand new) teaching role, and also given the presumed newness of the WAW content for many GTAs, (how) can GTAs responsibly be expected to teach WAW in FYW, especially during their first year? And what happens when they do? Our work here aims to (begin to) answer these questions.

GTAs and Writing about Writing at a Midwest State University

In their 2013 article reflecting on WAW, Wardle and Downs study the impact of hiring eighteen instructors, from a range of English disciplines, whom they describe as "enthusiastic, smart teachers willing to read and learn and try new things." They note that as a result of this hiring, they were able to "design a training course and encourage teachers to become familiar with the relevant content of writing studies, and to embrace that field as their own." Noting similarities between the professional development program Downs and Wardle describe and our English department's approach to GTA preparation, we conducted an IRB-approved, mixed-methods study of thirteen GTAs at a midwestern research institution in order to explore how these graduate students pursuing a range of degrees from the English subdisciplines (MA in literature, MFA in creative writing, and PhD in rhetoric and composition) learn to teach—and teach to learn—writing through a WAW curriculum.

Midwest State University Context

All first-year GTAs in the English Department at Midwest State University[2] enroll in a practicum course, the Composition Instructor's Workshop, during their first semester teaching FYW 101: Introduction to Academic Writing. As part of the Composition Instructor's Workshop they also prepare to teach the second course, FYW 102: Academic Writing, the following semester. So, in fall 2017, as the first-year GTAs who participated in our study enrolled in the semester-long Composition Instructor's Workshop, they taught their very first section of FYW 101, and they prepared for their spring 2018 FYW 102 teaching assignment. While it is possible that these GTAs might teach FYW for more than one year, they are only required to enroll in the Composition Instructor's Workshop and teach the common curriculum (WAW) for one semester.

As part of the required preparation for their teaching assignment, all of the first-year GTAs participated in a one-week Graduate Student Orientation (GSO) where they were provided with a WAW curriculum for their FYW 101 course. In our roles as graduate student writing program administrators we developed the curriculum, which included readings from journals in writing studies (see appendix for the full reading list) as well as six writing assignments.[3] Following Wardle and Downs's suggestion that "there is no Wardle and Downs approach" to writing about writing—that the approach focuses on teaching writing studies content to students "and there are myriad pedagogical strategies for teaching this content" (2013)—we supplied the GTAs with writing studies content and assignments. The GTAs enrolled in the practicum were expected to teach the WAW curriculum during their first semester teaching, with the understanding that they would have more flexibility in designing their FYW 102 syllabus. During the GSO week and then more thoroughly throughout the semester, the GTAs were introduced to each writing project on the syllabus. As they learned about each writing project, they read the accompanying reading assignments and example student submissions, as well as additional articles from writing studies and readings from Adler-Kassner and Wardle's *Naming What We Know*.

Methods and Participants

We began this study with an initial research question: What happens when GTAs at Midwest State University, from a range of English subdisciplines, teach a WAW curriculum in FYW? More specifically, we were interested in understanding what GTAs learn about the discipline of writing studies from teaching a WAW-approached FYW course, and whether educators can responsibly ask GTAs to teach writing studies content even if those GTAs do not identify as compositionists. To address these questions we conducted a mixed methods study of GTAs who taught FYW 101 at Midwest State University in fall 2017. First, we sent a survey to all GTAs (first-year and beyond) who taught FYW 101 that semester. The survey included questions about the GTAs' FYW 101 course content as well as their perceptions of their own and their students' learning about writing. We purposely asked GTAs to describe their curriculum, anticipating that some of the first-year GTAs could have altered it to fit their or their students' needs. We also asked these questions because we sent the survey to all of the GTAs who taught FYW 101 in fall 2017, including returning GTAs who were not required to teach the WAW curriculum.

The thirteen GTAs who responded to the survey represent all of Midwest State University's English Department's subdisciplines—MA in literature, MFA in creative writing, and PhD in rhetoric and composition. Twelve of the thirteen respondents were first-year GTAs in fall 2017, meaning they taught the WAW curriculum and participated in the Composition Instructors' Workshop that semester. One respondent was a returning GTA, and so had taught FYW 101 at least one time prior to fall 2017 and had enrolled in the Composition Instructors' Workshop a previous year, but not in fall 2017. That participant was not required to teach the WAW curriculum in fall 2017. Six GTAs were PhD students in rhetoric and composition, three were MFA fiction students (out of five total, and no students on the poetry track responded to the survey); three were enrolled in the MA literature program (out of six total); and the one returning instructor did not list their degree program. The six PhD students who responded to the survey represent the entire population of PhD students enrolled in the Composition Instructors' Workshop in fall 2017. The respondents to this survey (n=13) represent a little over half of the twenty-two students enrolled in the Composition Instructor's Workshop in fall 2017, a response rate of 59%.

At the end of the survey we invited GTAs to indicate interest in participating in a follow-up group interview. We conducted two group interviews with a total of four first-year GTAs—Lynne (rhetoric and composition), Sabrina (literature), Frank (rhetoric and composition), and James (rhetoric and composition). During the interviews, we asked the GTAs questions about their experience teaching the WAW curriculum in fall 2017, including what they and their students learned about writing and what they would change if they were to teach a WAW curriculum again.

Data Analysis

To analyze the survey data, we separately qualitatively coded GTAs' responses to two survey questions related to the subject of this chapter: How would you describe the focus of your FYW 101 class? And, what did you learn about writing from teaching your FYW 101 class? Using the *in vivo* method, we individually coded the responses to those two questions. Then we individually sorted the *in vivo* codes into themes and compared the results for the two sets of answers. We worked together to name the common themes we identified individually. The codes we discuss in this section are represented in table 5.1. For the first question about the focus of FYW 101, we identified two overall themes—"**Pedagogy**" or "**Content**," to signal whether the GTA's response focused on pedagogy—the *how* of teaching; content—the *what* of teaching; or both. Responses that discussed content were further coded for the type of content, either "**Content: Explicit WAW**" content or "**Content: Abstract WAW**" (vague ideas about writing). Upon reviewing and coding the group interviews (discussed later in this section), we saw a strong connection between how the GTAs described the focus of their class and how they identified their expertise. That is, the GTAs who described the pedagogical focus of their FYW 101 class identified as strong teachers, but not necessarily as writing studies content experts; whereas the GTAs who described the content of their FYW 101 class identified as writing studies experts. Thus, we came to understand these codes as reflecting the (self-identified) source of the GTAs' expertise.

We took a similar approach in theming responses to the next question, on what GTAs learned about writing from teaching their FYW 101 course. We categorized those responses according to three themes, whether they expressed *learning to teach, learning about writing studies,* or *learning about both*. Then, we further organized the responses categorized as *learning about writing studies* according to whether the GTA expressed having gained new writing studies knowledge (**"New"**), confirmed their prior knowledge (**"Prior"**), or "**Mislearned**" (i.e., expressed having learned something about writing studies that we noted as inaccurate according to writing studies research). We further discuss the nuances of these codes, in context with our findings, below.

Finally, after coding the survey results, we used the same themes (pedagogy and content, learning about teaching and learning about writing) as lenses through which to read the interview transcripts. We noted occurrences of these themes across the interview data, which largely reinforced and expanded on the GTAs' survey responses. We also applied *in vivo* coding to the interview data, which was an important step in guiding our results: our interest in specific participants and themes comes from the distinct language they used as they discussed their teaching and learning about writing.

Findings

We organize this discussion according to three significant findings from our case study. First, we discuss how GTAs *learned to teach* by teaching the

Table 5.1. Overview of GTA Participants Teaching Experience and Degree Program

GTA	Degree Program	Prior Teaching Experience	Source of Expertise (Code)	Teaching to Learn (Code)
Carla	MA in literature	No	—	—
Sabrina		Yes	Content: Abstract WAW pedagogy	Mislearned
Violet		No	Content: Abstract WAW pedagogy	Prior
Eliza	MFA in creative writing	No	Content: Explicit WAW	"New"
"H"		No	—	—
Kara		No	Content: Explicit WAW	"New"
Frank	PhD in rhetoric and composition	Yes	Content: Explicit WAW	—
James		Yes	Pedagogy	Prior
Lynne		Yes	Pedagogy	—
Marie		Yes	Content: Explicit WAW	—
Molly		No	Content: Abstract WAW	"New"
Rita		Yes	Content: Abstract WAW pedagogy	—
Glenn	Unknown	Yes*	Content: Abstract WAW	—

*Taught FYW 101 previously.

Note. Overview of GTA participants' degree program, teaching experience, whether GTA's expertise was found in content or pedagogy, and whether GTAs (mis)learned writing studies content.

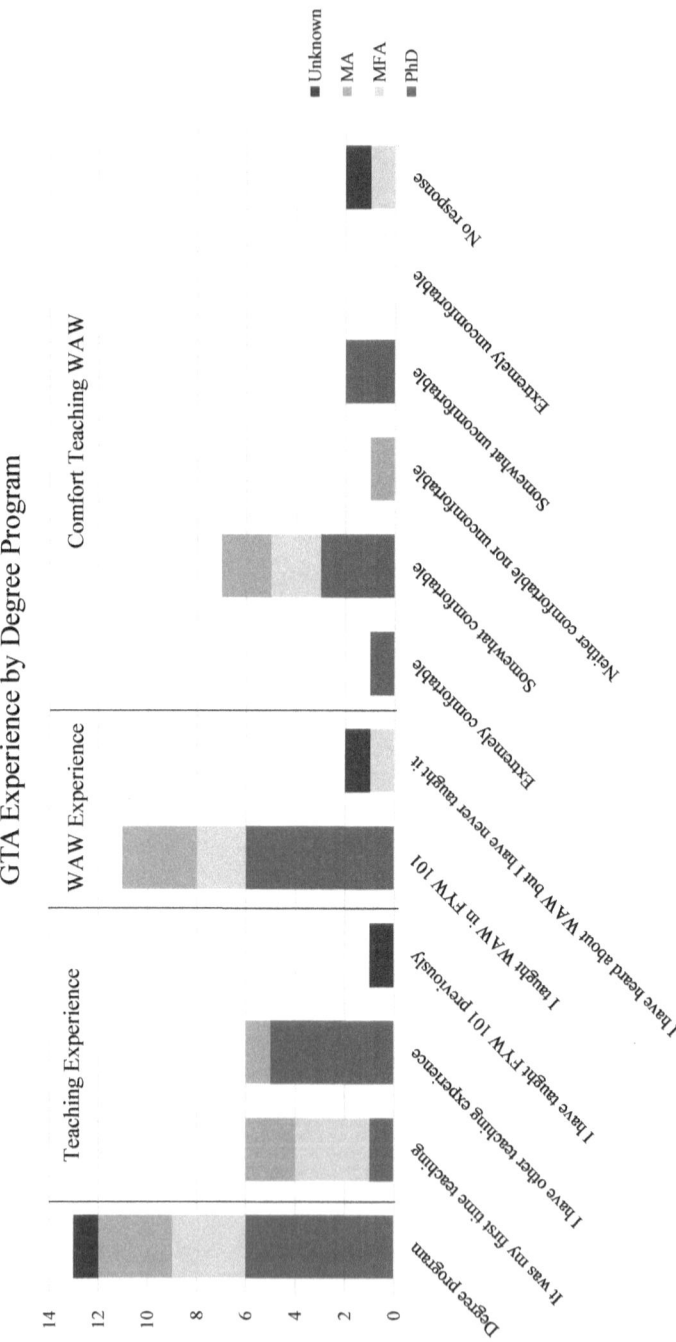

Figure 5.1, GTA teaching experience and comfort teaching WAW by degree program.

WAW curriculum in FYW 101, centering the GTAs who focused more on pedagogy in their responses and who described learning to teach. Next, we explore responses from the GTAs who discussed WAW content and responded as having learned about writing studies, which we categorize as *teaching to learn*. Finally, we conclude the discussion of our findings by locating the sources of our GTAs' expertise according to the reported focus of their FYW 101 course. Table 5.1 lists each of our GTA participants alongside their degree program, their prior teaching experience, and the codes we assigned to their two survey question answers, and figure 5.1 displays the GTAs' responses to questions about their teaching experience, WAW, and their comfort teaching WAW according to their degree program.

Learning to Teach

Once we analyzed the survey and interview data, we were eager to learn whether the GTAs' prior experience or degree program had any correlation with their comfort teaching the WAW curriculum. Of the first-year GTAs we surveyed, six indicated that fall 2017 was their first time teaching and six said that they had teaching experience at a different institution prior to teaching FYW 101. Though only half of the participants were experienced teachers, eight of the GTAs indicated that they felt comfortable teaching the WAW curriculum in FYW 101, and one (Sabrina) indicated feeling neither comfortable nor uncomfortable. Additionally, none of the non–rhetoric and composition students (i.e., those from literature and creative writing) reported feeling uncomfortable teaching the WAW curriculum. Four reported feeling "somewhat comfortable," one was neither comfortable nor uncomfortable, and one did not respond. In terms of this study, the survey responses don't show a connection between GTAs' prior experience or degree program and their comfort teaching WAW. Although all of the respondents who claimed prior experience indicated that their prior experience came from teaching at another institution, in her survey response Sabrina clarified that her previous teaching experience was from serving as "a tutor in undergrad for three years" and that during one of those years she "was an embedded writing tutor in a Comp II class and worked only with the students in that class." Though Sabrina saw herself as having previous teaching experience, her experience differed from that of the other experienced GTAs, who had all served as instructors of record at their previous institutions.

The GTAs' experience became especially important in this research because it did not directly correlate, as we might have expected initially, with the GTAs' comfort teaching the WAW curriculum. That is, we expected that GTAs with prior experience teaching first year writing would feel more comfortable teaching the WAW curriculum, but that was not necessarily the case. Only one participant indicated feeling "extremely comfortable" teaching the WAW curriculum (Frank, a rhetoric and composition student with prior teaching experience). Furthermore, we expected that the GTAs from the rhetoric and composition PhD program would be the most comfortable with the WAW curriculum, as the content directly aligns with their course of study. However, both of the GTAs who reported feeling "somewhat uncomfortable" teaching the WAW curriculum were PhD students—Molly, the only rhetoric and composition student who was also a first-time teacher, and Lynne, who had prior teaching experience.

Lynne provided some additional insight to her discomfort with teaching WAW during the group interview. She explained that a writing about writing curriculum

> introduces you to how complex it is to teach composition. Because, depending on where you're coming from, your experience, if you have no experience then you're only relying on your own memory of what your classes were. And if you have experience, you're relying entirely on that experience, and that can be very limited depending on where you were teaching. So I think for me what it really introduced me to is the fact that there's so much within writing studies that you can do. Like, it's kind of an overwhelming amount of options for how to teach at this level. (Lynne and Sabrina 2018)

For Lynne, the WAW curriculum "overwhelm[ed]" her teaching confidence: she had "limited" experience to rely on, but the curriculum opened her eyes to the (too) many possibilities for teaching first year writing. It is quite possible, then, that Lynne's prior experience contributed to her feeling "somewhat uncomfortable" toward the WAW curriculum, because it was so different from how she had previously taught first year writing—she had to (re-)learn how to teach composition at Midwest State University. By contrast, most of the inexperienced GTAs, who had to learn to teach composition for the first time, reported feeling comfortable teaching the WAW curriculum.

We stated earlier that one result of our survey indicated no connection between GTAs' prior (teaching) experience or their degree program and their comfort teaching the WAW curriculum. In his study of new GTAs' writing insecurities, Dryer came to a similar finding, noting that GTAs "who had served in a 'support' role in teaching"—like Sabrina—"were much more sanguine about teaching than those who had had sole responsibility for a classroom" (2012, 430). Dryer also found that "prior tutoring experience corresponds with a heightened self-awareness as writers, stronger feelings of readiness for academic writing, and greater confidence as teachers" (430). Though we didn't ask the GTAs about their confidence in themselves as teachers, as Dryer did in his study, five of the GTAs in our study discussed their teaching when we asked them what they learned about writing. Since these five responses did not explicitly mention *writing studies* content, we took these responses as an indication of greater confidence in their pedagogy, rather than comfort with the WAW curriculum. Given the responses, we determined that the GTAs likely talked about their teaching (though we asked them what they learned about writing) because they felt greater confidence in themselves as teachers and discomfort with the content.

Teaching to Learn

The GTAs who participated in our study came to understand and theorize the discipline of writing studies based on their classroom practices. In other words, they taught (writing) to learn (about writing studies). Specifically, the GTAs demonstrated their understanding of the discipline in one of three ways in their survey responses, which described: learning "new" writing studies content, confirming prior knowledge they held about writing, or mislearning writing studies content (figure 5.2).

The first way that GTAs taught to learn was by learning "new" (to them) writing studies content. Three participants, Eliza, Molly, and Kara, reported learning writing studies content through teaching the WAW curriculum. Figure 5.2 represents the GTAs' responses to the question "What did you learn about writing from teaching your FYW 101 class?" While ten GTAs responded to that question, here we depict the six responses that answered the question about writing—the other three GTAs responded with what they learned about teaching. As new teachers, Eliza, Molly, and Kara were encountering "new" writing studies content for the first time as they were teaching. Molly (a PhD student in rhetoric and composition), for example, was reading *Naming What We Know* for the first time, which "provided [her] with numerous opportunities to learn about threshold concepts and introduce them in [her] classroom." Similarly, Kara (an MFA student) appreciated the idea of threshold concepts and the projects she taught in 101 "looked at the process of writing from different angles." Eliza (MFA) suggested that teaching FYW helped her "approach [writing] more like a process that could be learned and taught, rather than an in-

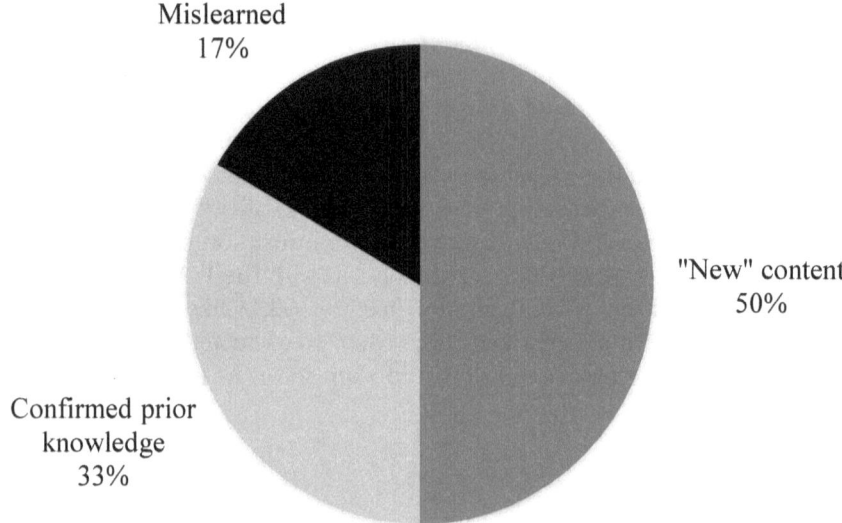

Figure 5.2, GTA participants' writing knowledge learned, mislearned, or confirmed as prior knowledge.

stinctive thing." We expected graduate students to learn about writing as they taught the WAW curriculum, but were somewhat surprised that only three participants reported learning something new about writing.

The second way in which GTAs taught to learn, based on our coding of survey data, was by confirming prior knowledge they held about writing. Violet, an MA student, reported that she "always knew that there wasn't a sole and correct way to write, but being a teacher really confirmed that." James, on the other hand, had previous teaching experience and "learned even more than I'd somewhat known how great reflection is for writing." For both of these GTAs, teaching the WAW curriculum reinforced beliefs they already held about writing.

Finally, the third way that GTAs taught to learn was through mislearning threshold concepts about writing. Sabrina, an MA student, focused on "basics" and "good writing," emphasizing that she "learned how important it is to consider the basics of writing when you write, even when you are a teacher or in grad school, because if you can't do the basics well then you are not going to be a very good writer" (Lynne and Sabrina 2018). Sabrina further explained that teaching writing "reminded me of the importance of focusing on some of those—just some of the stylistic stuff that you need to focus on in whatever writing you do" (Lynne and Sabrina 2018). Her responses evidenced common misunderstandings about writing—despite teaching a writing studies curriculum, at the time of our study Sabrina still didn't understand writing as "an activity and a subject of study" (Wardle and Adler-Kassner 2015, 15). Sabrina's emphasis on the "basics of writing" and being a "good writer" was evidence to us that she seemed to be focused on product, rather than process, and believed that there is only one "good" way to write. In addition to the misconceptions about "basics of writing" and "good writers," Sabrina also suggested that there are "naturally good writers," indicating that English majors are generally "good writers" because, for "a lot of them, it just came so naturally. Because, I mean, you're in English." Again, Sabrina seemed to mislearn another threshold concept, "writing is not natural" (Dryer 2015, 29).[4]

What's more, responses suggest that the GTAs' learning of writing studies content through their teaching was influenced by their graduate degree program. The GTAs from degree programs in writing, whether in creative writing or rhetoric and composition, demonstrated more openness to learning about writing through their teaching, whereas the students from literature were less open to learning new content about writing. For Violet (MA student in literature), teaching first year writing confirmed something she "always knew" about writing, as noted earlier. She didn't report learning anything new about writing. And Sabrina (also an MA student in literature), as we discussed, mislearned a threshold concept despite reading *Naming What We Know* in the practicum. They both reported learning something about writing, but the new (or confirmed) knowledge was not writing studies content represented in the WAW curriculum. Therefore, we suggest that these two GTAs in fact were not open to learning more about writing studies content, whereas the GTAs representing the other two degree programs reported changes in their thinking about writing studies content. For example, James (PhD student in rhetoric and composition) "learned even more than [he'd] somewhat known" about reflection—he confirmed and built upon his prior knowledge, whereas Violet described her students' writing as an example of knowledge she already held. While this finding isn't conclusive in its own right, it leaves us wondering to what extent a GTA's degree program influences their openness to learning about writing studies content, even within the scope of the same department.

Performing Expertise

Another emerging theme from our survey of GTAs suggests that GTAs claim expertise by discussing explicit WAW content, abstract WAW con-

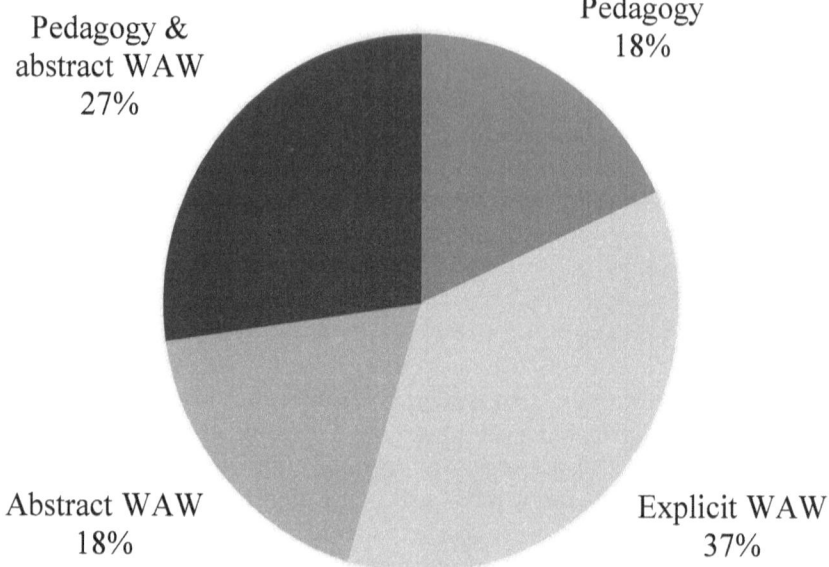

Figure 5.3, How GTA participants sourced their WAW expertise through references to pedagogy, abstract references to pedagogy, explicit references to WAW, or abstract references to WAW.

tent, or their pedagogy. When we asked GTAs about the focus of their FYW 101 course, five (out of eleven respondents) described their approach in terms of their pedagogy and/or abstract writing knowledge (see fig. 5.4). That is, they claimed expertise through *how* they taught and/or performed writing, but they didn't explicitly name concepts they learned from WAW. Four GTAs, however, did claim WAW expertise—they used key terms from the WAW curriculum to describe the focus of their FYW 101 course. Ultimately, as figure 5.3 depicts, when talking about the focus of their FYW 101 classes, the GTAs privileged their teaching knowledge (which we coded as pedagogy) over (writing studies) content knowledge. Two GTAs described the focus of their courses in terms of only their pedagogy, and an additional three GTAs mentioned both pedagogy and abstract writing content. This emphasis on pedagogy suggests that new GTAs are just as likely to claim expertise through their teaching styles as through content of the FYW classes they teach.

When discussing their expertise in WAW content, GTAs drew on explicit WAW knowledge, such as Kara (MFA student), who "focused on talking about writing as a recursive process, rather than a linear checklist."

Marie, Frank, and Eliza also reported teaching specific ideas. Marie (PhD student in rhetoric and composition) discussed focusing "on revision and development of transferable skills and understandings, so that was where I tried to place the focus of the course." Frank focused "on the eight habits of mind, especially metacognition," which he "find[s] to be instrumental in acquiring the other seven habits" (Frank and James 2018). (The "habits of mind" here refer to the Council of Writing Program Administrators' *Framework for Success in Postsecondary Writing* (2011), which one of the assignments in our WAW curriculum focused on.) Eliza (MFA student) similarly focused "on the habits of mind" but added that she was "kind of going along with what we were covering in pedagogy class" (the Composition Instructor's Workshop). Interestingly, although Eliza was explicit with her WAW expertise, she indicated in the survey that she had never taught WAW previously (including in fall 2017), even though she was a first year GTA enrolled in the Composition Instructors' Workshop. Eliza grasps the writing studies' content knowledge, but she doesn't name it as such or seem to recognize that she has taught it. These four GTAs made clear connections between the content of their FYW 101 course and what they learned in the Composition Instructor's Workshop—they demonstrated emerging expertise in writing studies content.

In addition to claiming expertise by discussing explicit WAW content, four GTAs mentioned abstract WAW concepts without explicitly naming them as WAW-related. Glenn, for example, focused his class on "learning how to write in the academic context and how it applies to [students'] lives," which was more student-centered. Similarly, Violet explained how her FYW 101 class "was focused on helping the students discover the topics and ideas they wanted to be most vocal about and figuring out how to channel that into essay writing." She continued, "Writing is a reflection of oneself, and that first year in a university setting is when many students learn the most about themselves." Rita (PhD student in rhetoric and composition) was another GTA who focused on students, noting that she "prioritized student agency and student passions" and that she "wanted them to select project topics that they were engaged by." Rita noted the importance of connecting to students' own expertise and "tried to ground them in a familiar thing they love as we diversify and expand what they know." Molly (another PhD student) also explained that the focus of her FYW 101 class was "on student writing, often in a personal way that incorporated some academic conventions as a way of acclimating them to writing in a university setting." Although Glenn, Violet, Rita, and Molly all focused on the personal nature of student writing, they specifically discuss the importance of focusing on writing content without explicitly naming that content. We find these responses significant, then, because the GTAs' thinking about writing seems aligned with Wardle's (2009) concept of "mutt genres," which focus more on "acclimating" to academic writing vaguely defined than on exploring writing studies content. In this sense, these GTAs claim expertise in writing as an *activity*, but not quite as a subject of study (see Wardle and Adler-Kassner 2015).

Even as the GTAs we coded as demonstrating abstract knowledge of writing displayed a disconnect between their teaching and writing studies content, Sabrina (MA student in literature) mentioned WAW by name but did not provide any specific examples of writing studies content she taught in FYW 101. Sabrina wrote that she "focused on teaching the WAW material in a way that made it fun and understandable for [her] students." Unlike her peers who demonstrated abstract knowledge of writing studies content, Sabrina named the curriculum—she knows that she taught WAW—but she didn't explain it in a way that would demonstrate ownership of the field. Some of Sabrina's other responses shed light on why she might not have claimed writing studies expertise: she didn't understand some of the assignments and concepts from the WAW curriculum. When we asked the GTAs what they would do differently if they were to teach FYW 101 again, Sabrina wrote, "I would change the discourse communities paper to be just a standard research paper on a topic that interests them, because both my students and I had trouble understanding discourse communities." Instead of claiming expertise in a field she didn't feel she fully understood or owned, Sabrina drew direct comparisons between her prior tutoring experience and her teaching (which made her familiar with how to teach genres like research papers). Noting the overlap between the essays she tutored at her previous institution and what she taught in FYW 101, she said she had done "a personal narrative essay, so essentially a literacy narrative. . . . A rhetorical analysis, and . . . a final theory of writing type paper" (Lynne and Sabrina 2018). Teaching these three FYW 101 projects came easily to Sabrina because she had experience guiding students through them before. But other projects in the WAW curriculum, like the discourse community paper she mentioned, made her uneasy. Sabrina was most interested in teaching the projects she was familiar with or had tutored in the past, and she was uncomfortable with the new-to-her content (i.e., the WAW content) that she didn't understand.

Sabrina perhaps wasn't wrong to question the writing studies content she was unfamiliar with. As a literature MA student, writing studies, by her definition, didn't have much to do with her degree program. Furthermore, a long-standing divide between writing studies and other English subdisciplines (e.g., literature and creative writing) often results in scholars and students misunderstanding one another, or even undervaluing each other's work. This divide certainly exists at Midwest State University, and so it might have been an influence for Sabrina as well. During the group interviews we asked the GTAs to share what relationships they saw between their degree program and teaching FYW. Sabrina tried to see the value in teaching writing studies as content in FYW 101, but explained that "literature people are more concerned with literature, and they don't see writing, like writing classes, as being as important or as content-based" (Lynne and Sabrina 2018). Yet she viewed herself differently from others in her field of study because she "see[s] the benefit of teaching composition because I know wherever I end up I'll have to teach composition" (Lynne and Sabrina 2018). She continued to explain that she "value[s] it, but a lot of other people don't. Which is sad, because composition is important" (Lynne and Sabrina 2018). Sabrina perceived value in composition and understood its importance, but she didn't fully locate the content of writing studies or a WAW curriculum within that frame.

While Sabrina (perhaps understandably) saw little connection between her own degree program and writing studies, Frank, James, and Lynne (all rhetoric and composition PhD students) saw more direct connections between their coursework and teaching WAW. James and Frank discussed similarities between WAW and their exam reading list and mentioned that concepts such as the rhetorical situation, which James said is "eventually what we address in FYW," were "explored directly and in detail in just about every course I've taken so far" (Frank and James 2018). Similarly, Lynne said, "so much of what we talk about in FYW 101, like discourse communities for example, is something that came up in other coursework after that" (Lynne and Sabrina 2018). Additionally, James suggested that the doctoral program is set up so that "it can promote and help us with our teaching. A lot of things that we're doing in FYW are based on, or tweaked by, or informed, or just aided by what we're learning and doing in the doctoral program" (Frank and James 2018). Ultimately, James was glad that his "work and study patterns are linked" (Frank and James 2018). For James, Frank, and Lynne, any writing studies expertise they gained from teaching the WAW curriculum was reinforced by the content they studied in their doctoral program.

Though the rhetoric and composition students could easily identify a strong relationship between teaching FYW and their degree program, not all of the GTAs identified their expertise in terms of their writing knowledge. Two of the eleven GTAs who responded to the question about the focus of their FYW 101 course identified expertise solely through *how* they taught their class (their pedagogy) and not through *what* they were teaching (the content), while three GTAs identified expertise through a combination of their pedagogy and abstract references to content. These three GTAs described their course in terms of how they taught it, specifically with concern for students' attitudes toward writing. Lynne, Violet, James, and Rita were concerned with changing student perceptions toward writing and student agency. The focus of Lynne's FYW 101 class was "on getting students to feel more comfortable with writing and seeing themselves as writers." Similarly, Violet wanted "students to discover that writing an essay is not simply about impressing an instructor or repeating what you think that instructor wants to hear." James was focused on "trying to sneak in, or enhance, a love of or at least comfort toward writing." Rita explained that she "prioritized student agency and student passions." With the survey data alone, it seems as though these GTAs claimed expertise by describing their pedagogy, not by their writing studies content knowledge. Lynne, James, and Rita's responses were particularly surprising because, as students in the rhetoric and composition program ourselves, we would have thought they'd be the first to share their disciplinary knowledge. (In James and Lynne's cases, we know that they do own their writing studies knowledge based on their responses during the group interviews.) Similarly, the five GTAs who expressed expertise in terms of pedagogy had various levels of teaching experience—only one of the five was a first-time instructor in fall 2017. We might have expected that more first-time instructors would respond by describing their expertise in terms of pedagogy when asked about the focus of their FYW 101 class.

In "On Learning to Teach," Reid (2016) claims that GTAs must simultaneously undertake declarative, procedural, and metacognitive knowledge about writing and the teaching of writing in order to effectively perform their roles as instructors. The findings from our survey support Reid's claim in that the GTAs we studied often seemed unable to separate their writing content knowledge from their pedagogical knowledge. They were, in Reid's words, "learning everything at once" (246). Our participant Lynne speaks to the difficulty of simultaneously taking on all of this new knowledge:

> The concepts that we're talking about in writing about writing, for almost every GTA, are brand new. So they're learning it as they're teaching it. . . . A lot of people are coming from a background where they maybe didn't have *Writing about Writing*, or have a full writing about writing curriculum; so it's not even similar to something they've done in many cases. It's like a brand-new curriculum. . . . You're kind of having to learn everything at once, and

then feeling confident enough to then present that, and because it's so many new projects and so many new concepts, and you're planning all of that while teaching for the first time, and then trying to plan 102—it's just very overwhelming. (Lynne and Sabrina 2018)

Given that the GTAs are tasked with learning so many new concepts at once, and that teaching is just one aspect of an often-overwhelming graduate student role, we recommend that writing program administrators ensure that GTAs are adequately prepared to teach a WAW curriculum.

Concluding Implications: Privileging Time in GTA Preparation

We began this research wanting to understand what happens when GTAs are tasked with teaching a WAW curriculum, and how GTA educators might responsibly prepare GTAs to teach such content. We determined that, when GTAs teach a WAW curriculum, they are shaped by their "understanding of composition as a discipline," whether that understanding comes from content—new knowledge or prior knowledge—or pedagogy (Restaino 2012, 2). While a case study of one composition program certainly can't create large-scale answers, from our findings we provide a few recommendations for how GTAs might responsibly be expected to teach WAW content, especially as new (or non-) compositionists. Wardle and Downs suggest that instructors without expertise in writing studies cannot be expected to effectively teach WAW; however, they advocate for rich professional development programs that can help prepare instructors to teach writing studies content. It follows, then, that what GTAs need most to effectively teach writing about writing is adequate preparation, including time, mentorship, and professional development, in order to not only learn the writing studies content they'll teach but to "embrace that field as their own" (Wardle and Downs 2013). While GTA preparation continues to be impacted by the COVID-19 pandemic that began after this research was conducted, we advocate that TA education programs consider the needs of their GTAs and students. Small and incremental moves toward writing about writing can be just as effective as the broad changes we suggest in this chapter.

In order for GTAs to cultivate ownership of WAW content, we suggest first that they are given more time to prepare for their teaching role prior to the first semester in the classroom. For example, for English department GTAs at Midwest State University, first-year GTAs experienced a one-week GSO prior to the first week of the fall semester, which was their first semester in the classroom. In an ideal revision of this approach, we would recommend that GTAs are given an alternative assistantship during the first semester, so that they could enroll in a semester-long pedagogy course before teaching. An alternative to this approach that would still provide GTAs with more time could be to enroll GTAs in an online pedagogy course during the summer prior to their teaching assistantship. While several universities already provide GTAs with a semester or more of preparation prior to the teaching assignment, we think this extra time is especially integral when GTAs are teaching WAW: they need *time*—time to learn the writing studies content and feel ownership of that content before they step into the classroom.

Lynne spoke to the need for content ownership during the group interview: "I think the premise of writing about writing is that you have people who are more 'experts' of that subject teaching it, but if people are coming in and they have no clue what it is, then that kind of benefit is sort of lost" (Lynne and Sabrina 2018). Lynne is right. Wardle and Downs (2013) are also right when they argue that "we are a field and we know things and should teach them." In order to reconcile the reality of new GTAs teaching composition without losing the benefit of WAW experts teaching FYW 101, GTAs *do* need additional time, but part of the onus is also on the GTAs to be open and "willing to read and learn and try new things" (Wardle and Downs 2013). This isn't to say that the GTAs in this study weren't open and willing to learn new things (even if they resisted new writing studies knowledge, as was sometimes the case); nor is it to say that the GTAs underperformed in their classrooms. But GTA educators must prepare for instances when, sometimes, GTAs' understanding of composition does not align with current trends in writing studies. Expecting GTAs to teach WAW is also expecting them to identify with composition as a field—it requires commitment on the part of the program and the GTAs themselves.

Notes

1. Though we use the term "graduate teaching assistant," note that we are specifically referring to graduate students who perform as the instructor of record for their first-year writing courses.

2. Midwest State University, course titles, and participant names are pseudonyms.

3. The writing projects were: Literacy Narrative, Habits of Mind Project, Writing in Communities, Rhetorical Analysis, Revision Project, and Theory of Writing.

4. Reid (2009, 201) notes that positions like Sabrina's are common among English-major GTAs: "Students who become English majors are often 'naturally'

good writers. The composition pedagogy class may thus be students' first opportunity to experience writing as a difficult task."

Works Cited

Adler-Kassner, Linda, and Elizabeth Wardle, eds. 2015. *Naming What We Know: Threshold Concepts of Writing Studies.* Boulder: University Press of Colorado.
Bishop, Wendy., ed. 2003. *The Subject Is Writing: Essays by Teachers and Students,* 3rd ed. Portsmouth, NH: Boynton/Cook.
Council of Writing Program Administrators. 2014. "WPA Outcomes Statement for First-Year Composition (3.0)." Approved July 17, 2014. https://wpacouncil.org/aws/CWPA/pt/sd/news_article/243055/_PARENT/layout_details/false.
Council of Writing Program Administrators, National Council of Teachers of English, and National Writing Project. 2011. *Framework for Success in Postsecondary Writing.* https://wpacouncil.org/aws/CWPA/pt/sd/news_article/242845/_self/layout_details/false.
Dew, Deborah Frank. 2003. "Language Matters: Rhetoric and Writing I as Course Content." *WPA: Writing Program Administration* 26, no. 3 (Spring): 87–104.
Dobrin, Sidney I., ed. 2005. *Don't Call It That: The Composition Practicum.* Urbana, IL: National Council of Teachers of English.
Downs, Douglas, and Elizabeth Wardle. 2007. "Teaching about Writing, Righting Misconceptions: (Re)Envisioning 'First-Year Composition' as 'Introduction to Writing Studies.'" *College Composition and Communication* 58, no. 4 (June): 552–584.
Dryer, Dylan B. 2012. "At a Mirror, Darkly: The Imagined Undergraduate Writers of Ten Novice Composition Instructors." *College Composition and Communication* 63, no. 3 (February): 420–452.
———. 2015. "Writing Is Not Natural." In Adler-Kassner and Wardle 2015, 27–29.
Estrem, Heidi, and E. Shelley Reid. 2012. "What New Writing Teachers Talk about When They Talk about Teaching." *Pedagogy* 12, no. 3 (Fall): 449–480.
Frank and James. 2018. Interview by authors. Video recording. August 15, 2018.
Lynne and Sabrina. 2018. Interview by authors. Video recording. December 14, 2018.
Reid, E. Shelley. 2009. "Teaching Writing Teachers Writing: Difficulty, Exploration, and Critical Reflection." *College Composition and Communication* 61, no. 2 (December): 197–221.
———. 2016. "What Is TA Education?." In *A Rhetoric for Writing Program Administrators,* 2nd ed., edited by Rita Malenczyk, 245–257. Anderson, SC: Parlor Press.
———. 2017. "On Learning to Teach: Letter to a New TA." *WPA: Writing Program Administration* 40, no. 2 (Spring): 129–145.
Reid, E. Shelley, and Heidi Estrem, with Marcia Belcheir. 2012. "The Effects of Writing Pedagogy Education on Graduate Teaching Assistants' Approaches to Teaching Composition." *WPA: Writing Program Administration* 36, no. 1 (Fall): 32–73.
Restaino, Jessica. 2012. *First Semester: Graduate Students, Teaching Writing, and the Challenge of Middle Ground.* Urbana: Southern Illinois University Press.

Wardle, Elizabeth. 2009. "'Mutt Genres' and the Goal of FYC: Can We Help Students Write the Genres of the University?" *College Composition and Communication* 40, no. 4 (June): 765–789.

Wardle, Elizabeth, and Doug Downs. 2013. "Reflecting Back and Looking Forward: Revisiting 'Teaching about Writing, Righting Misconceptions' Five Years On." *Composition Forum*, 27 (Spring). https://compositionforum.com/issue/27/reflecting-back.php.

Wardle, Elizabeth, and Linda Adler-Kassner. 2015. "Writing Is an Activity and a Subject of Study." In Adler-Kassner and Wardle 2015, *Naming What We Know*, 15–16.

Yancey, Kathleen Blake. 2002. "The Professionalization of TA Development Programs: A Heuristic for Curriculum Design." In *Preparing College Teachers of Writing: Histories, Theories, Programs, Practices*, edited by Betty P. Pytlik and Sarah Liggett, 63–74. New York: Oxford University Press.

Zoch, Melody, Joy Myers, Claire Lambert, Amy Vetter, and Colleen Fairbanks. 2016. "Reimagining Instructional Practices: Exploring the Identity Work of Teachers of Writing." *Teaching/Writing: The Journal of Writing Teacher Education* 5, no. 1 (Fall): 1–23.

Appendix: Reading Lists

FYW 101 Reading List

Brandt, Deborah. 1998. "Sponsors of Literacy." *College Composition and Communication* 49, no. 2 (May): 165–185.

Carroll, Laura Bolin. 2010. "Backpacks vs. Briefcases: Steps toward Rhetorical Analysis." In Lowe and Zemliansky, *Writing Spaces*, 45–58.

Council of Writing Program Administrators, National Council of Teachers of English, and National Writing Project. 2011. "Framework for Success in Postsecondary Writing." Council of Writing Program Administrators, http://wpacouncil.org/files/framework-for-success-postsecondary-writing.pdf.

Gee, James Paul. 1989. "Literacy, Discourse, and Linguistics: Introduction." *Journal of Education* 171 (1): 5–17.

Giles, Sandra L. 2010. "Reflective Writing and the Revision Process; What Were You Thinking?" In Lowe and Zemliansky, *Writing Spaces*, 191–204.

Grant-Davie, Keith. 1997. "Rhetorical Situations and Their Constituents." *Rhetoric Review* 15, no. 2, (Spring): 264–279.

Hinton, Corrine E. 2010. "So You've Got a Writing Assignment. Now What?" In Lowe and Zemliansky, *Writing Spaces*, 18–33.

Irvin, L. Lennie. 2010. "What Is 'Academic' Writing?" In Lowe and Zemliansky, *Writing Spaces*, 3–17.

Johns, Ann M. 1997. "Discourse Communities and Communities of Practice: Membership, Conflict, and Diversity." In *Text, Role, and Context: Developing Academic Literacies*, 51–70. New York: Cambridge University Press.

Lamott, Anne. 1994. "Shitty First Drafts." In *Bird by Bird: Some Instructions on Writing and Life*, 21–27. New York: Anchor Books.

Losh, Elizabeth, Jonathan Alexander, Kevin Cannon, and Zander Cannon. 2014. "Why Rhetoric?" In *Understanding Rhetoric: A Graphic Guide to Writing*, 35–66. New York: Bedford St. Martin's.

———. 2014. "Rethinking Revision." In *Understanding Rhetoric*, 217–244.

Lowe, Charles, and Pavel Zemliansky. *Writing Spaces: Readings on Writing*. Vol. 1. West Lafayette, IN: Parlor Press.

Mellix, Barbara. 1987. "From Outside, In." *Georgia Review* 41 (2): 258–267.

Murray, Donald M. 1991. "All Writing Is Autobiography." *College Composition and Communication* 42, no. 1 (February): 66–74.

Robertson, Liane, Kara Taczak, and Kathleen Blake Yancey. 2012. "Notes toward a Theory of Prior Knowledge and Its Role in College Composers' Transfer of Knowledge and Practice." *Composition Forum* 26 (Fall). http://www.composition-forum.com/issue/26/prior-knowledge-transfer.php.

Rose, Mike. 1980. "Rigid Rules, Inflexible Plans, and the Stifling of Language: A Cognitivist Analysis of Writer's Block." *College Composition and Communication* 31, no. 4 (December): 389–401.

Selzer, Jack. 2004. "Rhetorical Analysis: Understanding How Texts Persuade Readers." In *What Writing Does and How It Does It: An Introduction to Analyzing Texts and Textual Practices*, edited by Charles Bazerman and Paul Prior, 279–307. Mahwah, NJ: Lawrence Erlbaum Associates.

Swales, John. 1990. "The Concept of Discourse Community." In *Genre Analysis: English in Academic and Research Settings*, 21–32. Boston, MA: Cambridge University Press.

Trim, Michelle D., and Megan Lynn Isaac. 2010. "Reinventing Invention: Discovery and Investment in Writing." In Lowe and Zemliansky, *Writing Spaces*, 107–125.

Composition Instructors' Workshop Reading List

Adler-Kassner, Linda, and Elizabeth Wardle, eds. 2015. *Naming What We Know: Threshold Concepts of Writing Studies*. Boulder: University Press of Colorado.

Conference on College Composition and Communication. 2015. "Principles for the Postsecondary Teaching of Writing." National Council of Teachers of English. https://ncte.org/statement/postsecondarywriting/.

Council of Writing Program Administrators. 2014. "WPA Outcomes Statement for First-Year Composition." http://wpacouncil.org/positions/outcomes.html.

Council of Writing Program Administrators, National Council of Teachers of English, and National Writing Project. 2011. "Framework for Success in Postsecondary Writing." Council of Writing Program Administrators. https://wpacouncil.org/aws/CWPA/pt/sd/news_article/242845/_self/layout_details/false.

Dartmouth Institute for Writing and Rhetoric. 2016. "Syllabus and Assignment Design." April 15, 2016. https://writing-speech.dartmouth.edu/teaching/first-year-writing-pedagogies-methods-design/syllabus-and-assignment-design.

Downs, Douglas, and Elizabeth Wardle. 2007. "Teaching about Writing, Righting Misconceptions: (Re)Envisioning 'First-Year Composition' as 'Introduction to Writing Studies.'" *College Composition and Communication* 58, no. 4 (June): 552–584.

Driscoll, Dana Lynn, and Jennifer Wells. 2012. "Beyond Knowledge and Skills: Writing Transfer and the Role of Student Dispositions." *Composition Forum* 26 (Fall). http://compositionforum.com/issue/26/beyond-knowledge-skills.php.

Duffy, John. 2017. "Post-Truth and First-Year Writing." *Inside Higher Ed*, May 8, 2017. https://www.insidehighered.com/views/2017/05/08/first-year-writing-classes-can-teach-students-how-make-fact-based-arguments-essay.

Gardner, Traci. 2015. "Converting to a More Visual Syllabus." *Bedford Bits* (blog). July 2, 2015. https://community.macmillanlearning.com/t5/bits-blog/converting-to-a-more-visual-syllabus/ba-p/2873.

Gayle Morris Sweetland Center for Writing. 2017. "Using Peer Review to Improve Student Writing." University of Michigan. https://lsa.umich.edu/content/dam/sweetland-assets/sweetland-documents/teachingresources/UsingPeerReviewToImproveStudentWriting/UsingPeerReviewtoImproveStudentWriting.pdf.

Gee, James Paul. 1989. "Literacy, Discourse, and Linguistics: Introduction." *Journal of Education* 171 (1): 5–17.

Kent State University. 2017. "Assessing Student Multimodal Work." https://www.kent.edu/english/assessing-multimodal-student-work.

Massachusetts Institute of Technology. 2011."No One Writes Alone: Peer Review in the Classroom, A Guide for Instructors." *MIT Tech TV*, 2011. Video, 6:40. https://techtv.mit.edu/videos/5c1490f7951645d99c2884d3fdc9f03a/.

Reiff, Mary Jo, and Anis Bawarshi. 2011. "Tracing Discursive Resources: How Students Use Prior Genre Knowledge to Negotiate New Writing Contexts in First-Year Composition." *Written Communication* 28, no. 3 (July): 312–337.

Sasser, Tanya. 2014. "Teaching Revision vs. Editing." *Remixing College English*, February 24, 2014. https://remixingcollegeenglish.wordpress.com/2014/02/24/teaching-revision-vs-editing/.

Sommers, Nancy. 1982. "Responding to Student Writing." *College Composition and Communication* 33, no. 2 (May): 148–156.

———. 1980. "Revision Strategies of Student Writers and Experienced Adult Writers." *College Composition and Communication* 31, no. 4 (December): 378–388.

Takayoshi, Pamela, and Cynthia L. Selfe. 2007. "Thinking about Multimodality." In *Multimodal Composition: Resources for Teachers*, edited by Cynthia L. Selfe, 1–12. Cresskill, NJ: Hampton Press.

Wardle, Elizabeth, and Doug Downs. 2013. "Reflecting Back and Looking Forward: Revisiting 'Teaching about Writing, Righting Misconceptions' Five Years On." *Composition Forum*, 27 (Spring). https://compositionforum.com/issue/27/reflecting-back.php.

Interlude 6

Mothering and Laboring as a Graduate Student and Teacher

Alma Villanueva

It was my second semester in the PhD program. I was all alone, with an infant, at a conservative, Southern, historically military and all-male university. It was a hostile environment for people of color, for queer persons, for mothers. In our department alone, there were attacks on any mode of teaching or doing scholarship—any existence of an *identity*—that diverged from the status quo. I had to fight every step of the way just to exist in what ended up being conflicting roles as a graduate student–graduate teacher and a de facto single parent in a strange new place thousands of miles away from any family. But I was determined to hold true to the supposed feminist stance that "I could do it all"—I simply had no choice. There was no support, no structural accommodations for parent graduate students.

Between breastfeeding and pumping in my shared office around the clock for an infant who remained in the ninety-fifth percentile in weight for quite some time and the stress of coursework and teaching, within a few months after delivering, my bodyweight dropped fifteen pounds below what it was before I got pregnant. I was having crying spells and found myself sleeping with my eyes open while sitting straight up as I stared blankly at the words in books and on the computer screen. I was experiencing the usual "fourth-trimester" emotions from changes in my body coupled with the sleep deprivation that comes from caring for an infant, yet I was also being hazed into a new academic role.

I was constantly filled with fear—fear of not being able to live up to the neoliberal mandates of academic success. On a day when I was supposed to present and facilitate discussion, I finally gave in. Right before the class, I emailed the professor to let her know I couldn't make it. In response, the teacher pressured me to drop her course. "Not everyone is going to cater to you just because you had a baby," she told me. In another class, I missed two consecutive sessions early on in the semester because my infant was ill. With the support of the graduate director, that professor wanted me to take the course alternatively, to meet with her one on one instead of attending the regular class. Since I had an infant at home, she reasoned, it was likely that I would miss further classes. For some reason she thought my absences would be disruptive to the other students in the class. Repeatedly, there were attempts to make invisible the maternal labor that I had to perform outside of academia. When I "overstepped" by refusing to work outside of the official term period of a summer assistantship because my partner was visiting us from overseas that week, having not seen his own child for over half a year, an administrator told me I was "testing the good graces of my department."

Eventually, I could no longer afford to please the department. I had to become selective with which professors I'd try to impress. Some courses wouldn't get As. The service and publication sections of my CV wouldn't match those of my peers. But as I reluctantly let go of the "do it all" narrative that graduate school mandates, I was introduced to another narrative, in a course on cultural studies through a race and gender lens. It was a small class, all women, most of color, though I was the only parent. We read a book by Diane Negra on "post-feminism," which argues that popular media sells women the idea that it's empowering to choose leaving their professions or reducing their paid workloads in order to better care for their children (2009). And yet, thinking of my baby whom I yearned to be with more, I shared with the class that I kept finding myself to have similar desires. Another woman in the class nodded her head, saying, "I know, me too!"—as if we were agreeing that even we, women who do intersectional feminist work, get pulled into such "anti-feminist" desires. Yet, I take issue not only with post-feminism, even though it purports to value the work of caring for family, but with critiques of post-feminism that risk denouncing or undervaluing maternal labor in general. How could a feminist politic discuss mothering only in terms of a supposed regression of feminism?

Nearly all of the punitive actions taken against me in my program came from women, mothers, people whose scholarship focuses on feminisms. I remember as I took classes in my late pregnancy, when my belly was protruding, and then after when my bodyweight dipped to as low as it had been when I was a preadolescent, how strange it was to read theories of affect and embodiment that were entirely void of discussions of pregnancy, or mothers, or mothering labor. Later I found some solace in Sekile Nzinga-Johnson's edited collection, *Laboring Positions: Black Women, Mothering and the Academy* (2013). While the collection's focus is on Black women's experiences in particular, the collection speaks to the maternal labor performed within academia even by people who may not be biological or legal mothers. This got me thinking: we don't just need to talk about intersectionality in mother studies, but mother studies needs to permeate into our feminisms even when the subject or subjects at the center do not themselves identify as mothers. As someone in love with the intense and rigorous production and circulation of knowledge that academia can cultivate, I wonder about the potential impact of centering theories of mothering in feminist praxis to create spaces where academics' maternal labor could be visible, valued, allowed to flourish, and be challenged.

Now, as a doctoral candidate and parent of an amazing eleven-year-old and two-year-old, with another child on the way, I live in the conflicting, rewarding, yet heartbreaking dual privilege and disadvantage of pulling back from academia, no longer grounded in an academic institution with all its resources and intellectual community, while also free of its exploitive working hours and conditions.

Works Cited

Negra, Diane. 2009. *What a Girl Wants? Fantasizing the Reclamation of Self in Postfeminism*. London: Routledge.

Nzinga-Johnson, Sekile, ed. 2013. *Laboring Positions: Black Women, Mothering and the Academy*. Ontario: Demeter Press.

Interlude 7

Parenting while Researching?
It Takes Support, Kid-Friendly Systems, and a Lot of Luck

Jacqueline Kory-Westlund

I started a family during grad school. I worked in an immersive, high-performing research lab, the Personal Robots Group at the MIT Media Lab, led by Cynthia Breazeal. I wasn't the first in my lab to get married or have a baby, but I may have been unusual in planning my wedding while running a two-month field study at a local school and writing my master's thesis. No one else was six months pregnant with their second kid while defending their dissertation, either. Balancing my family with lab life was challenging, but doable for a few key reasons. My husband was supportive. My advisor and department were supportive. My lab was more kid-friendly than most. And I was lucky.

Cynthia cultivated a lab where differing ideas and perspectives could flourish. As a fellow student explained to me in my first week, "There should be no 'squashing' of ideas, unless it has been done before, in which case gently point your colleague to the work already done." In other words, be positive. Be game. Don't dismiss ideas off the bat. Cynthia actively cultivated an accepting and supportive lab. My infant received a tiny t-shirt emblazoned with our lab's logo. Besides being a brilliant scientist and engineer, Cynthia was a mother of three herself. She understood the difficulty of the family balancing act, and after I gave birth for the first time, she gave me leeway to work remotely as needed. This kind of personal support led to increased comfort, productivity, and collaboration in the lab. More of this support is needed at all levels of graduate school in the United States, as Alma Villaneuva points out elsewhere in this volume.

Part of the collaborative atmosphere was due to our field and our lab. We had a habit of calling our research in human-robot interaction (HRI) a "team sport" since it is highly interdisciplinary (drawing on computer science, psychology, cognitive science, robotics, philosophy, education, and more). Generally speaking, no one can be an expert in all aspects of HRI. Collaboration is a given. Cynthia had a compelling vision for how we could use social robots to help humans flourish. Much of our research while I was in the lab focused on using social robots to support young children's early language development—which meant we often brought three- and four-year-olds into the lab to play with whatever technology we were testing. The lab, as such, was relatively kid-friendly.

The lab's kid-friendliness was very important. My husband and I have a parenting philosophy that emphasizes children's rights (such as their right to their parents, especially very young children's right to their mothers), frugality, learning, and love. We both come from white, middle-class families with multiple siblings, mothers who stayed home, and fathers who worked. I was homeschooled, and even before COVID, we intended to homeschool our kids. We didn't want to outsource child care. Plus, child care is very expensive in Boston, and we were saving all the pennies we didn't spend on rice and beans to buy a house when I finished school. All of this meant I needed to be able to bring my first baby, and my husband, to the lab sometimes. Fortunately, my husband is a computer engineer who worked from home on his startup and on contract work for MIT, so his hours were very flexible and he was often on campus anyway. I shared an office with another graduate student mother, which afforded privacy for breastfeeding. We were lucky our son was generally happy and calm.

At the MIT Media Lab, research is the main event. Students are immersed from day one in a project-based, hands-on, learning-by-doing research culture. The ramp-up time is short. Taking classes often feels like a sideshow. As part of this structure, students in both the master's and PhD programs are funded through research assistantships. About half our time is officially allotted for research activities rather than a heavy course load. When I gave birth in my fourth year, I was finished with formal classwork entirely, enabling me to sculpt my schedule around baby feedings and naptimes. Since our research was predominantly grant-funded, everyone in the lab had to work on grant projects as well as their own courses and research. Usually, our interests were pretty well aligned with the grant projects we had to work on, since the grants always related to the lab's vision. I primarily worked on a series of experimental studies for a five-year grant investigating the use of social robots in children's early literacy education. I prepared and ran a study, or two, each year. I wrote experimental protocols, developed learning games, programmed robots, created new assessments for measuring kids' learning or social behavior, recruited participants at local schools, interacted with kids, teleoperated robots, coded and analyzed data, drafted papers, and attended no small number of meetings. Fortunately, my professors provided excellent mentoring and feedback throughout this process. I gained a lot of experience designing and running experimental studies. I was lead author on multiple papers. In addition, I did my own, separate, master's and PhD projects. Each built on and referenced the work I did for our grants, using those projects as a cornerstone for my own explorations.

Balancing a baby with research was made easier because my department was trying hard to be a positive place for student parents. I benefited from several brave pioneers before me (who were likely much like Alex Hanson, writing in this volume) who had championed an extra month of maternity leave for women in my department. The department installed a Mamava pod on the fifth floor so we wouldn't have to walk to the basement in the next building over to nurse or pump. Even so, I felt like I was asking for extra accommodations or burdening my labmates and colleagues, even though they assured me everything was fine and that the baby improved morale. I couldn't work as much as I had before. As Andrew Hollinger wrote in this volume, balancing labor as a student with the labor of being a parent isn't easy. I opted out of most on-campus events, especially evening events, and stopped traveling out of town to conferences and workshops. I worried I wasn't keeping up academically, even though I published papers and had spent part of my maternity leave trying to work on my dissertation proposal.

Perhaps I worked more than was strictly necessary because I was afraid of falling into the stereotype of the working mother who scales back to spend more time with her family. No: I was dedicated to my research! I had to show it. So I showed up: leading those studies, organizing a conference workshop while pregnant, never missing a lab meeting. Perhaps I could have gotten away with doing less. But I couldn't do less. Even with the support I had and luck on my side, I felt I had something to prove, to myself, to the rest of the academic world: mothers belong in research, too, and we'll work hard to show it.

PART III

THE LABOR OF "PROFESSIONALIZATION"

Interlude 8

The Professoriate Is a Job

Sarah Welsh

I graduated from college with no idea how hard it was going to be to find a job I liked. I loved writing so I tried journalism, which was engaging but didn't pay enough. I tried freelance writing, which made it difficult to earn a steady paycheck, and I also tried marketing, which paid slightly more but didn't allow me to do the kind of writing I wanted to do. After a few bad jobs, I decided graduate school would fix this very common problem of failing to secure meaningful work.

As an English PhD student, I spent six years working on a dissertation that felt meaningful to me, in a great city, where I made lifelong friends. I earned $28,000 a year by maxing out the allowed working hours; this was only slightly less than I had been making in entry-level jobs anyway. I managed to graduate with no debt by receiving help from my family when I needed it and by living frugally. I felt lucky to have enough support to continue pursuing something that made me happy, all the while realizing that nothing was guaranteed. I thought often of the jobs I left behind.

During my graduate program, I took a class that helped PhD students navigate the job market. It involved a series of talks by both former graduate students who had become professors and former students who had chosen other paths, like marketing, research, or university administration. The speakers who left academia were consistently asked questions about their own happiness: are you happy outside of academia? These questions were not asked of guest speakers on the tenure-track, because their happiness was assumed. It was always understood that graduate school was supposed to be a "direct rout to the professoriate," as Brown describes in the introduction to this collection (3).

In *Work Won't Love You Back*, Sarah Jaffe (2021) explains that creative fields like journalism, organizations with an emphasis on helping others (like nonprofits), and industries that are traditionally "women's work" (like teaching) have a high propensity for exploiting the people who choose to join them. It is the emphasis on meaning that holds us in working environments where we accept lower standards of living because we are pursuing a vocation. We choose to accept positions with low pay, with limited to no benefits, with known dismal job prospects that we think we'll overcome if we are "good enough." Academia is not the only industry where this is the case.

In graduate school I sought out advisors who were open to varied perspectives on career options, who would support me in those possibilities, and who did not see nonacademic options as failures. I surrounded myself with people who were open-minded and realistic, and I talked to lots of people who had jobs *outside* of academia. I found other professions to explore with other benefits, other freedoms, other ways to teach, and better benefits. This was a great way to start building a network, while also learning about other work.

As Chris Caterine (2020) reiterates, tenure-track jobs are the absolute exception within academia, not the norm. And as Kupsh and McDonald and others in this volume explain time and again, "payoff" in the form of a tenure-track job is simply unlikely. Professors have learned how to train graduate students for a very specific kind of job, but they are also part of the system that perpetuates a lack of these jobs. As such, they have a responsibility to their students to do their best to adapt to shifting norms and expectations. Mentors can help graduate student workers by being open and even encouraging them to explore other kinds of work. What can you encourage or accept as academic credit that students can incorporate into their own professionalization? How can you widen the definition of "professionalization"? Can you advocate for related department course offerings or even workshops or talks about other kinds of jobs? Tell your graduate students what your job is really like.

I finished my doctorate in the midst of COVID-19, but even before the pandemic was raging, I decided to apply for both academic and nonacademic positions. When I told people about my decision to pursue all kinds of work, it struck me that graduate students in the humanities, and many professors, did not really see professorships as one of many kinds of careers; rather, they saw it as a kind of vocation apart from base careerism. Reframing the professoriate as a job, rather than a vocation, has made me more confident in my potential, but it has also helped me set boundaries around what I am willing to tolerate. This reframing has been a critical part of my transition out of grad school.

Like many graduate students before me, I have built a skill set that is incredibly valuable to many different kinds of companies: research, writing, teaching, and presentations, to name a few. These are great skills for fields like public policy, communications, user experience research, corporate consulting, marketing, public relations, learning design, and more. Resources like ImaginePh.D. have helped me immensely in learning about other options, but I have also done a lot of research in this area myself. After all, that's what we know best.

Books that have helped me in my nonacademic job search include *Leaving Academia*, by Christopher Caterine (2020); *Putting the Humanities Ph.D. to Work* by Katina Rogers (2020); Jaffe's *Work Won't Love You Back*; and *The 2-Hour Job Search*, by Steve Dalton (2020). Each of these books provides different kinds of practical advice and helped me reframe ideas and emotions around this thing that we call "work." Caterine and Rogers have lots of advice on how to translate all the work you've been doing as a grad student into other kinds of work that you might even find meaningful. But as Jaffe's book suggests, you might find more meaning by pulling apart the myth that you should be looking for it in the first place.

And if you are reading this essay and staring down another dismal market year, remember that whatever job you end up with will be a job that will require you to work.

Works Cited

Caterine, Chris. 2020. *Leaving Academia: A Practical Guide*. Princeton, NJ: Princeton University Press.
Dalton, Steve. 2020. *The 2-Hour Job Search: Using Technology to Get the Right Job Faster*. Berkeley, CA: Ten Speed Press.
Jaffe, Sarah. 2021. *Work Won't Love You Back: How Devotion to Our Jobs Keeps Us Exploited, Exhausted, and Alone*. New York: Bold Type Books.
Rogers, Katina. 2020. *Putting the Humanities Ph.D. to Work*. Princeton, NJ: Princeton University Press.

6 | Scholar-Selves in the Managerial University
The Hidden Labor of Disciplinary Identity Formation in the Doctoral Journey

Adam Haley

Three years into my tenure-track job search, as I digested the latest in a long procession of advice columns calling for new PhDs to embrace the tactics of self-promotion, I experienced a moment of simultaneous identity crisis and structural clarity: Who exactly was this scholarly self I was supposed to be promoting? Where, in the chaotic multiplicity of academic and institutional roles I cycled through daily, did that self reside? When was he supposed to have emerged, and what was he made of? What relationship did he have to the teacher-self I inhabited much more readily, or to the student-self still slightly visible in the rear-view mirror? Every well-intentioned proffer of wisdom about how to craft an academic brand or scholarly persona seemed to rest on the assumption that over the course of a doctorate, one's interests and values and achievements would organically cohere into some sort of singular academic identity, which could then be strategically packaged and circulated. The problem, apparently, was that young PhDs, intimidated by the apocalyptically desolate academic hiring market, weren't doing the right things to sell those selves; if we could just market our scholarly identities more sharply, commodify them more effectively, "begin taking control of [our] own PR" (Van Wyck 2015), these articles seemed to suggest, our chances of sustainable academic employment would improve substantially.

In practice, though, I had no idea where—amid the kaleidoscopic pile of cover letters, research statements, and tailored CVs, not to mention the existential panic and impostor syndrome brought on by the academic hunger games—to find that identity, that marketable academic selfhood on which my professional future apparently depended. Graduate school had been profoundly transformative for me in any number of ways, and I left with both a well-developed pedagogy and an ambitious research agenda, but the strategic development and articulation of a cohesive, independent scholarly identity, tacitly assumed to be something candidates developed along their doctoral journeys, had slipped through the cracks in my experience. If identity is, as Ken Hyland suggests, "how we create meanings while engaging with others" (2012, x), then a vital mechanism of academic and disciplinary meaning-making seemed to have gone unattended in my doctoral education, leaving me struggling to articulate my place within the field to prospective employers. Whether the failure was my own, my graduate program's, or somewhere in between, what became excruciatingly clear to me as I treaded water amid a sea of job applications was that this high-stakes self-fashioning was more central to graduate education and professional development than I had ever realized. Needless to say, this belated realization was not a pleasant one.

    I offer this reflection not because I see it as definitive evidence of widespread curricular or advising failure, nor because I imagine my own bafflement to be generalizable across recent doctoral grads' experiences. Rather, I mean to suggest that the exigencies of collapsing job markets and intensifying academic capitalism have a way of making visible certain tacit assumptions and structures of graduate education—in this case, the subterranean processes of scholarly identity formation and the intimidatingly high stakes thereof. In this chapter, I explore the increasingly prominent role of these identity formation processes in the academic and professional development of graduate students, particularly at the doctoral level. Through a constellation of theories of identity traced across critical university/labor studies, writing and composition studies, and social theory more broadly, I map the contours of disciplinary identity formation as an important site of graduate student labor, fraught with internal tensions, contradictions, and unacknowledged burdens. Though recent decades have seen a rise in critical discussion of identity in the wake of postmodern and anti-essentialist critiques, the processes underlying identity formation have rarely been interrogated as a site of academic labor. Given the importance of asserting an independent scholarly identity within and against the disciplinary enculturation processes through which one enters academia, I suggest that much of the hidden curriculum of doctoral education falls within the undertheorized orbit of scholarly identity formation. Ultimately, I argue not only that the production of identity is a nexus of significant but unacknowledged intellectual, emotional, and relational labor by graduate students and early career scholars but also that it offers a crucial vantage point on the widening gap between the expectations laid on graduate students' shoulders and the institutional support made—or not made—available to them. The escalating demands of identity production in the ruins of the austerity-era university have drastically reshaped graduate student subjectivity, I contend, in ways that institutions, graduate directors, and advisors have yet to fully reckon with. Put another way: more and more, what developing doctoral students are most aggressively pressured to do is, precisely, to *become*.

Identity Work and Neoliberal Academia

The burdens of identity production and maintenance have been noted in broader discussions of modernization, postmodernity, and late capitalism. Most pointedly, Zygmunt Bauman diagnoses the individualization endemic to modernity, asserting that "needing to *become* what one is is the feature of modern living" (2001, 124, emphasis in original). Where identity had once been imagined as ontologically stable, psychoanalytic and postmodern destabilizations of selfhood (Butler 1990; Butler 1993; Foucault 1977; Foucault 1990a; Foucault 1990b; Lyotard 1984) in conjunction with postindustrial reconfigurations of labor (Bell 1973; Castells 1976) made it instead an object of necessary work, a perpetual and individualized obligation to maintain, perform, and circulate a commodifiable self. Noting the burden imposed by this obligation in the absence of institutional support or compensation for that work, sociolinguist James Paul Gee declares it "a particularly 'modern' plight that people must negotiate and sustain a number of crucial identities without overt support from traditional, stable, or 'official' institutions" (2000–2001, 105). These claims resonate with Anthony Giddens's account of "the reflexive project of the self," which frames modern self-identity as "something that has to be routinely created and sustained in the reflexive activities of the individual" (1991, 52). Rather than identity emerging from ostensibly stable external sources like nature, God, or the state, the burden for calling forth an identity through discourse, affiliation, or performance now falls on each of us.

Diverging from optimistic appraisals of the modern/postmodern fracturing of identity and performative selfhood as liberatory, which see possibility in postmodernism's radically expanded routes for self-creation, affinity, and identification, these accounts instead emphasize the transformation of identity into yet another site of compulsory labor. Though such liberatory possibilities may indeed have been unlocked, the dissolution of "an integral, originary, and unified identity" (Hall 1996, 1) brings not only the potential to fashion the self but the *responsibility* to do so on a continual basis; "individualisation consists in transforming human identity from a given into a task" (Bauman 2001, 124), and the reflexive work of producing identity becomes another recurring item on the to-do list—sometimes explicitly recognized or mandated as such, but just as often tacitly imposed. Like all the worst tasks, though, the production of identity can never be crossed off the list. As a "never-ending, always incomplete, unfinished and open-ended activity" (Bauman 2001, 129) rather than a sturdy foundation for agency and action, identity gives way to identification—is *only ever* identification, "a construction, a process never completed—always 'in process'" (Hall 1996, 2).

In an institutional context like present-day neoliberal academia, the stakes of these ongoing identification processes are particularly high. In academia as elsewhere in what Gee and others call "the new capitalism," an institution "tends to highly value fluidity, flexibility, and multiple identities and not stability, narrow focus, and inflexible identities defined in traditional terms" (Gee 2000–2001, 120). Where faculty members in earlier eras of higher education "enjoyed optimal conditions for the formation and maintenance of distinct, stable, and legitimizing identities" (Henkel 2010, 4) and could thus cumulatively scaffold their professional identities over the course of a career, the managerial structures of accountability and performativity governing today's universities ensure that "successful, authentic academic identities are rendered insecure, temporary and risky" (Archer 2008, 392). A successful academic must continue to produce and perform, in accordance with the constantly shifting metrics and standards that characterize contexts in which "process rather than stability is the nature of the institutional reality" (Delanty 2008, 127). Importantly, the managerial demands for regular, quantifiable achievement don't replace or crowd out considerations of identity but rather reconfigure and rearticulate them. In academic hiring and promotion, for example, the "intangible assets" of "identity capital" (Côte and Levine 2002) not representable on a CV or research activity report remain integral to success; where the tangible assets of publications and fellowships might earn one a first-round interview, the intangible assets of personality and sociality strongly influence the outcome of a final on-campus interview. Though the stability of identity may have dissolved, the stakes of performing it in specific moments and contexts remain dizzyingly high.

Meanwhile, the austerity policies that accompany the incursion of consumerism, bottom-line decision making, and corporate management styles into higher education leave academics with less time and funding with which to meet these moving standards—and thus to assert the identities demanded by their institutional contexts. Andrew Ross has suggested that these shifts mark the emergence of "a mode of production marked by a quasi-convergence of the academy and the knowledge corporation," a key consequence of which is that "a public commons unobtrusively segues into a marketplace of ideas, and careers secured by stable professional norms morph into contract-driven livelihoods hedged by entrepreneurial risks" (2009, 205). From the standpoint of academic identity, the end result of this convergence of educational institutions and economic logics is that "traditional notions of academic freedom, autonomy and purpose, which have been central signifiers of academic identity, no longer hold" (Harris 2005, 421). Just as the previously solid, traditional sources of identity writ large melted into air under the onslaught of modernization (Berman 1981), so have the established building blocks of academic identity crumbled under the weight of the corporatization of higher education, the burdens of self-creation and self-maintenance thus redistributed as individual responsibilities, albeit responsibilities not to be enumerated on faculty activity reports. The stable academic identities that characterized earlier eras are thereby displaced by the "continual reconstruction and revising of the academic" (Billot 2010, 718), and the academic workforce becomes increasingly precarious in terms of not only material welfare but also the sense of professional self.

This intensifying burden for academics to constantly perform identity work even as their tools for doing so erode and evaporate represents more than just another predictable iteration of the same "do more with less" ethos that university administrators constantly impose on faculty both on and off the tenure track. Because "exploitation within the contemporary Academy operates in and through technologies of selfhood that are producing new kinds of labouring subject" (Gill 2013, 13), Rosalind Gill argues that to bring academics properly within the sights of critical labor studies, "we need to develop a psychosocial understanding . . . of the way in which power is operating through new labouring subjectivities" (2013, 25). Among other things, such an understanding would aim to make visible the means by which "the terms of identity building are being rendered diffuse" (Delanty 2008, 131), destabilizing not only traditional academic identities themselves but also the mechanisms of their production, through the "constant slippage between process and product" (Davies and Petersen 2005, 81). That is, as stable academic identity is displaced by shifting expectations, precarious material circumstances, and "the priority of process over form" (Delanty 2008, 127) that increasingly govern institutions of higher education, the production of identity is channeled ever more aggressively into the self-management and self-monitoring characteristic of neoliberal subjectivities. The individualizing discourses of managerialism in turn work to obscure these forces, naturalizing certain technologies of selfhood by mandating their constant enactment: because there is only ever the performance of self, the fact of that performance recedes into the background of impact factors, productivity reports, and curricula vitae. Given its socializing and enculturating functions, I contend that graduate education is ground zero for these operations of power—a testing ground and assembly line for the "new labouring subjectivities" that facilitate the exploitation endemic to modern academe. Understanding these subjectivities, the means of their propagation, and the forms of labor they naturalize is therefore vital for those aspiring to help graduate students and early career scholars navigate this increasingly hostile terrain.

Writing Identities

Though Gee claims that "the modern need for recognition . . . places a particular importance on discourse and dialogue" as the engines of identity production (2000–2001, 112), this connection between discourse and identity formation may be particularly intense in the context of academia, which locates textual production "at the core of negotiating the interactive relationships among the members of academic communities and claiming and constructing academic identities" (Flowerdew and Wang 2015, 82). With regard to academic writing broadly conceived, Roz Ivanič distinguishes between the autobiographical self, the self as author, and what she calls the "discoursal self," or "the impression—often multiple, sometimes contradictory—which [a writer] consciously or unconsciously conveys of themself in a particular written text" (1998, 25). Though Ivanič observes this distinction among adult undergraduates who first enter higher education after the age of twenty-five, the notion of the discoursal self has been widely adopted in research on identity development in academic writing to explain the interrelations between what we write, who we are, and how we are perceived by readers. As artifacts-in-activity (Prior 2006), academic texts constitute vital sites of identity production, through which "academic voice appears as a 'trace-in-activity' of the researcher's social identity as an academic writer" (Castelló and Iñesta 2012, 184). As Hyland notes, "writing as an academic often means the construction of individuals by texts, rather than the other way round" (2012, x), what Barbara Kamler and Pat Thomson have aptly dubbed "textwork/identitywork" (2014). In light of the managerial structures governing contemporary academia and "the fluidity between writing, thinking and developing a research identity" (Carter 2011, 727), the production of academic identity through academic writing takes on particular urgency in the earlier stages of an academic's career, when their positions within their discipline and their institution are not yet firmly established.

Crucially, writing is also—again, particularly within academia—an interface between an individual's established sense of self and the social and institutional environments through which that self moves. In this way, writing is "a complex negotiation of a sense of identity and the institutional regulation of meaning-making" (Hyland 2012, 20), mediating between a writer and the institutional/disciplinary discourses that shape the "socially available possibilities for selfhood" (Burgess and Ivanič 2010), i.e., the possible identities to which that writer might lay claim. Although the pressures exerted by institutional and disciplinary forces on these possibilities for selfhood are considerable, this high-stakes social identity borderland is a space of mutual determination, a "structuration" meeting point between the structure of disciplinary institutions and the agency of the research writer (Giddens 1984), where the discursive formations of a discipline shape the possibilities of identity just as the discoursal self conjured by a text speaks back to those discursive formations. Summarizing the research on identity in academic careers, Meghan Pifer and Vicki Baker note that "scholars have moved away from considering just how contexts shape identity and toward the use of identity as a foothold for making sense of rapidly changing contexts" (2013, 120). Rather than a purely deterministic account in which the possibilities for academic identity are straightforwardly dictated by surrounding institutional structures, recent scholarship emphasizes "the ways in which individual entrants are mutually influencing and influenced by the conditions of the academic career" (Pifer and Baker 2013, 118). Because "professional identity develops where agency and structure . . . , or the self and context, interact" (Billot 2010, 712), it is exactly at this interface, in which identities live as "points of temporary attachment to the subject positions which discursive practices construct for us" (Hall 1996, 6), that developing academics must be most attuned to the processes of identity formation and the rhetorical strategies for navigating those processes.

The Paradox of Independent Research

Although the rhetoric of graduate education (especially at the doctoral level) often emphasizes transformation, namely, from student to candidate to scholar, its structures frequently reinforce tropes that belie the complexity of identity formation and the weight of the labor it entails for graduate students. This tension between the transformative aspirations of graduate education and its increasingly transactional realities constitutes a significant barrier to graduate students' successful development, especially as the latter dimension comes to dominate graduate pedagogy, supervision, and curriculum. Taking aim at the language of *transferable skills* that saturates the discourse of doctoral development, especially in the wake of the 2008 global financial crisis's decimation of an already sparse academic job market, Robyn Barnacle contends that "an account of Doctoral becoming that treats the learning outcomes purely as a commodity is impoverished, and misses the real import of the learning experience: that it is transformative" (2005, 187). In advocating the reprioritization of transformation over transaction, Barnacle echoes Bill Green's oft-cited assertion that "doctoral pedagogy is as much about the production of identity, then, as it is the production of knowledge" (2005, 162). Unlike other degrees and certificates that index a student's preparedness to transition to some more advanced role, the attainment of the doctoral degree itself marks a transition that has ostensibly already taken place—not only the accumulation of skills and competencies but the transformation into expert and scholar, with all the complex identity development implied therein. Without facilitating the transformative identity work comprising that transition, doctoral supervision will fail to meet the intended goals of doctoral education; the market-oriented pragmatism of transferable skills and learning-outcome-as-commodity, however well-intentioned on the part of graduate programs and advisors responding to shrinking job markets and evaporating budgets, threatens to unravel the guiding ethos of graduate education.

I would argue, moreover, that the common evaluative criterion of a *significant original contribution to research*—typically the key distinguishing feature between doctoral and master's learning objectives—presumes not only the completion of a specific research product (usually a thesis/dissertation) but the establishment of a research identity that constitutes one's access point to the disciplinary discourses through which knowledge production is authorized and legitimated. Somewhat tautologically, the notion of expert or insider knowledge indexed by the *significant original contribution to research* criterion characterizes knowledge by knower, doing by being: an artifact of knowledge production qualifies one for the doctoral degree if it is recognized by experts/insiders to signal the writer's transformation into expert/insider. One becomes authorized as a disciplinary expert, that is, not only through producing and communicating knowledge of a certain caliber but through developing and articulating an expert identity as knowledge-producer. In this way, textwork/identity-work is at the heart of the transformation that comprises the doctoral journey. This accords with the definitive assessment at the end of the doctoral journey, the defense, in which the thesis or dissertation is evaluated not only for the significance of its contribution or the soundness of its methods but for the relationship it establishes between the candidate and her discipline.

To get to that transformational culmination point, though, requires a doctoral candidate to overcome what might be described as the paradox of independent research: "the contradiction between attempting to break new disciplinary or methodological ground in their research that may lead to creating new activities while at the same time adhering to current norms for validity of research methods operating within status quo activities" (Lundell and Beach 2002, 488). This necessity of balancing innovation and legibility may constitute, per Lundell and Beach, an internal contradiction within the research itself, or it may point to a larger tension between disciplinary structure and researcher agency, "between the disciplinary community's expectations for individual members to display proximity to or conform to certain rules and conventions, on the one hand, and individual scholars' desire to claim their agency and develop their uniqueness, on the other" (Flowerdew and Wang 2015, 83). Either way, doctoral candidates are faced with the difficulty of "negotiating a representation of self from the standardising conventions of disciplinary discourses" (Hyland 2012, 20)—that is, of asserting an identity in the midst of disciplinary forces that, especially in STEM fields, tend to militate toward the effacement of identity in knowledge production,[1] even as the demands of academic capitalism make the strategic articulation of scholarly identity a precondition of securing stable academic employment. Fundamentally, disciplines *discipline*, shaping both the knowledge produced therein and its producers (Foucault 1977); of the many juggling acts that comprise doctoral education, the most fraught for graduate students may be navigating between the disciplinary enculturation that enables one to participate and the independence necessary to push that discipline forward. With identity development in mind, then, this *in it but not of it* positioning may be a particularly significant consideration in research design and framing, and graduate curricula and supervisory pedagogies should be carefully designed to support these processes. Indeed, as Hyland suggests, identity is ultimately how students "simultaneously achieve credibility as insiders and reputations as individuals" (2012, 20), and navigating this duality is a key hurdle to transcending the paradox of independent research.

Another way to think about the burgeoning academic's vexed negotiation between novelty and convention is through the lens of creativity, as contrasted with the conformity so often emphasized by graduate curricula and advising. Barbara Lovitts has explored the role of creativity in the graduate student's transition to independent researcher, a widely emphasized outcome of doctoral education (Lovitts 2005; Lovitts 2008; Wang, Xiong, and Ye, this volume). Examining the transition from the earlier phases of coursework and exams to the later stages of independent research, Lovitts diagnoses a significant disconnect between, on the one hand, the implicit (and sometimes explicit) valorization of creativity and, on the other, "the educational system's overvaluation of analytical intelligence and other norms in graduate education that promote intellectual conformity" (2008, 322). In its admission processes, its curriculum, and even its funding structures (as when fellowships are determined by standardized test scores or research assistantships are distributed based on performance in coursework), graduate education—like, many would argue, its tertiary, secondary, and primary antecedents—generally rewards forms of intelligence altogether distinct from the creativity needed to pursue an independent research agenda. Although "creativity is inherent in and integral to graduate education" (Lovitts 2005, 140), curricular and institutional structures often push against the formation of autonomous academic identity and the transition to independent research—doctoral education's ostensible goals. Encapsulating this contradiction, Isabelle Skakni asks "what is concretely attested by a Ph.D. diploma when doctoral studies are mainly based on the student's capacity to understand and follow implicit rules, norms, and expectations" (2018, 15). In a study of doctoral education and researcher development in six Australian universities, Angela Brew, David Boud, and Sang Un Namgung (2011) found no evidence that doctoral study had a strong influence on candidates' preparedness for independent research, indicative of the very disconnect Lovitts identified—and suggesting, moreover, that the structures of graduate education may in fact blunt or obstruct the creative dimensions of identity development. Indeed, a chapter in this volume by Wang, Xiong, and Ye emphasizes Chinese doctoral students' desire for more extensive preparation in research methods from their American institutions, the lack of which may prevent them from confidently claiming a researcher identity.

Beyond the internal contradictions in doctoral programs' purported development of independent researchers, there is some evidence to suggest that the fixation on researcher independence may itself be detrimental to transitions both into and within graduate education, imposing further emotional labor burdens on already-overburdened graduate students and otherwise impeding their development. Jane Tobbell and Victoria O'Donnell argue that graduate study's emphasis on independence "promotes feelings of isolation in students and may undermine confidence and shape transition trajectories in particular ways" (2013, 124). During key developmental stages, the unattainable asymptote of independence may be less motivational than disheartening, preventing students from seeking support. This possibility is reflected in the complex dynamics of doctoral advising. Nickola Overall, Kelsey Deane, and Elizabeth Peterson (2011) call particular attention to the challenge of giving students sufficient guidance to develop necessary research skills (academic support) while also facilitating students' burgeoning independence as researchers (autonomy support). Researcher independence, like creativity, involves a delicate balance between the familiarity of established knowledge, skills, and methods and the challenge of the new and unknown. Interestingly, although Overall, Deane, and Peterson found no strong association between student satisfaction and autonomy support from supervisors, they did find that increased autonomy support predicted higher research self-efficacy, leading to their recommendation that supervisors "provide a balance of directly helping students to complete research tasks and providing students with the room to make their own research decisions" (2011, 801–802).

The Interdependence of the Researcher

The emphasis on independence as a desired outcome and an index of doctoral achievement may also be at odds with the larger relational structures of both research education and research itself, masking "the social nature of researcher identification and development" (Mantai 2017, 2) and compromising candidates' preparedness to assert a scholarly identity within the social and institutional contexts of knowledge production. Jennifer Sinclair, Robyn Barnacle, and Denise Cuthbert suggest that, developmentally, "an emphasis on candidates' transition to independence . . . may obscure what is in fact an inter-dependent relation between advisor and candidate" (2014, 4). This echoes Inger Mewburn's (2011) broader characterization of PhD candidature as an "assemblage" as well as Barnacle and Mewburn's contention that "a doctoral candidate can be understood as a 'knowing location' in a doctoral actor-network" (2010, 434). Active and successful researchers, in other words, may not be the same as independent researchers; despite academia's persistent fixation on the trope of the researcher as isolated genius, in fact the processes of research and researcher development are inescapably social, relational, and interdependent, constituting a complex disciplinary ecology. Indeed, given increasing trends toward collaboration and interdisciplinarity, Marian Jazvac-Martek, Shuhua Chen, and Lynn McAlpine argue that "supporting doctoral students in developing their ability to negotiate intentions and extend and maintain a network of relationships may serve them better in their academic futures" (2011, 35). This call echoes sociocultural and developmental network accounts of doctoral development (Baker and Lattuca 2010; Baker and Pifer 2011), which draw attention to the situatedness of doctoral learning and identity formation within a constellation of social and relational contexts. These relationships and networks, Baker and Pifer contend, are precisely what "provide meaning, efficacy, and identity development" along the doctoral journey (2011, 15).

Neglecting or downplaying these relational dimensions at curricular and supervisory levels comes at a significant cost to doctoral candidates' development and effectiveness as researchers and scholarly peers, increasing the emotional and rhetorical labor graduate students must undertake while also eroding their tools for performing that labor—but it likely does particular damage to the development of scholarly selfhood. Emphasizing "the distributed nature of identity formation within doctoral education," Barnacle and Mewburn (2010, 433) explore the actor-networks of doctoral candidates' broader "research landscape"—relational contexts and dependencies that may be just as determinative of a candidate's success or failure as intelligence, work ethic, or emotional durability—concluding that researcher development must take into account "how both knowledge and the candidate themselves are being situated within research contexts and practices" (2010, 442). A central feature of the "research education ontologies" that shape doctoral becoming (Barnacle 2005) is the precarity and contingency of knowledge and knowledge production. Yet doctoral education's fixation on independence and on the narrower student-supervisor dyad compromises candidates' ability to fully engage with these precarious networks of knowledge production. A failure to contend with the situatedness of both knowledge and knowledge producer can thereby stymie a doctoral candidate's ability to articulate their identity in relation to larger disciplinary networks without being subsumed by them.

Given that "the relational level of socialization may be the most central to the student's professional identity development" (Smith and Hatmaker 2014, 557), Green urges us to reconceive doctoral supervision and development in ecosocial terms, "as a total environment within which postgraduate research activity (study) is realised" (2005, 153). Similarly, David Boud and Alison Lee (2005) advocate deemphasizing the (fiction of the) transition to independence, proposing instead the notion of "becoming peer" as a better guide to navigating the interdependent social ecologies of disciplines and academic institutions. As a model for both theorizing researcher identity in relation to the networks of disciplinary knowledge production and facilitating researcher development in its social and relational dimensions, "peerness" may better capture candidates' modes of relation to these networks, as well as the actual practices and relationships they make recourse to during difficult and formative moments, like peer writing groups or informal "troubles talk" (Mewburn 2011). Such a reframing helps to broaden researcher development beyond the supervisory dyad—which Lilia Mantai found to be a relatively minor factor in doctoral candidates' researcher identification, compared to informal settings and nonacademic connections (2017, 12). Peerness instead accounts for the broader networks of colleagues, friends, family, and peers without which many doctoral candidates would not complete their degrees, let alone develop the identity and disciplinary standing necessary for postdegree success.

Of course, because these informal developmental networks are often composed of other graduate students, this peer support constitutes another site of significant intellectual and emotional labor on the part of students, generally neither acknowledged nor compensated by departments or institutions. Writing in this volume, April Cobos and Megan Mize describe a blended learning doctoral program in which local and distance students "often work in small ways to support each other," mitigating the failures of the institution to support distance students, who reported that "in the absence of willing faculty [relationships,] they turned towards each other for support" (102). While providing such support is not mandated of graduate students, horizontal mentorship is nevertheless a common facet of graduate student development, and one that graduate institutions rely on to fill the gaps between institutionally sanctioned modes of support. (We might see this peer support as akin to mutual aid networks compensating for the erosion of governmental welfare provisions.) Further, Cobos and Mize reveal the troubling ways institutions not only rely upon but coopt credit for these informal peer support structures. Specifically, they recount Mize's creation of a successful dissertation bootcamp which one graduate program director, uninvolved in its development and support, hoped to include "on the official program website as an example of a unique resource *the program* offers" (95), suggesting the ways that the peer-to-peer labor of horizontal mentorship is invisibilized and exploited by the same institutions that increasingly rely on said labor. A cursory glance at any dissertation acknowledgments section reveals the *it takes a village* foundation upon which doctoral education's house of cards stands.

Bringing this village within the scope of our theories and practices of doctoral development is essential to supporting the complex identity labor of doctoral candidates learning how to relate to their disciplinary communities—and helping each other do so.

Identity Tension and the Contradictions of Doctoral Development

Doctoral student identity formation may be both vital and uniquely difficult to theorize and facilitate in large part because of the many dualities that comprise doctoral students' role(s) and labor. Baker and Pifer, for instance, hint at the dizzyingly complex work underlying doctoral identity formation, bifurcated into a "parallel identity development process that requires [students] to master the student role and corresponding identity, while simultaneously beginning to accept and enact the identity of scholar and academic" (2011, 14). In other words, rather than gradually progressing along an experience/expertise spectrum from student to scholar, doctoral students must work to simultaneously hone identities in both dimensions, becoming increasingly adept both as students and as scholars—given that both roles are determinative of the outcomes of doctoral education. Along the same lines, M. J. Curry notes that graduate education is

> a context that positions [students] as learners, yet also asks them to develop and display specialized disciplinary knowledge. In fact, as students write the dissertation, they ideally take on highly expert stances, possibly more expert than their evaluators in their area. This subtle yet crucial careening from one identity position (novice, student) to another (expert, scholar), often within a matter of semesters, poses challenges to students' identities and often to their confidence in their writing abilities—not least because until the end of their programs, students are being evaluated by faculty members with institutional power. (2016, 87)

This constant movement between ostensibly opposed identity positions with differing relationships to disciplinary and institutional power, which Jazvac-Martek refers to as "oscillating role identities" (2009), is a significant source of "the vulnerability, emotional angst and elation at stake in scholarly identity formation" (Kamler and Thomson 2014, 29). This identity tension and the intense emotional labor arising from it can be especially acute for students undertaking a professional doctorate or coming to a graduate program from an established professional career, like the education doctoral students Jazvac-Martek interviewed, who often have already established strong professional identities that are then put under pressure by the novice/student positions they suddenly inhabit in their graduate programs.

Far from being either irrelevant or impediments to doctoral becoming, Lynn McAlpine and Lisa Lucas argue that "these personally distinct *past* experiences of intention, affect and action influence *present* intentions and aspirations and how individuals will engage in present academic experiences as well as *future* imagined possibilities" (2011, 695, italics in original). Thus, to incorporate these identities and positionalities into doctoral development discourses that often ignore or erase them, McAlpine and others (McAlpine, Amundsen, and Turner 2014; McAlpine, Jazvac-Martek, and Hopwood 2009; McAlpine and Turner 2012) have proposed the framework of *identity-trajectory*, or "the individual's integration of past-present-future in the experience of academic work, and the individual's desire to enact intentions and hopes through time" (McAlpine and Lucas 2011, 695). In contrast to narratives of socialization, which tend to position graduate students as passive recipients of insider knowledge and enculturation from experienced figures of academic authority, the identity-trajectory framework emphasizes individual student agency in the process of identity development. Additionally, McAlpine and Lucas frame identity-trajectory as a synthesis of the binaries of academic/personal and positive/negative affect—work and life, successes and failures—"both of which [dyads] influence agency and commitment to academic work" (2011, 696). Identity-trajectory thus provides a more integrative account of how academic selves are woven together from varied, even seemingly incompatible elements, responding to external exigencies but actively driven by the agency of the doctoral student.

As these theories suggest, graduate students live at the intersection of a series of oppositions that destabilize graduate student identity in relation to its institutional contexts, leaving them especially ripe for exploitation. Michael Gallope makes the labor implications of these split identities clear, critiquing the rhetorical and administrative entrapment of graduate students within "a series of insufficient oppositions: student/worker, student/employee, academic/economic, and so on" and arguing that "the work performed by academic labor entirely exceeds the possibility of these strict distinctions" (2007, 32). These oppositions manifest most frequently in contexts where graduate student identity, agency, and positionality are contested by university administrations or legal institutions, highly visible in the decades-long fight for unionization. In these contests, administrators often insist on graduate students' roles as students, apprentices, or trainees, rejecting their self-definitions as workers, with the attendant benefits and protections such a status would rightly entail (see Brown; Welsh; Isaac; Cox, all this volume). From the institutional standpoint, graduate students are generally treated as students when it's to the institution's advantage to classify them as such but as employees when that would be more advantageous, indicating that the development of scholarly identity is profoundly shaped by institutional power.

Given that "power is an important discursively constructed dimension of identity" (Flowerdew and Wang 2015, 90), the formation of graduate student identity, while not wholly determined by discursive and institutional power, is certainly shaped by that power and by the relations it regulates. Considering power as "a productive network which runs through the whole social body, much more than as a negative instance whose function is repression" (Foucault 1980, 19), provides another reminder that this identity tension marks not the destruction or erasure of identity but rather its rerouting into the managerial domain of task and performance—another domain for uncompensated labor, its burdens multiplied onto individual students. As Stuart Hall has argued, identities "emerge within the play of specific modalities of power, and thus are more the product of the marking of difference and exclusion, than they are the sign of an identical, naturally-constituted unity" (1996, 4). In the case of graduate student identity, these markings of difference and exclusion are often internal to the category of graduate student—an identity position largely defined, as outlined above, by its own internal contradictions. In the definitional unsettling at the heart of being a graduate student we therefore see the confluence not only of novice and expert or student and scholar but of the multiple vectors of power and agency that shape graduate student subjectivity. From this perspective, the politics of academic labor are a primary catalyst generating and amplifying identity tension, identity confusion, and the fragmenting of academic identity as the default condition of doctoral becoming.

Textual Performances of Scholarly Authority in the Dissertation Genre

Many of these tensions and contradictions come to a head within the genre of the thesis/dissertation, which, as Susan Carter notes, characteristically mediates its writer's student and scholar subjectivities:

> The thesis showcases textual generic performance. Its task is multiple, including creating and occupying a gap in existing knowledge, making an original contribution that is accepted by its community, demonstrating an internationally recognisable standard of presentation and transforming its author from novice to licensed practitioner. As a form of literature it weaves its author's social identity, while weaving its new knowledge into existing knowledge. (Carter 2011, 730)

In this multifaceted rhetorical performance, the doctoral dissertation merges the student task of *writing to learn* and the scholarly task of *writing to communicate*, meeting supervisory, departmental, and institutional learning outcomes as well as professional research requirements of novelty, originality, and presentation (see Austin and Moreland in this volume for more on this dynamic as it plays out in graduate student teaching). This student/scholar juggling act is especially dizzying in the increasingly common thesis-by-article dissertation form, in which a dissertation is comprised of several article manuscripts, bookended by general introduction and conclusion chapters that frame the manuscripts as a cohesive body of work. Writing in this format, doctoral candidates must navigate between the supervisory/institutional standards of the dissertation as a learning document and the disciplinary/rhetorical standards of article manuscripts as professional scholarly documents. In theory, the former should be gauged by the persuasiveness of the latter—that is, a dissertation manifests the appropriate learning achievement if it convincingly inhabits the professional scholarly mode. Some departments even formalize this proxy standard, requiring that doctoral candidates have a certain number of manuscript chapters submitted and/or accepted for publication in order for the degree to be conferred, thereby letting the judgment of the larger disciplinary community stand in for, or at least mediate, the judgment of the committee and institution.

In practice, the lines between writing to learn and writing to communicate in the dissertation can be much more slippery, not least because the more pressing exigency for the student is, ultimately, to satisfy the demands of the committee, department, and institution so as to complete the requirements for the degree. Although these evaluators hold both institutional and disciplinary authority over a doctoral candidate, given the firmly specialist emphasis of doctoral education, a doctoral candidate may well be—should be, in many cases—the expert on her specific topic from a disciplinary point of view by the time of the defense, potentially more knowledgeable than even her committee members or advisor. Despite its nominal function as the culmination of doctoral transformation and the official marker of scholarly attainment, the dissertation can thus be an internally contradictory genre when it comes to identity formation and the emergence of a student's scholarly voice, effectively trapping writers in a state of doctoral liminality (Keefer 2015).

Whether considered in terms of local (i.e., committee/department) or broader disciplinary audiences, the dissertation is a document whose primary task is in tension with the power dynamics in which it is embedded: through it, a doctoral candidate manifests the authoritative voice of an expert peer, but its legitimating audiences hold hierarchical institutional and disciplinary power over the author. Barnacle and Gloria Dall'Alba ask, "What is the doctoral thesis if not the site in which an author establishes credibility as just that: an authoritative author?" (2014, 2). I want to emphasize here that this fundamental task of authorizing oneself is fraught with tensions of identity, power, and authority whose resolution falls, as so many burdens do, almost entirely on graduate student writers. As Kamler and Thomson put it, "writing a text *and* writing a self at the same time is hard labour" (2014, 16, emphasis in original).

Disciplining Identity, Forming Subjects

Because "the need to acknowledge the discourse community one is entering as a doctoral student is essential to the genre of the thesis" (Carter 2011, 730), theses and dissertations constitute a potent site for textwork/identitywork in relation to disciplinary discourse communities. As Anthony Paré, Doreen Starke-Meyerring, and Lynn McAlpine remind us, the writing of theses and dissertations is "a project of rhetorical subject formation that reproduces world views, epistemologies, ideologies, and ontologies that sustain disciplinary knowledge-making practices" (2011, 232). Writing a thesis/dissertation in a discipline—even a thesis/dissertation that puts pressure on disciplinary norms—necessarily embodies and iterates the knowledge production practices of that discipline, (re)producing both knowledge and knowledge-producing subject. Dacia Dressen-Hammouda similarly emphasizes this connection between writing and disciplinary identity, arguing that "gaining specialized knowledge of a disciplinary community's genres and mastering them presupposes taking on the discipline's identity" (2014, 234); to fully and expertly participate in disciplinary knowledge production requires one to inhabit a legible approximation of that discipline's identity. Disciplinary discourses themselves thus operate as technologies of selfhood whose norms and conventions "both restrict how something can be said and authorise the writer as someone competent to say it" (Hyland 2012, 16), simultaneously constraining and enabling both articulation and identity formation. In other words, just as academic selfhood is primarily discursively produced, so too do the discursive conventions and expectations of disciplines and institutional bodies shape subject formation and the possibilities of selfhood. If the function of ideology is, per Althusser, to reproduce the social relations of production (1971), then we might say that the function of disciplinary discourse is to reproduce the social relations of knowledge production.

These processes of subject formation take place at multiple levels and within multiple, sometimes competing activity systems (Lundell and Beach 2002): through the thesis/dissertation and other genres and everyday practices (McAlpine, Jazvac-Martek, and Hopwood 2009), doctoral candidates are socialized and enculturated as departmental subjects, institutional subjects, disciplinary subjects, and so on. At an institutional level, "regulations and practices intersect in significant ways with student opportunities for exploring and developing disciplinary identities," as when institutions mandate the inclusion of external committee members or departments require particular courses (Paré, Starke-Meyerring, and McAlpine 2011, 224). At a disciplinary level, the discourse practices of a discipline shape the possibilities of selfhood, and thus the discoursal self, available to a graduate student writer. For example, many disciplinary discourses stigmatize or altogether disallow explicit self-mention (i.e., self-citation and/or use of the first person), whereas other disciplines carry the expectation of a certain amount of self-mention as ethos-building, signaling, and/or acknowledgment of subjectivity. Avoidance of self-mention does not mean that a self is not being constructed, performed, and circulated (see endnote 1). In many STEM disciplines, refraining from self-mention signals that a writer "has a commitment to universalistic knowledge motivated by conceptual issues" (Hyland 2012, 18) and is thus properly aligned with disciplinary values and epistemologies. Students and scholars across disciplines thus have significantly different toolkits of discursive self-construction available to them and potentially differing levels of awareness of and access to those toolkits. Feedback from an advisor can also exert a particularly strong force on subject formation. While Mewburn writes that "the supervisor's marks on the paper are a way of guiding student subjectification and encouraging a 'correct' (or legible) academic to emerge" (2011, 323), given a dissertation advisor's degree-conferring power (along with the committee's), these marks are more than mere "encouragement"; rather, they set decisive standards students must meet in order to have their dissertation accepted and their degree conferred.

Together, this multiplicity of levels and systems constitutes the complex discursive structure doctoral writers must navigate, finding ways to assert a distinctive academic identity, legible within a discipline but also innovating and thus not merely reproducing that discipline. As disciplinary newcomers, graduate students "must define and redefine ourselves in orthodoxical terms or risk being labeled transgressive to disciplines of which we wish to be participatory members" (Di Leo 2003, 104). However, the careful manipulation of these orthodoxical terms affords the possibility of agency and individuation within the hegemony of disciplinary knowledge production:

> Disciplinary discourses are cultural models which index relationships with others. They take on a hegemonic dimension because sharing these models reflects, recreates and reinforces the discourses which underpin them. However, in the process of using and reproducing texts, actors also elaborate and manipulate them, shaping what they have to say to their own proclivities and preferences within the boundaries of community expectations of how meanings should be conveyed, arguments constructed and relationships negotiated. (Hyland 2012, 197–198)

Enculturation into these disciplinary discourses involves not only the remaking of both the writer and the discipline but also "the renegotiation of broader social identities and power" (Prior and Bilbro 2012, 22). The pressure one exerts on a discipline's status quo by deviating methodologically or rhetorically is thus related to the pressure exerted on disciplinary old guards by the incursion of new participants with demographically, socioculturally, and linguistically different identities—who carry with them not just their identities but their culturally instantiated ways of "saying-doing-being-valuing-believing" (Gee 1989, 6), even in the sciences. In this way, the neoliberal fracturing of traditional academic identity (which was also strongly marked by whiteness, patriarchy, cisheterosexuality, wealth, ablebodiedness, and so on) is also a potential vehicle for disciplinary change, with the evolving conjunction of social and disciplinary identity opening up new possibilities for ways of knowing, doing, and being (Carter 2007) within contemporary academia.

Professionalization and the Futures of Identity

As I suggested at the outset of this chapter, the stakes of navigating identity formation processes become glaringly obvious when viewed in the harsh lights of professionalization and the academic job market. The "academic superhero" imagined by tenure-track job ads is "a multi-talented, always ready and available worker . . . capable of being everything to everyone and leaping over 24 KSC [key search criteria] in a single job application" (Pitt and Mewburn 2016, 99). Given the realities of dwindling academic job openings and the mounting expectations of candidates for those few openings, developing an assertive but flexible, cohesive but multifaceted scholarly identity is increasingly a prerequisite for acquiring gainful academic employment within "a field of practice and identity that renews itself by eating its young" (Green 2005, 152). Failing to develop such an identity can consign one to the contingent labor pool on which those vanishingly few research scholar jobs depend so heavily—or at least can appear to do so, since achieving the desired position depends as much on luck as on any mode of preparation. This pressure provides the subtext to what Gallope calls the "hegemonic ideology of graduate student professionalism" (2007, 34), wherein departments and advisors, haunted by the specter of a terrible job market, urge students to present, publish, and network as early as possible in their program timelines. Graduate students are thus expected to "profess, perform and produce as active scholars" (Gallope 2007, 34)—for minimal compensation beyond marginally improved professional prospects, enthusiastically oversold by well-intentioned advisors and job placement officers—even as they are still supposed to be *learning*. In taking on this impossible labor and its many internal contradictions, graduate students subsidize the research work of tenure-line faculty and advance institutional reputations while accruing little to no professional or material benefit themselves, invisibly carrying the very burdens for which they are ostensibly being trained but in which they will likely not find long-term professional academic employment after graduation. By acculturating graduate students to become professionals from day one, graduate programs paradoxically prevent them from *becoming*, full stop, leaving young academics in indefinite limbo between student and scholar, novice and professional, afforded neither the support warranted by the former nor the respect and compensation due the latter. The tensions and contradictions of graduate student identity formation, this is to say, constitute not only a considerable burden of emotional, intellectual, and rhetorical labor but also a powerful machinery of labor extraction under the beneficent guise of mentorship and professional development.

Of course, there is no lack of individualizing advice about what graduate students can do to escape this limbo. One common theme is broadening and expanding one's skill sets and institutional fluencies (*Learn to code! Write a grant! Serve on a committee! Work a nonacademic job on the side!*[2]) to diversify one's identity-portfolio and prepare for alt- and para-academic possibilities: "Doctoral scientists must be prepared for many possible future selves; nomadic knowledge workers operating amidst global competition and financial austerity" (Hancock and Walsh 2016, 8). This advice, though, marks another key internal contradiction within imaginings of twenty-first-century academic identity. Doctoral study has historically been predicated on a logic of hyperspecialization, on the attainment of identity through being the world's foremost expert on a tiny but consequential sliver of a niche of a subfield of a discipline. But neoliberal academia's increasing fixation on just-in-time, flexible-on-demand professional scholarly identity (Nealon 2012), filtered through a job market in which traditional research faculty jobs are increasingly scarce, accords with Terry Caesar's assertion that "we cannot go back to a time when the career of specialization existed for more than a few. That time will probably exist no more" (2003, 172). The structures and pedagogies of doctoral education persist in creating subjects for whom there is no room in the academic labor market, churning out specialist pegs left with no choice but to try to fit into generalist holes (which, in the anachronistic prestige economy of academia, typically accrue considerably less respect, less compensation, less job security, less bargaining power, and so on). In this context, ostensibly well-intentioned calls for graduate students to carve out more generalist identities within specialist structures inject yet another unresolvable contradiction into the dynamics of graduate student identity formation.

Here, I firmly echo Sue Monk and Loraine McKay's warning that "a focus on identity created through individual agency alone obscures the shifting terrain upon which notions of identity are constructed" (Monk and McKay 2017, 228). Responding to the ongoing reconfiguration of academia by piling new obligations and expectations on an already overburdened population merely intensifies the "individualised, toxic, self-blaming discourses that are characteristic of academics in the neoliberal University" (Gill 2013, 13). In this sense, I concur with Mike Neary and Joss Winn that "the concept of academic identity is not adequate to the critical task for which it is utilised as it fails to deal with the real nature of work in capitalist society" (2016, 409). Specifically, the discourse of identity formation as it is often invoked runs the danger of individualizing a complex set of structural dynamics, inadvertently absolving higher education institutions of accounting for academia's transformations in any robustly systematic or infrastructural way. Although "the system of governance that has evolved in higher education is one that has been reflexively incorporated into the actual practice of academic work" (Delanty 2008, 130), the changes that have reshaped academia and eviscerated its labor market are nonetheless systemic rather than individual, structurally altering the possibilities of selfhood and propagating the "new labouring subjectivities" to which Gill (2013) alludes. Any programmatic response to these changes that neglects this structural register in favor of individual professionalization will thus amplify the associated structural problems and exacerbate the already escalating pressures on graduate student identity formation.

What, then, is to be done? First and foremost, any attempts to ameliorate doctoral graduates' short-term struggles on the job market must avoid accelerating the longer-term trends catalyzing those struggles. This means that adaptations to doctoral education and professional development should take place at institutional, programmatic, and curricular levels, rather than the extracurricular and hidden-curricular levels on which much of the current frantic adaptation takes place, and which disingenuously individualize systemic issues and multiply the burdens placed on individual graduate students. The graduate curriculum provides "a set of cultural, linguistic and social resources . . . in relation to which (among others) students constantly construct, reconstruct and transform their subjectivity" (Kress 2003, 16), and these resources should be designed to enable, not erode, graduate student agency within the rapidly evolving subjectivities of twenty-first-century academic life. As Khadeidra Billingsley argues at the beginning of this volume, "the extensive and complex hierarchical lines that separate graduate students and the administrators who hold the power to make literal life-changing decisions about our lives seem to convolute the perception of what we do and who we are" (29). Graduate curricula and support structures built without a clear-eyed recognition of the full labor expected of graduate students ("what we do") and the complex identity formation processes they must undertake ("who we are") will only set graduate students up for failure, compounding the already considerable stresses and burdens of graduate student life and the overwhelming pressures of the unforgiving labor market awaiting graduate students if they successfully complete their programs.

Towards this end, I would enthusiastically echo the myriad researchers advocating for incorporation of identity theory and related considerations into the structures of doctoral education, advising, and mentorship (Hall and Burns 2009; Jawitz 2009; Lovitts 2005; Lovitts 2008; Overall, Deane, and Peterson 2011; Trede, Macklin, and Bridges 2012). The hidden expectations and contradictions of identity formation need to be made explicit and engaged with directly and thoughtfully in the course of training graduate students; the full labor of formulating a scholarly identity and becoming a scholarly peer needs to be accounted for in the structures of graduate pedagogy, assessment, and support. As Lundell and

Beach have suggested, "student advising and mentoring needs to honestly acknowledge the inevitable double binds created by contradictory objects of different systems" (2002, 508), instead of expecting students to resolve these contradictions themselves, on their own time and with little to no guidance. Notwithstanding "the crucial role of emergent and unstructured experiences in doctoral students' learning" (Hopwood 2010, 840), much of the tacit knowledge of disciplinary development could be made visible and explicit by "treating mentoring relationships explicitly as processes of identity formation and negotiation" (Hall and Burns 2009, 50). Incorporating "critical engagement in the rhetorical nature of subject formation" (Paré, Starke-Meyerring, and McAlpine 2011, 232) may help strengthen student agency and mitigate identity-related anxieties and impostor phenomenon by empowering students to assert a discoursal self that matches the identity-trajectory they envision for themselves.

Doctoral education is at a perilous crossroads, its function as a specialization machine made obsolete by the demands for flexible, generalist, interdisciplinary knowledge workers. Graduate programs need to make careful, reflective decisions about their programmatic and disciplinary goals and adjust accordingly; neither they nor their graduates can be all things to all people, even if neoliberal academia idolizes (the fantasy of) the infinitely adaptable researcher. If indeed doctoral education aims primarily to produce autonomous, creative researchers, then programs must prioritize the elements proven to facilitate this transformation, many of which are inhibited by current curricula and pedagogies: "practical and creative intelligence, informal knowledge, perseverance in the face of frustration/failure, tolerance of ambiguity, self-direction, a willingness to take risks, and intrinsic motivation" (Lovitts 2008, 323). Research has surfaced some promising alternative supervision models and pedagogies that may better foster autonomy, integrate structures of collegiality, and facilitate the goal of *becoming peer*, such as the collaborative cohort model (Burnett 1999), in which faculty members within a discipline facilitate a collaborative learning environment broader than the advisor-student dyad, and the dissertation house model (Carter-Veale et al. 2016), which broadens this collaboration to include multiple disciplines as well as external coaching and mentorship. Ultimately, higher education institutions have a responsibility to resolve the unfunded mandate of graduate student identity formation, providing students support that enables them not only to do the difficult work of academia but to become the scholarly selves toward which they aspire.

Notes

1. Importantly, the disavowal of explicit authorial presence or acknowledgment of subjectivity in scientific writing is not a rejection of the rhetorical construction of identity but rather a *requirement* of it in certain disciplinary contexts; by avoiding self-mention and thereby presenting method and analysis as independent of the subject performing them, a writer in the physical or natural sciences implicitly signals their adherence to disciplinary epistemologies that value objectivity, reproducibility, and scientific method. That is, the discoursal self can be crafted as much by avoiding explicit authorial presence as by embracing it.

2. Elsewhere in this volume, Jaclyn Fiscus-Cannaday and Allison Hutchison offer vital pushback against the way this advice multiplies the litany of burdens graduate students must carry, instead urging graduate students to "do something, but not *all* the things"—a message I very much wish I could pass on to my younger, unbearably overwhelmed graduate student self.

Works Cited

Althusser, Louis. 1971. *Lenin and Philosophy and Other Essays.* London: New Left Books.

Archer, Louise. 2008. "Younger Academics' Constructions of 'Authenticity,' 'Success' and Professional Identity." *Studies in Higher Education* 33, no. 4 (August): 385–403.

Baker, Vicki L., and Lisa R. Lattuca. 2010. "Developmental Networks and Learning: Toward an Interdisciplinary Perspective on Identity Development during Doctoral Study." *Studies in Higher Education* 35, no. 7 (November): 807–827.

Baker, Vicki L., and Meghan J. Pifer. 2011. "The Role of Relationships in the Transition from Doctoral Student to Independent Scholar." *Studies in Continuing Education* 33, no. 1 (March): 5–17.

Barnacle, Robyn. 2005. "Research Education Ontologies: Exploring Doctoral Becoming." *Higher Education Research and Development* 24, no. 2 (May): 179–188.

Barnacle, Robyn, and Gloria Dall'Alba. 2014. "Beyond Skills: Embodying Writerly Practices through the Doctorate." *Studies in Higher Education* 39 (7): 1139–1149.

Barnacle, Robyn, and Inger Mewburn. 2010. "Learning Networks and the Journey of 'Becoming Doctor.'" *Studies in Higher Education* 35, no. 4 (June): 433–444.

Bauman, Zygmunt. 2001. "Identity in the Globalising World." *Social Anthropology* 9, no. 2 (June): 121–129.

Bell, Daniel. 1973. *The Coming of Post-Industrial Society: A Venture in Social Forecasting.* New York: Basic Books.

Berman, Marshall. 1981. *All That Is Solid Melts into Air: The Experience of Modernity.* New York: Simon and Schuster.

Billot, Jennie. 2010. "The Imagined and the Real: Identifying the Tensions for Academic Identity." *Higher Education Research and Development* 29, no. 6 (December): 709–721.

Boud, David, and Alison Lee. 2005. "'Peer Learning' as Pedagogic Discourse for Research Education." *Studies in Higher Education* 30, no. 5 (October): 501–516.

Brew, Angela, David Boud, and Sang Un Namgung. 2011. "Influences on the Formation of Academics: The Role of the Doctorate and Structured Development Opportunities." *Studies in Continuing Education* 33 (1): 51–66.
Burgess, Amy, and Roz Ivanič. 2010. "Writing and Being Written: Issues of Identity across Timescales." *Written Communication* 27 (2): 228–255.
Burnett, Paul C. 1999. "The Supervision of Doctoral Dissertations Using a Collaborative Cohort Model." *Counselor Education and Supervision* 39, no. 1 (September): 46–52.
Butler, Judith. 1990. *Gender Trouble: Feminism and the Subversion of Identity.* New York: Routledge.
———. 1993. *Bodies That Matter: On the Discursive Limits of Sex.* New York: Routledge.
Caesar, Terry. 2003. "Affiliation and Mourning in a Career of Specialization." In *Affiliations: Identity in Academic Culture*, edited by Jeffrey R. Di Leo, 156–174. Lincoln: University of Nebraska Press.
Carter, Michael. 2007. "Ways of Knowing, Doing, and Writing in the Disciplines." *College Composition and Communication* 58, no. 3 (February): 385–418.
Carter, Susan. 2011. "Doctorate as Genre: Supporting Thesis Writing across Campus." *Higher Education Research and Development* 30 (6): 725–736.
Carter-Veale, Wendy Y., Renetta G. Tull, Janet C. Rutledge, and Lenisa N. Joseph. 2016. "The Dissertation House Model: Doctoral Student Experiences Coping and Writing in a Shared Knowledge Community." *CBE—Life Sciences Education* 15, no. 3 (Fall): 1–12.
Castelló, Montserrat, and Anna Iñesta. 2012. "Texts as Artifacts-in-Activity: Developing Authorial Identity and Academic Voice in Writing Academic Research Papers." In *University Writing*, 179–200.
Castelló, Montserrat, and Christiane Donahue, eds. 2012. *University Writing: Selves and Texts in Academic Societies.* Bingley, UK: Emerald Group.
Castells, Manuel. 1976. "The Service Economy and Postindustrial Society: A Sociological Critique." *International Journal of Health Services* 6 (4): 595–607.
Côte, James E., and Charles G. Levine. 2002. *Identity Formation, Agency, and Culture: A Social Psychological Synthesis.* Mahwah, NJ: Lawrence Erlbaum Associates.
Curry, Mary Jane. 2016. "More Than Language: Graduate Student Writing as 'Disciplinary Becoming.'" In *Supporting Graduate Student Writers: Research, Curriculum, and Program Design*, edited by Steve Simpson et al., 78–96. Ann Arbor: University of Michigan Press.
Davies, Bronwyn, and Eva Bendix Petersen. 2005. "Neo-Liberal Discourse in the Academy: The Forestalling of (Collective) Resistance." *LATISS: Learning and Teaching in the Social Sciences* 2, no. 2 (August): 77–98.
Delanty, Gerard. 2008. "Academic Identities and Institutional Change." In *Changing Identities in Higher Education: Voicing Perspectives*, edited by Ronald Barnett and Roberto Di Napoli, 124–133. London: Routledge.
Di Leo, Jeffrey R. 2003. "On Becoming and Being Affiliated." In *Affiliations: Identity in Academic Culture*, edited by Jeffrey R. Di Leo, 101–114. Lincoln: University of Nebraska Press.
Dressen-Hammouda, Dacia. 2014. "Place and Space as Shapers of Disciplinary Identity: The Role of Indexicality in the Emergence of Disciplinary Writing Exper-

tise." In *Space, Place and the Discursive Construction of Identity*, edited by Julia Bamford, Franca Poppo, and Davide Mazzi, 71–106. Bern: Peter Lang.

Flowerdew, John, and Simon Ho Wang. 2015. "Identity in Academic Discourse." *Annual Review of Applied Linguistics* 35:81–99.

Foucault, Michel. 1977. *Discipline and Punish: The Birth of the Prison*, trans. Alan Sheridan. New York: Random House.

———. 1980. "Truth and Power." In *Power/Knowledge: Selected Interviews and Other Writings, 1972–1977*, edited by Colin Gordon, 109–133. New York: Pantheon Books.

———. 1990a. *The History of Sexuality*. Vol. 1. *An Introduction*. New York: Vintage.

———. 1990b. *The History of Sexuality*. Vol. 2. *The Use of Pleasure*. New York: Vintage.

Gallope, Michael. 2007. "The Professionalizing of Graduate 'Students.'" *Workplace: A Journal for Academic Labor* 14:31–39.

Gee, James Paul. 1989. "Literacy, Discourse, and Linguistics: Introduction." *Journal of Education* 171 (1): 5–15.

———. 2000–2001. "Identity as an Analytic Lens for Research in Education." *Review of Research in Education* 25:99–125.

Giddens, Anthony. 1984. *The Constitution of Society: Outline of the Theory of Structuration*. Cambridge, UK: Polity Press.

———. 1991. *Modernity and Self-Identity: Self and Society in the Late Modern Age*. Cambridge, UK: Polity Press.

Gill, Rosalind. 2013. "Academics, Cultural Workers and Critical Labour Studies." *Journal of Cultural Economy* 7 (1): 12–30.

Green, Bill. 2005. "Unfinished Business: Subjectivity and Supervision." *Higher Education Research and Development* 24, no. 2 (May): 151–163.

Hall, Leigh A., and Leslie D. Burns. 2009. "Identity Development and Mentoring in Doctoral Education." *Harvard Educational Review* 79, no. 1 (April): 49–70.

Hall, Stuart. 1996. "Introduction: Who Needs 'Identity'?" In *Questions of Cultural Identity*, edited by Stuart Hall and Paul du Gay, 1–17. London: Sage.

Hancock, Sally, and Elaine Walsh. 2016. "Beyond Knowledge and Skills: Rethinking the Development of Professional Identity during the STEM Doctorate." *Studies in Higher Education* 41 (1): 37–50.

Harris, Suzy. 2005. "Rethinking Academic Identities in Neo-Liberal Times." *Teaching in Higher Education* 10, no. 4 (October): 421–433.

Henkel, Mary. 2010. "Introduction: Change and Continuity in Academic and Professional Identities." In *Academic and Professional Identities in Higher Education: The Challenges of a Diversifying Workforce*, edited by George Gordon and Celia Whitechurch, 3–12. New York: Routledge.

Hopwood, Nick. 2010. "Doctoral Experience and Learning from a Sociocultural Perspective." *Studies in Higher Education* 35, no. 7 (November): 829–843.

Hyland, Ken. 2012. *Disciplinary Identities: Individuality and Community in Academic Discourse*. Cambridge, UK: Cambridge University Press.

Ivanič, Roz. 1998. *Writing and Identity: The Discoursal Construction of Identity in Academic Writing*. Amsterdam: John Benjamins.

Jawitz, Jeff. 2009. "Academic Identities and Communities of Practice in a Professional Discipline." *Teaching in Higher Education* 14, no. 3 (June): 241–251.

Jazvac-Martek, Marian. 2009. "Oscillating Role Identities: The Academic Experiences of Education Doctoral Students." *Innovations in Education and Teaching International* 46, no. 3 (August): 253–264.

Jazvac-Martek, Marian, Shuhua Chen, and Lynn McAlpine. 2011. "Tracking the Doctoral Student Experience over Time: Cultivating Agency in Diverse Spaces." In *Doctoral Education: Research-Based Strategies for Doctoral Students, Supervisors and Administrators*, edited by Lynn McAlpine and Cheryl Amundsen, 17–36. Dordrecht: Springer Netherlands.

Kamler, Barbara, and Pat Thomson. 2014. "Writing the Doctorate, Writing the Scholar." In *Helping Doctoral Students Write: Pedagogies for Supervision*, 2nd ed., edited by Barbara Kamler and Pat Thomson, 14–29. London: Routledge.

Keefer, Jeffrey M. 2015. "Experiencing Doctoral Liminality as a Conceptual Threshold and How Supervisors Can Use It." *Innovations in Education and Teaching International* 52 (1): 17–28.

Kress, Gunther. 2003. "Representational Resources and the Production of Subjectivity: Questions for the Theoretical Development of Critical Discourse Analysis in a Multicultural Society." In *Texts and Practices: Readings in Critical Discourse Analysis*, edited by Carmen Rosa Caldas-Coulthard and Malcolm Coulthard, 15–31. London: Routledge.

Lovitts, Barbara E. 2005. "Being a Good Course-Taker Is Not Enough: A Theoretical Perspective on the Transition to Independent Research." *Studies in Higher Education* 30, no. 2 (April): 137–154.

———. 2008. "The Transition to Independent Research: Who Makes It, Who Doesn't, and Why." *Journal of Higher Education* 79, no. 3 (May–June): 296–325.

Lundell, Dana Britt, and Richard Beach. 2002. "Dissertation Writers' Negotiations with Competing Activity Systems." In *Writing Selves/Writing Societies: Research from Activity Perspectives*, edited by Charles Bazerman and David R. Russell, 483–514. Fort Collins, CO: WAC Clearinghouse.

Lyotard, Jean-François. 1984. *The Postmodern Condition: A Report on Knowledge*. Translated by Geoff Bennington and Brian Massumi. Minneapolis: University of Minnesota Press.

Mantai, Lilia. 2017. "Feeling Like a Researcher: Experiences of Early Doctoral Students in Australia." *Studies in Higher Education* 42 (4): 636–650.

McAlpine, Lynn, and Gill Turner. 2012. "Imagined and Emerging Career Patterns: Perceptions of Doctoral Students and Research Staff." *Journal of Further and Higher Education* 36 (4): 535–548.

McAlpine, Lynn, and Lisa Lucas. 2011. "Different Places, Different Specialisms: Similar Questions of Doctoral Identities under Construction." *Teaching in Higher Education* 16 (6): 695–706.

McAlpine, Lynn, Cheryl Amundsen, and Gill Turner. 2014. "Identity-Trajectory: Reframing Early Career Academic Experience." *British Educational Research Journal* 40, no. 6 (December): 952–969.

McAlpine, Lynn, Marian Jazvac-Martek, and Nick Hopwood. 2009. "Doctoral Student Experience in Education: Activities and Difficulties Influencing Identity Development." *International Journal for Researcher Development* 1, no. 1 (April): 97–109.

Mewburn, Inger. 2011. "Troubling Talk: Assembling the Ph.D. Candidate." *Studies in Continuing Education* 33 (3): 321–332.

Monk, Sue, and Robin McKay. 2017. "Developing Identity and Agency as an Early Career Academic: Lessons from Alice." *International Journal for Academic Development* 22 (3): 223–230.

Nealon, Jeffrey. 2012. *Post-Postmodernism or, The Cultural Logic of Just-in-Time Capitalism*. Stanford, CA: Stanford University Press.

Neary, Mike, and Joss Winn. 2016. "Against Academic Identity." *Higher Education Research and Development* 35 (2): 409–412.

Overall, Nickola C., Kelsey L. Deane, and Elizabeth R. Peterson. 2011. "Promoting Doctoral Students' Research Self-Efficacy: Combining Academic Guidance with Autonomy Support." *Higher Education Research and Development* 30 (6): 791–805.

Paré, Anthony, Doreen Starke-Meyerring, and Lynn McAlpine. 2011. "Knowledge and Identity Work in the Supervision of Doctoral Student Writing: Shaping Rhetorical Subjects." In *Writing in Knowledge Societies*, edited by Doreen Starke-Meyerring et al., 215–236. Fort Collins, CO: WAC Clearinghouse.

Pifer, Meghan, and Vicki Baker. 2013. "Identity as a Theoretical Construct in Research about Academic Careers." In *Theory and Method in Higher Education Research: International Perspectives on Higher Education Research*, edited by Jeroen Huisman and Malcolm Tight, 115–132. Bingley, UK: Emerald Group.

Pitt, Rachael, and Inger Mewburn. 2016. "Academic Superheroes? A Critical Analysis of Academic Job Descriptions." *Journal of Higher Education Policy and Management* 38 (1): 88–101.

Prior, Paul. 2006. "A Sociocultural Theory of Writing." In *Handbook of Writing Research*, edited by Charles A. MacArthur, Steve Graham, and Jill Fitzgerald, 54–65. New York: Guilford Press.

Prior, Paul, and Rebecca Bilbro. 2012. "Academic Enculturation: Developing Literate Practices and Disciplinary Identities." In Castelló and Donahue, *University Writing*, 19–31.

Ross, Andrew. 2009. *Nice Work If You Can Get It: Life and Labor in Precarious Times*. New York: New York University Press.

Sinclair, Jennifer, Robyn Barnacle, and Denise Cuthbert. 2014. "How the Doctorate Contributes to the Formation of Active Researchers: What the Research Tells Us." *Studies in Higher Education* 39 (10): 1972–1986.

Skakni, Isabelle. 2018. "Doctoral Studies as an Initiatory Trial: Expected and Taken-for-Granted Practices That Impede Ph.D. Students' Progress." *Teaching in Higher Education* 23 (8): 927–944.

Smith, Amy E., and Deneen M. Hatmaker. 2014. "Knowing, Doing, and Becoming: Professional Identity Construction among Public Affairs Doctoral Students." *Journal of Public Affairs Education* 20, no. 4 (Fall): 545–564.

Tobbell, Jane, and Victoria L. O'Donnell. 2013. "Transition to Postgraduate Study: Postgraduate Ecological Systems and Identity." *Cambridge Journal of Education* 43 (1): 123–138.

Trede, Franziska, Rob Macklin, and Donna Bridges. 2012. "Professional Identity Development: A Review of the Higher Education Literature." *Studies in Higher Education* 37 (3): 365–384.

Van Wyck, James M. 2015. "Grad Student: You Are Your Own Spokesperson." *Inside Higher Ed*, November 16, 2015. https://www.insidehighered.com/advice/2015/11/16/how-grad-students-can-best-present-themselves-during-job-searches-essay.

Interlude 9

Ethically Honoring Graduate Student Expertise through Joy Projects

Jaclyn Fiscus-Cannaday and Allison Hutchison

Dear Graduate Students,

 You're going to have an obscene amount of work to do in graduate school, and let's be honest: everyone knows the job market is competitive, so you want to accrue a few accolades and accomplishments for your CV. First of all, remember that you were accepted to graduate school because you're smart and motivated. You may feel inclined to apply to conferences, submit to publication CFPs, join school- and field-related organizations, and just generally do all the things. Inadvertently or otherwise, graduate programs abuse the system, treating graduate student instructors (GSIs) as a low-cost, renewable labor force (Bosquet and Nelson 2008). We're writing to provide some advice on how to (1) narrow down the possibilities of activities to get involved with, and (2) assert your expertise—all while being mindful of how graduate school is prime territory for labor exploitation.

 As graduate students in writing studies doctoral programs, we both witnessed and experienced unethical labor conditions. Because of these experiences, we became co-chairs of the Labor Census Task Force, a group affiliated with the Writing Program Administrators Graduate Organization (WPA-GO). Our task force investigated the conditions of writing studies graduate student instructors by conducting a nationwide survey. The Labor Census Task Force's report (Osorio et al. 2019), which surveyed 344 graduate students in writing studies programs in fall 2017, found that the majority of graduate students (62.8%) worked more hours per week than their contract dictates. Meanwhile, 71.65% of graduate students indicated that their stipends did not satisfy their living needs. GSIs also detailed a general lack of benefits: inadequate medical insurance, as well as low to no personal or parental leave policies. We see these working conditions as unethical for two reasons: (1) graduate students are underpaid and overworked, and (2) these conditions impede their ability to finish their degrees. We hope our report will help you organize for better labor conditions—especially because graduate student labor has become even more precarious during the COVID-19 pandemic. In fact, several graduate student labor unions in 2020 bargained for additional benefits to support stressors related to COVID-19 (St. Amour 2020). Beyond using our report itself, we also hope that sharing our experiences of doing this unpaid, time-intensive task force work will offer insight into how to ethically honor your expertise to select your own joy project.

One of our biggest takeaways from our experience as co-chairs is to trust our own expertise as graduate students. Graduate students too often are relegated to the apprenticeship role of aiding faculty in their research because the assumption is that we lack expertise. Instead, we believe faculty in all disciplines can include graduate students in research projects as a part of professionalization to create important and invaluable learning experiences—but it is just as important to provide space, support, and compensation for graduate student-led research projects like the one that we experienced. Whether you conduct research with a faculty member, independently, or as a group, we encourage you to value your labor by bargaining for compensation and/or recognition. And, as you do that, be strategic; narrowing your focus is a way of valuing your expertise. As Khadeidra Billingsley suggests in the first interlude in this collection, graduate students experience layers of emotional, professional, and economic stressors that impact labor and working conditions—so we need to be wary of adding more to an already overburdened workload.

Do Something, but Not All the Things

Our first recommendation is to not do "all the things." Be selective. Be willing to say no. But also be willing to say yes, to yourself: that is, find your "joy project." A joy project is some kind of labor that falls outside the scope of what is required of you in your role as a graduate student, but you do anyway because it brings you joy. Joy projects are an important step in figuring out what the job market might look like for you—inspiring you to look at opportunities that exist both inside and outside the academy. As we know, the harsh reality is that the academic job market is reeling; 650,000 academics lost their jobs between February 2020 and February 2021 (Kroger 2021). Your joy project could qualify you for opportunities outside academia. For instance, based upon the kind of work you love, you could consider positions in research institutions, think tanks, politics, non-profits or administration, educational technology, or textbook development.

Select a Joy Project

For both of us, our joy project was the Labor Census Task Force with WPA-GO. For Allison, the decision to join was based upon her previous experience as an adjunct instructor at a few institutions before she returned to graduate school. Meanwhile, Jaclyn got involved because of her experiences as a graduate student struggling to find timely, adequate mental health care that was covered in her benefits package. Though we came to this project with different interests, it helped us determine what kind of work we wanted to do in the future, all while bolstering one of the oft-forgotten areas of the CV: service. We enjoyed the project so much because we felt empowered by creating a resource that graduate students could use to advocate for labor change.

Advocate for Recognition and Compensation

Once you've vetted a joy project, make sure your work carries a title that you can put on your CV. For us, that meant making sure that our positions on the task force were named as "co-chairs" and supported by WPA-GO and therefore codified as "national service." We were not compensated monetarily, but we were given credit for our labor in a tangible, documented way. Our experience leads us to recommend that if you are asked by someone in your department to participate in an activity outside of your labor contract, ask what your title will be and if there is any compensation. If the service or leadership opportunity does not carry a title, suggest one to the organizers or fellow collaborators. We felt that because the Labor Census Task Force was affiliated with a national organization in the field, our involvement was worthwhile despite it not offering financial compensation. At the same time, our decisions to do this unpaid work was shaped by the support of other income streams in each of our families. Not everyone has access to these resources, so your context should be a factor in your decision making. Further, compensation does not always have to be monetary: you can ask for a reference, a recommendation letter, a meal, or a teaching observation in exchange for your work.

Use Your Joy Project to Move Forward

Here is how we each represented our work in our CVs. Allison listed her involvement under the heading "Professional Activities and Service," and Jaclyn added hers to "Service."

Co-Chair, Labor Census Task Force, Writing Program Administrators Graduate Organization [Allison]

- Developed and conducted national survey on graduate student instructor labor conditions in collaboration with task force members
- Organized meetings and created reports for CWPA Executive Board
- Coded qualitative survey data results

Co-Chair, Labor Census Task Force, WPA-GO [Jaclyn]

- Co-developed a national survey on graduate student labor conditions in writing studies; facilitated task force meetings, deadlines, and labor-distribution to achieve task force goals; co-wrote progress reports to WPA-GO to keep the organization appraised of progress.

In both of these examples, we named and showcased our joy project as valuable by documenting the expertise gained from this experience. This was useful to us on the job market, becoming something that helped us give examples of our administrative prowess, aptitude for service, and feminist identities. Allison now serves as a senior lecturer in the Engineering Communications Program at Cornell University, and Jaclyn is an assistant professor in the English Department at Florida State University. Our experience with this project influences how we are allies to GSIs, adjunct instructors, and lecturers in negotiations on campus; inspires us to be advocates for self-care; and grounds our support for fair and ethical labor conditions across the university and beyond.

Good luck finding your joy project. Trust your expertise. Call out the unethical and exploitative behavior of those around you. And, know we're here if you need us.

In Solidarity,

Jaclyn and Allison

Works Cited

Bosquet, Marc, and Cary Nelson. 2008. *How the University Works*. New York: NYU Press.

Kroger, John. 2021. "650,000 Colleagues Have Lost Their Jobs: A Moral Issue for Higher Education." *Inside Higher Ed*, February 19, 2021. https://www.insidehighered.com/blogs/leadership-higher-education/650000-colleagues-have-lost-their-jobs.

Osorio, Ruth, Allison Hutchison, Jaclyn Fiscus-Cannaday, Sarah Primeau, Molly Ubbesen, Alexander Champoux, Julianna Edmonds, Leah Heilig, Laura Matravers, and Katie McWain et al. 2019. "Labor Census Survey Data on Graduate Student Instructors in Writing Studies." https://sites.google.com/cornell.edu/gsi-laborcensus-writingstudies/home.

St. Amour, Madeline. 2020. "Organizing for Help in a Pandemic: When COVID-19 Hit, Graduate Student Workers Organized to Win Basic Protections and Extensions." *Inside Higher Ed*, June 16, 2020. https://www.insidehighered.com/news/2020/06/16/graduate-student-workers-organized-win-covid-19-protections.

7 | Chinese Doctoral Students' Perceptions of Employability in the United States
Cultivating Preparedness for a Challenging World

Xueshuang Wang, Weiyan Xiong, and Huiyuan Ye

Introduction

Doctoral education originated in Germany in the nineteenth century. Traditionally, it has cultivated academic and research talents for the professoriate. With the advent of the knowledge economy, especially the trend of globalization and the expansion of various labor market demands, doctoral education has become diversified in the types of talents trained (Mok 2017). For example, in addition to academic and professional doctorates, there are new types of doctoral degrees, such as the practice-based doctorate in the United Kingdom and the doctorate by publication (Quality Assurance Agency for Higher Education 2011). In Australia, to systematically integrate employability into doctoral programs, some public universities have reformed their doctor of philosophy (PhD) programs, such as the "Monash PhD" of Monash University and the "Career Advantage PhD" of the University of Queensland (Molla and Cuthbert 2015). The value of cultivating the employability of doctoral students has been widely recognized by developed countries. The United States, as a significant provider of doctoral education, has been exploring ways to reshape and reform doctoral education in order to match doctoral graduates' skills with labor market needs.

Doctoral education in the United States is mature and stable, and its development is at the forefront of the world. But since the 1990s, many US universities have begun to change their doctoral programs to deal with a series of problems. The number of faculty positions at colleges and

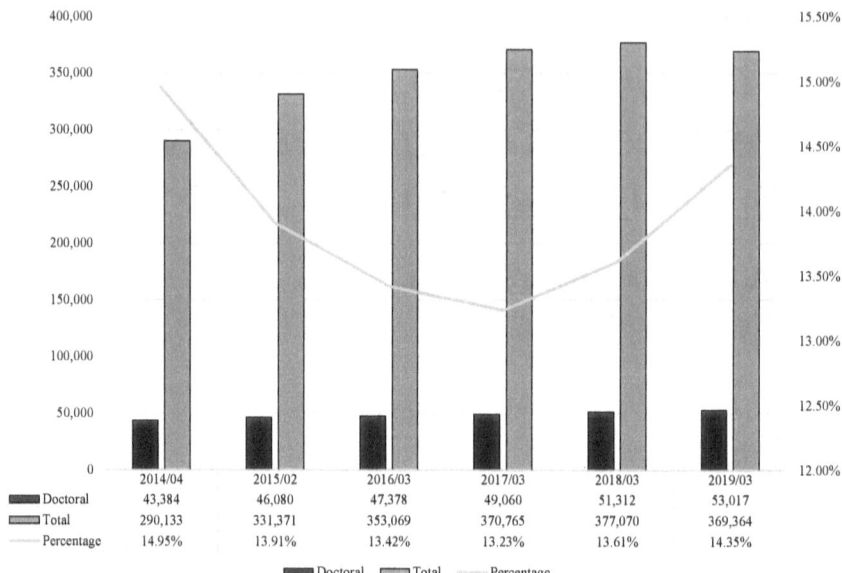

Figure 7.1, Chinese doctoral students in the United States with active visa status, 2014–2019. Source: US Department of Homeland Security (2019), https://studyinthestates.dhs.gov/sevis-by-the-numbers/sevis-by-the-numbers-data.

universities has remained limited, while the number of doctoral graduates is rapidly increasing (Benderly 2018). Moreover, due to the reduction of public education funds and the corporatization of higher education, US colleges and universities are increasingly hiring temporary and adjunct faculty members to reduce financial expenses (Brennan and Magness 2018). When doctoral graduates attempt to seek employment outside academia, they often fail to meet job requirements because they lack critical abilities and the skills required by industry (Hancock and Walsh 2016). In this context, we can see that US doctoral education is still facing the challenges of the academic and wider labor markets, and that the reformation of doctoral programs to cultivate students' employability inside and outside academia is quite in demand (Allum, Kent, and McCarthy 2014). Therefore, it is of great practical significance to explore how to enhance the employability of doctoral students at the institutional level in the United States.

The changing landscape of doctoral education in the United States is also influencing Chinese international students who are pursuing their graduate degrees. Currently, China is the top country of origin for international students coming to the United States. In the 2017–2018 academic year, 363,341 Chinese students were studying in the country, of whom 36% were studying at the graduate level (IEE 2018). As figure 7.1 depicts, in March 2019, 53,017 Chinese students were pursuing their doctoral degrees at US universities. From 2014 to March of 2019, around 14% of all Chinese international students in the US were enrolled in doctoral programs. Some studies of Chinese graduate students in the United States have focused on Chinese graduate students' academic experiences (e.g., Le and Gardner 2010; Li and Collins 2014; Zhang 2016; Zhou 2014). However, little research exists about Chinese doctoral students' perceptions of employability, which evolves continuously in a fast-changing job market. Moreover, it is worth exploring Chinese doctoral students' working experiences as graduate employees like research assistants or teaching assistants while finishing their doctoral programs. Following Kupsch and McDonald's attention in this volume to graduate student life, this study provides an international perspective on Chinese graduate student life in US higher education.

Literature Review

Definitions of Employability

Employability is a complex concept with multiple definitions (Cole and Tibby 2013). Hillage and Pollard (1998) suggest that employability should include knowledge and quality in addition to skills. Specifically, they argue that employability should include four elements: (1) "assets" in terms of knowledge, skills, and attitudes; (2) "deployment" regarding the ability to use the assets; (3) the abilities of presenting and demonstrating employability; and (4) "context" including personal circumstances and labor markets (Hillage and Pollard 1998, x).

Another widely recognized definition is Knight and Yorke's (2004), which defines employability as a set of abilities and skills that will benefit both individuals in terms of achieving a successful career, and the labor market and society as well. What needs to be clarified here is that employability and employment are two different concepts. Employment means having a job, while employability means having the qualities to maintain employment and progress at work (Lees 2002). In this study, following Knight and Yorke's (2014) definition, employability refers to the range of knowledge, skills, abilities, and personal qualities acquired by individuals which makes them more likely to obtain jobs and succeed in their chosen career, benefiting themselves, employers, and wider economic development.

Employability and Higher Education

In recent years, many countries and regions have emphasized employability as a crucial element in promoting economic prosperity and improving workers' quality of life. Globally, various governments have set the goal of improving graduate employability for their national higher education systems (Bui and Nguyen 2019; Yorke 2006). At the same time, universities and colleges have begun to explore effective ways to cultivate and enhance students' employability in order to serve the institutional goals of improving the quality of education. In the United Kingdom, employability has long been a core part of the strategic direction of the Department for Education and Employment (Hillage and Pollard 1998). Moreover, employability has been an important goal of the European Higher Education Area, and member countries are required to enhance the employability of their citizens in order to face changes in social and employment environments. To deal with dramatically changing labor markets caused by digitalization and automation, the "Skills Strategy" section of the OECD identifies life-long learning as an essential part of the future of work and employability (OECD 2019, 15).

Given the reality that the employment environment has changed, some developed countries, including the United States, are continually improving their doctoral programs to enhance their graduates' employability (Allum et al. 2014). European nations in particular have made collective efforts through the platform of the European Union. Since 2001 the European Commission has focused on the career development of researchers as a vital part of establishing the European Research Area (e.g., "One Profession, Multiple Careers" and "Realizing a Single Labor Market for Research") (Commission of the European Communities 2003; European Commission 2008). At the same time, as part of the European partnership, the European Commission has developed the "European Framework for Research Careers" in cooperation with its member states and has established principles for innovative doctoral development (European Commission 2011).

Employability plays a central role in the European Commission's reform of higher education. At the same time, universities themselves are increasingly aware of the importance of ensuring that graduates have the right job skills (European Commission/EACE/Eurydice 2014). The employability of graduates has been widely emphasized by a range of higher education stakeholders, increasingly becoming part of the functions and responsibilities of colleges and universities. Yet despite such emphasis on the parts of governments and universities, it appears that college graduates are still not able to meet the skills requirements of the labor market, especially in the current knowledge economy (Cuthbert and Molla 2015). "Companies still complain about the employability of graduates . . . [D]espite the cash, government pressure and numerous initiatives, many believe that universities are neglecting the employability factor" (Utley 2003, 10). As Brown's introduction to this volume indicates, graduate study in the United States has tended to accept the assumption that all doctoral students will become professors. However, with the development of the knowledge economy and the changes in the labor market, while many PhD graduates are still seeking jobs in academia, academic positions are limited and decreasing (Duke and Denicolo 2017; Gibbs, McGready, and Griffin 2015; Johnson and Parmenter 2017). Thus, preparing graduate students for employability beyond academia is more important than ever.

In China, the relationship between employability and higher education has been emphasized by the ministry of education, which is reflected by the application-oriented reform of undergraduate programs since 2015 (China's Ministry of Education, National Development and Reform Commission, and China's Ministry of Finance 2015). As such, practical career and entrepreneurship training and industry-university collaboration have been prevailing trends in China's higher education sector (Li and Xia 2018). However, this nation-wide application-oriented emphasis from the central government does not cover doctoral students, so doctoral training in China is still academically oriented, and issues similar to those in US PhD training also appear in China (Qing and Liang 2019). Therefore, a growing number of universities in China are seeking to reform PhD training with accentuated emphasis on employability training.

International and Chinese Doctoral Students in the United States

The United States has long been a top destination for students from all over the world to pursue their doctoral degrees because of its colleges and universities' reputation for high-quality graduate education (Kim, Roh, and de Barroso 2018). According to the Institute for International Education (2019), in the 2018/19 academic year, 132,581 international doctoral students were studying in the country. These students play a significant role in US graduate education in terms of enrollment and graduation (Kim, Roh, and de Barroso 2018). There are especially high proportions of international doctorates from Asian countries like China, India, and South Korea, especially in the sciences and engineering, and abundant research discusses their motivations, learning experiences, and postgraduation plans in the United States (e.g., Hoh 2015; Kim, Roh and de Barroso 2018; Wu et al. 2020; Zhang 2016; Zhou 2014). Because of the supportive policy of the Chinese government and the Chinese Scholarship Council (CSC), increasing numbers of Chinese doctoral students in the United States are funded by the Chinese state, in addition to self-financed doctoral students and institutional scholarship recipients (CSC 2020). This governmental support has been recognized by some Chinese doctoral students as a great facilitator of their educational attainment in the United States (Wu et al. 2020). These CSC-funded students sign a contract with a deposit, indicating that they will return to China to work for no less than two years after obtaining their doctoral degrees (CSC 2018).

International doctoral students from different countries and regions have unique living and learning experiences in the United States (Ugwu and Adamuti-Trache 2017). In addition to the challenges faced by international students in general, including language barriers for non-English speakers and cultural and social adjustment barriers (Campbell 2015; Ugwu and Adamuti-Trache 2017; Zhang 2016), international doctoral students also face particular challenges due to their age and life stage, including maintaining family relationships and work-life balance (Campbell 2015). For Chinese doctoral students, they also face challenges arising from their cultural and social backgrounds, especially the Confucian cultural heritage and collectivist social context (Li and Collins 2014; Zhang 2016). In addition, Chinese doctoral students are treated as more mature than undergraduate students and have relatively fixed values, worldviews, and living styles, bringing more challenges for them in adapting to the US environment (Zhang 2016).

Many studies also discuss international doctoral students' postgraduation plans, especially the decision regarding whether to stay in the United States or return to their home countries (e.g., Finn and Pennington 2018; Kim et al. 2018; Roh 2015; Ugwu and Adamuti-Trache 2017). In general, international students' decisions are greatly influenced by broader policy environments at the host and home countries in addition to their personal considerations (Zhou 2016). Especially in the years preceding the Trump presidency, the United States did very well in attracting international doctorate recipients to stay. For instance, 70% of the doctoral graduates from 2007–2009 had remained in the United States as of 2013. Within that same cohort, Chinese doctoral students had the second-highest stay rate at 84%, slightly less than Indian students' at 86% (Finn and Pennington 2018). For Chinese doctoral students in particular, the advantages in employability brought by a US doctoral degree and the rapid development of the Chinese economy have been the major draws for returning to China (Zhou 2016). However, at a micro level, the perceptions of the employability of Chinese doctoral students in the United States are understudied, despite these perceptions' relevance to their decisions to stay or to return, as well as their future career development.

Research Questions and Research Design

As Chinese scholars who have had doctoral study and graduate employment experiences in US universities, the authors have observed and experienced the influences of changing job markets inside and outside academia on Chinese doctoral students' perceptions and cultivation of employability. This study selects as its case a department of the school of education at a public research university in the United States. Seven Chinese doctoral students and candidates from different programs were purposively selected. Semi-structured interviews were conducted to collect qualitative data on three aspects of employability, including career expectations, perceptions of doctoral employability, and cultivation of doctoral employability. This study aims to explore how these seven Chinese doctoral students from one US public university school of education conceptualized the relationship between employability and their doctoral programs, with a particular focus on their experiences as graduate student employees. The study addresses the following three research questions.

1. What are the career expectations of Chinese doctoral students at one US graduate school of education?
2. How do Chinese doctoral students at this school of education perceive the labor market's demands on their employability?
3. How do Chinese doctoral students at this school of education describe their experiences cultivating employability?

The design and implementation of this study were reviewed and approved by the Internal Review Board of the study-affiliated institution.

Research Participants, Data Collection, and Analysis

Seven Chinese doctoral students from the case university participated in this study. In order to better explore the specific experiences of Chinese doctoral students, researchers purposefully recruited participants in different years of their doctoral programs. Participants came from both the academically oriented PhD program and the professionally oriented doctor of education (EdD) program. All participants had graduate employment experiences as graduate student researchers or assistants. To ensure the confidentiality of the interviewees' information, each participant was assigned a unique code. Table 7.1 presents basic information on all seven interviewees.

Our interviews focused on three aspects of doctoral employability: "institution choice and career expectations," "perceptions of employability," and "cultivation of employability." In the interview, after the basic information section, a total of nine open-ended questions were asked regarding the three aspects of doctoral employability. The answers to these nine questions were then qualitatively coded in data analysis.

All interviews were recorded with the consent of interview participants. After transcription, all interview data were compiled, cleaned, coded, and analyzed using the NVivo qualitative research software. In the data analysis process, copies of the transcript of one interview were coded by all authors to triangulate the codes to validate the research findings. The three categories of research questions each had their own unique findings with significant overlaps, as presented in the discussion section. Our key findings were that participants' career expectations were characterized by diversity and competition; their perceptions of employability were that their doctoral training valuably improved their critical thinking,

Table 7.1. Interview Participants

Interviewee	Gender	Program	Year in Program	Major
DSE01	M	EdD	7th	higher education management
DSE02	M	PhD	2nd	higher education management
DSE03	F	PhD	6th	comparative education
DSE04	M	PhD	6th	comparative education
DSE05	M	PhD	2nd	comparative education
DSE06	F	PhD	1st	comparative education
DSE07	F	PhD	5th	comparative education

research skills, and socialization; and their employability was cultivated most directly through relationships with advisors.

Key Findings

Career Expectations: Diversity and Competition

In general, the reasons why interviewees chose to embark on their doctoral journeys were linked to their career expectations and subsequent career development. Some interviewees named their aspiration as becoming a university faculty member. In the current economy, they saw having a doctoral degree as indispensable to entering a good university as a faculty member. At the same time, interviewees felt that doctoral degrees could also help them secure a job in their research areas or a related field. As one participant said, "I feel that if I do not have a PhD in the field of international policy studies, it is difficult to continue my research. As for my future career, it is not enough to only have a master's degree. I must have a doctoral degree. Only sufficient systematic study and academic training can support me to find the work I like, so I chose this doctoral program" (DSE06–1). In the following communications, this interviewee indicated she did not intend to seek a faculty position but felt that a doctorate was crucial for her to become a researcher in her chosen field.

Interviewees had three categories of career expectations. The first was to work as a university-level teacher or researcher, the second was to work at an educational research institute, and the last was to work at an international organization such as the United Nations or World Bank. Moreover, due to the fierce competition in the US job market, several of them planned to return to China for work opportunities. All seven interviewees pointed out that their career expectations had changed since the beginning of their doctoral programs. This change was the result of a combination of various factors, including the job market, interactions with advisors and other professors, and individual experiences in the doctoral programs.

Regarding the job market, interviewees indicated that after examining the market demands, they changed their initial thoughts of career plans, like changing from theoretical work to practical fields. One interviewee remarked, "Although your career expectations are good, if there is no market, you cannot find the ideal job. For example, [the current job market] has a minimum demand for philosophy major graduates, and it might be useless to study philosophy" (DSE04–2).

Interactions with advisors and other professors also affected interviewees' career expectations. Some interviewees indicated that their advisors had given them significant guidance for future career development. For example, one interviewee (DSE02) shared that in the early stage of his program, his advisor asked him what career he wanted to pursue in order to help him cultivate relevant abilities. "I told my advisor I wished to engage in research and teaching at a university after graduation, and he began to let me join in several research projects and co-author with him in some publications. Also, he asked me to co-teach some courses with him to accumulate my teaching experience" (DSE02–3). Interactions with other professors also influenced interviewees' career expectations. Another interviewee described how his professors' experiences in the field impacted his desire to pursue the same:

> Now for economic and financial reasons, universities are competing with many other social sectors, and you need to understand [the knowledge out of universities] to better manage a university. Some of my professors [had] this kind of experiences [before joining the faculty] and have brought these experiences to us. Working with them has affected my career expectation [in] that I want to go out first to gain practical experiences [before returning to higher education]. (DSE01–3)

Thus, it seems that interviewees' career expectations were strongly shaped by interactions with their advisors and other professors. However, having this kind of interaction depended on whether interviewees could proactively seek advice from their advisors or other professors. Interviewees identified the freestyle advisory pattern in the United States as very different from the more parental instructional style in China. For example, one noted that "[in the United States], some professors are very willing to give guidance and share their experiences. Some professors are not, and they just let you do things by yourself. But my master's advisor in China is just like my mother and cared about everything in addition to study" (DSE04–6). This phenomenon is rooted in traditional Chinese culture, in which the teacher is highly respected. Yet this mindset can also leave Chinese doctoral students reluctant to say no to their advisors. As one interviewee shared, "My graduate research assistant contract says I cannot work more than 20 hours a week, but nobody counts my working hour, and I just take the tasks and finish them" (DSE02–7). This interviewee emphasized that he was not complaining; rather, he appreciated this position because it trained him in research and teaching skills, which would be critical for his future academic job search.

In this sense, interviewees understood their advisors played significant roles in their future career development, but they also had to navigate interactional challenges brought on by differences between US-style mentorship and what they had experienced in China.

Perceptions of Employability: Improved by Critical Thinking, Research Skills, and Socialization

When discussing employability, interviewees highlighted the importance of critical thinking, interdisciplinary vision, ethical conduct, and the ability to synthesize a large amount of information, in addition to traditionally recognized specialized knowledge, research skills, and writing.

The interviewees generally mentioned critical thinking as a centerpiece of doctoral employability. One interviewee in particular reflected on being trained in critical thinking during his own doctoral experience: "I remember the instructors of one core course encouraged everyone to begin with the concept of 'skill gap' and look for an educational issue from around the world. We were encouraged to hunt a phenomenon, a hypothesis, a problem, and a question grounded in a historical context" (DSE02–4). In the process of doctoral education, students were encouraged to deliberate educational phenomena from different perspectives derived from their respective backgrounds. Critical thinking was developed through rationalizing opinions of others and one's own in order to discover and solve practical problems.

Yet, Chinese doctoral students in this study realized that despite the significance of critical thinking for their employment after graduation, they should go beyond the concept and consider the larger contexts in which critical thinking skills would be applied. In particular, participants saw interdisciplinarity and ethical thinking as part of what made well-qualified researchers. One interviewee reflected on the increasingly interdisciplinary nature of real-world problems and stated that it was difficult for a single discipline to solve them. Therefore, in his understanding, critical thinking is a skill not only to be used within disciplines but also between them:

> Take environmental pollution as an example. First, it is an issue related to environmental engineering. Second, it is related to public policy. It may also be related to social sciences or urban studies. I think doctoral students should have the ability to connect, integrate, and apply knowledge. It is not enough to be experts in their own fields. They must be aware of what is happening in other disciplinary fields, what that means to the economy as well as policies, and then situate themselves in this giant map with the most-needed skills and qualities they can provide. (DSE01–4)

Critical thinking also manifests itself as the ability to think independently. This ability not only stays at the cognitive level but is also increasingly reflected at the moral level. Interviewees generally believe that the nature of doctoral training enables students to become proactive formulators, rather than passive recipients, of public opinions, preparing them for difficult situations in their work. One respondent further stated that doctoral students should be prepared to interpret and guard against ethical misconduct in the knowledge profession. Said another participant:

> The most cutting-edge scientific research in the world is undertaken by former doctoral students. Controversial issues in research often require advanced knowledge that only they may understand, which entails ethical concerns. Stem cell research is such a field that would require aspirant doctoral students [to possess] cognitive abilities as well as ethical qualifications in order to enter. That is simply because only they would be capable of both. (DSE01–4)

In addition to critical thinking, interdisciplinary visions, and ethical conduct, interviewees highlighted the ability to synthesize a large amount of information as key to their employability as doctoral students. The age of the internet and big data makes accessing knowledge and information easier. Thus, being knowledgeable is no longer enough to make doctoral students stand out. They must also have the abilities to select, synthesize, digest, and functionalize knowledge. According to one interviewee, "You must know better than non-PhDs about analyzing, organizing, and producing knowledge, making it more useful and efficient. Otherwise, it is hard to tell the difference a PhD can make" (DSE04–4).

All Chinese doctoral students in this study agreed that there were gaps between their training and the job market requirements that needed to be filled in order for them to become highly employable. Meanwhile, they expressed confidence that their respective programs would help them fill those gaps. The study also found that the interviewees paid attention to nuances in employability. For example, one interviewee's comments tended to revolve around the relationship with his advisor in explaining how his communication skills had improved. Compared with the interviewees who tended to focus on peer-to-peer communication in the form of project collaboration, this respondent seemed to be more concerned about developing skills to communicate with his future workplace supervisors.

In addition, interviewees highlighted their freedom to choose what aspects of employability they considered significant, given the richly independent and collaborative nature of doctoral education in the United States. According to one participant, "As long as you are willing, you can incorporate into your doctoral studies the much-needed enhancements of those employable skills" (DSE04–5). The relative autonomy of doctoral education also provided some flexibility for students to explore, interpret, and cultivate their skills. As another participant commented:

> You have a fair amount of time to spend outside formal studies because you have an average of four to six years for doctoral studies. After the coursework is finished and the dissertation phase begins, there is more liberty for investing your time. You can get to know the communities nearby and catch up with labor market trends and events. As an international student, it also enriches your experience by visiting with local cultures and faith groups as an important way to enhance your intercultural skills and abilities. (DSE01–5)

Surprisingly, only one Chinese doctoral student (DSE01) among all interviewees mentioned intercultural skills and abilities. After reviewing all skills mentioned by interviewees, we found that they focused the most on those skills obviously relevant to research or future academic work as researchers, rather than more general social skills. When participants discussed communication skills, they stressed interactions with their advisors. This focus gestures at the isolating nature of doctoral study, as well as the closed social circles of Chinese doctoral students in the United States. In summary, the independent nature of doctoral study and the closed Chinese student group, to some degree, influenced the perceptions to employability of the Chinese doctoral students in this study.

Cultivation of Employability: Shaped by Advisor Relationships

In terms of the cultivation of employability, the seven Chinese doctoral students emphasized the role of their advisors in the whole process of academic training and career development. In the interviewees' minds, the relationship, interaction, and cooperation between interviewees and their advisors significantly impacted their employability. Interviewees also recognized research capability as an important aspect of their employability, and they further emphasized that while conducting research with advisors significantly enhanced their research capabilities, research method courses in their respective programs could be strengthened. Finally, interviewees shared their perspectives on the advantages and disadvantages of their specific school of education in the cultivation of employability.

In the interviews, all participants emphasized the important role and critical influence of the advisors in their entire doctoral program. One participant shared that "in my work and study, I have much communication with my advisor because of my current job position at his institute. This is very helpful for improving my research ability because I can observe how he deals with work and research issues" (DSE02–6). In addition to the explicit influence that the advisors have on the students, the participants also mentioned the "hidden" impact of the advisors. "The hidden influences of advisors to doctoral students include their style of leadership and conducting research. Some professors are very willing to sit down and talk to you and tell you their experiences in a down-to-earth manner. I think this is very important for the training of doctoral students" (DSE04–6).

Taking part in advisors' research projects was considered by interviewees as an essential way to enhance their research capabilities. Interviewees described being assigned to a research task individually or as a team, and several believed that this approach was beneficial to the development of doctoral students' research and teamwork skills. As one participant put it, "The advisor does a research project with students in his course. I think it is very important, and I have benefited a lot. Actually, there are other teachers who also use this approach. I have taken several courses. Moreover, in the course of education evaluation, which also uses this teaching method, we can participate in and understand the whole real-life research project" (DSE02–7). From the perspective of employability, these projects do not merely become resumé items but also help interviewees understand and apply skills such as critical thinking and information synthesizing in a real work environment.

Interviewees argued that courses involving research projects and collaboration with advisors and peers were an important "platform" for them to improve research capacity and cultivate employability. "The abilities like research, writing, and project management depend on the curriculum, the training and collaboration with advisors and peer friends," said one interviewee. "They have served as a platform, and we can gain these capabilities through this platform" (DSE02–6). Moreover, interviewees generally commented that research method courses played an important role in doctoral students' training as researchers. One remarked that "I feel that [the program] should add more research method courses to the curriculums of the doctoral program, especially the combination of research methods and practices" (DSE03–6).

Interviewees thought that two-way communication with advisors was important, especially for international students. One participant suggested that, on the one hand, students should take the initiative to communicate with their advisors and instructors. On the other hand, this participant thought that instructors should also recognize international students' limitations in language and culture and be proactive when communicating with international students in particular:

> According to my observations, I think the relationship, interaction, and cooperation between advisors and students need to be further strengthened. On the one hand, students need to be more active in learning and more aggressively approaching their advisors. On the other hand, I think advisors should be keenly aware of the difficulties of non-US students or students whose native language is not English. (DSE01-7)

Interviewees also shared their perspectives on how the institution itself cultivated their employability. The most significant offerings, they said, were institutional resources, whether hardware and software resources for doctoral students, training and consulting services, or career development guidance. The disadvantages noted by interviewees included too many courses and the need to strengthen the communication between them and advisors. Said one participant, "I think this PhD program may be a bit too much in terms of coursework, because I have already had a master's degree in the same program, but I still need to take many courses. Although it is possible to transfer credits, I still find myself having to repeat some compulsory courses" (DSE02-7).

In summary, Chinese doctoral students in this study appreciated how their PhD training cultivated their research skills and also indicated that both the advisor and the school play important roles in facilitating their growth in academia. In addition, while graduate assistant positions provided employees with many opportunities to accumulate employment skills, their previous experiences in Chinese institutions brought them some frustrations in working with their advisors.

Discussion

Our findings illustrate that Chinese students' approaches to employability are shaped by their relationships to their advisors and their understanding of their own goals and the needs of academic and nonacademic labor markets. We find that Chinese doctoral students in this study pursue doctoral education as a way to support their career goals. In particular, we identify an emphasis on role models' significant influences on Chinese doctoral students regarding their choices of career fields and paths. This last finding echoes other scholarship suggesting that interactions between Chinese doctoral students and role models are a crucial part of how their doctoral experiences influence the trajectory of doctoral students' career plans (Porter and Phelps 2014).

Regarding the cultivation of Chinese doctoral students' employability, we argue the period of doctoral training played an irreplaceable role in fostering abilities in research, writing, and interpersonal interaction, which was widely recognized by Chinese doctoral students as a critical experience. At the same time, study participants recognized and emphasized the significant role of their advisors in their academic and professional development, which has been extensively discussed in the literature on doctoral education (Celik 2013; Porter and Phelps 2014; Zhao 2013). It seems that high-quality doctoral education is inseparable from a caring advisor who can expertly guide students through the journey (Fenge 2012). Meanwhile, the added value of pursuing doctoral education has been recognized by participants in this study, including the understanding of academia, networking with established colleagues in chosen fields, and the cultivation of character and vision. These added values have provided insights for both institution and doctoral students to make use of their doctoral experiences.

Second, socialization matters for success in a doctoral program as much as afterward. The findings suggest that doctoral socialization may be vertical (with superiors) and/or horizontal (with peers), indicating visions, strategies, and implications for future careers. It is interesting to learn that while some Chinese doctoral students in this study enjoy socializing with their advisors, others prefer to be with their peers. One interviewee mentioned that socializing with his advisor prepares him to work effectively with his future boss (DSE01). While both vertical and horizontal socializations suggest positive outcomes for job preparedness, we are tempted to wonder if either of these occur at the cost of the other. We do not yet have evidence as to whether vertical and horizontal socializations positively impact each other. If socialization (or communication) is deemed an important skill in the tech economy, we feel that it is another worthy topic for further research, especially in the current COVID-19 pandemic, in which face-to-face interactions are hindered. The sudden digitization of higher education teaching and learning has brought additional challenges to international doctoral students in both their training and their socialization, which offer opportunities for further study.

Ultimately, the seven Chinese doctoral students in our study valued their graduate student employment experiences because, in addition to the cultivation of relevant skills in academia, they enjoyed the time and opportunities to communicate and collaborate with their advisors. The frequent or regular meetings with advisors significantly shaped their doctoral studies and future career development. However, Chinese doctoral students are also profoundly influenced by the Confucian cultural beliefs that teachers are highly respected (Zhou 2014) and therefore, they feel bad or wrong when they say no to their advisors. In this sense, almost all interviewees in this study indicated that they worked far more than twenty hours per week, which is the time limit regulated by the graduate student employment contract at their university. On the one hand, some interviewees argued they felt grateful for these opportunities offered by their advisors, so the overtime work seemed a kind of payback. One the other hand, these interviewees clearly knew that if they did not take the offers of participating in research projects and co-authoring papers, these opportunities would go to others. Therefore, Chinese doctoral students in this study seem to hold a complex position regarding their graduate student employment experiences: while feeling exploited, they recognized that the exploitation contributed to their ultimate employability.

Conclusion and Recommendations

This case study of seven Chinese doctoral students from the school of education at one public US research university has presented a small-scale image of current Chinese doctoral students' perceptions and cultivation of employability. These students discussed their career aspirations and perceptions of employability based on their doctoral experiences and expectations of job markets. While most interviewees intended to pursue an academic or research career after graduation, their expectations were highly influenced by the advisors, mentors, and even peers. Interviewees treated critical thinking, interdisciplinary visions, ethical conduct, and information synthesizing ability as the major employment skills. In addition to the critical role of the advisors, Chinese doctoral students in this study highlighted the significance of real-life research and graduate employment experiences.

In the face of the increasing trend of the unionization of graduate student employees at US colleges and universities (Benderly 2018; Rogers, Eaton, and Voos 2014), our examination of the subjective views of Chinese doctoral students may provide some insights regarding the general topic of this book on the exploitation of graduate student employees in US higher education. Based on our study, we can offer four recommendations for the institution we studied as well as other US institutions' doctoral programs.

First, while providing high-quality career guidance services, the university should give full play to the successful experiences of alumni to help doctoral students find a suitable employment path and cultivate their employability in a range of fields. At the school or department level, the career service office could contact alumni, including international alumni, to give lectures to share their successes or failures in employment. For academic advisors, they could invite their former advisees working in different industries to share their experiences with current doctoral students.

Second, US universities need to further explore how to strengthen advisors' guidance to enhance doctoral students' academic and career performances. Some of the professors at the case school of education have created relevant internship positions in the process of advising their doctoral students, and they work with their advisees as colleagues to complete research projects and co-author publications.

Third, universities need to pay attention to doctoral students' sensitive knowledge of emerging employment opportunities. Sometimes, people who need to find a job know more about the job market than those who are happily employed. From this perspective, doctoral students' advisors might not be the best candidates for mentoring doctoral students in career development. Our study confirms the notion that some advisors see their doctoral students as predominantly research partners. In some cases, doctoral students holding a graduate employment position need to invest time and effort into research unrelated to their doctoral dissertation project, which may delay graduation. Therefore, universities should update the evaluation criteria of doctoral advisors to deemphasize research and emphasize teaching and one-to-one advising, including employment counseling, with doctoral students. This way, students can receive more relevant employment channels and counseling from their advisors.

Finally, in the process of cultivating doctoral students, it is necessary to strengthen the training in research methods. High-quality academic production is inseparable from effective and rigorous research methods. For doctoral students, the importance of the research method courses is self-evident, but according to the interviews, participants still desired further attention to the theory and practice of methods. Therefore, high-quality and practical methods instruction need to be further strengthened and systematized in doctoral education. This final finding emphasizes the irreplaceable training doctoral study offers in preparing researchers for academia and industry, underscoring the importance of effective and sustainable graduate opportunities for students globally.

Works Cited

Allum, Jeffrey R., Julia D. Kent, and Maureen T. McCarthy. 2014. *Understanding Ph.D. Career Pathways for Program Improvement: A CGS Report.* Washington, DC: Council of Graduate Schools.

Benderly, Beryl L. 2018. "The Push for Graduate Student Unions Signals a Deep Structural Shift in Academia." ScienceMag.org, June 6, 2018. https://www.science.org/content/article/push-graduate-student-unions-signals-deep-structural-shift-academia.

Brennan, Jason, and Phillip Magness. 2018. "Are Adjunct Faculty Exploited: Some Grounds for Skepticism." *Journal of Business Ethics* 152 (1): 53–71.

Bui, Hong T. M., and Hoa T. M. Nguyen. 2019. "Higher Education, Innovation and Employability." In *Innovate Higher Education to Enhance Graduate Employability: Rethinking the Possibilities*, edited by Hong T. M. Bui, Hoa T. M. Nguyen, and Doug Cole, 1–8. Abingdon, UK: Routledge.

Campbell, Throy A. 2015. "A Phenomenological Study on International Doctoral Students' Acculturation Experience at a U.S. University." *Journal of International Students* 5 (3): 285–299.

Celik, Kazim. 2013. "The Contribution of Supervisor to Doctoral Students in Doctoral Education: A Qualitative Study." *Creative Education* 4, no. 1 (January): 9–17. https://file.scrip.org/pdf/c.e._201301117025747.pdf.

China's Ministry of Education, National Development and Reform Commission, and China's Ministry of Finance. 2015. *Guidelines for Transforming Some Higher Education Institutions to Offer Application-Oriented Undergraduate Programs.* Beijing: China's Ministry of Education, National Development and Reform Commission, and China's Ministry of Finance. http://www.moe.gov.cn/srcsite/A03/moe_1892/moe_630/201511/t20151113_218942.html.

Chinese Scholarship Council (CSC). 2018. *Agreement for State-Funded Studying Abroad Programs.* Beijing: CSC. https://www.iloveocean.top/usr/uploads/2019/01/4227711101.pdf.

———. 2020. *Selection Guidance for State-Funded Studying abroad Programs.* Beijing: CSC. https://www.csc.edu.cn/article/1710.

Cole, Doug, and Maureen Tibby. 2013. *Defining and Developing Your Approach to Employability: A Framework for Higher Education Institutions.* York, UK: Higher Education Academy.

Commission of the European Communities. 2003. *Researchers in the European Research Area: One Profession, Multiple Careers.* Brussels: Commission of the European Communities. https://cdn1.euraxess.org/sites/default/files/policy_library/careercommunication_en.pdf.

Cuthbert, Denise, and Tebeje Molla. 2015. "The Politicization of the Ph.D. and the Employability of Doctoral Graduates: An Australian Case Study in a Global Context." In *Technology and Workplace Skills for the Twenty-First Century*, edited by Deane E. Neubauer and Kamila Ghazali, 95–111. New York: Palgrave Macmillan.

Duke, Dawn C., and Pam M. Denicolo. 2017. "What Supervisors and Universities Can Do to Enhance Doctoral Student Experience (and How They Can Help Themselves)?" *FEMS Microbiology Letters* 364, no. 9 (May): 1–7.

European Commission. 2008. *Realising a Single Labour Market for Researchers.* Brussels: European Commission. https://op.europa.eu/en/publication-detail/-/publication/dea5f8e7-6048-4fda-8437-af480d2815fd/language-en.

———. 2011. *Towards a European Framework for Research Careers.* Brussels: European Commission. https://cdn5.euraxess.org/sites/default/files/policy_library/towards_a_european_framework_for_research_careers_final.pdf.

European Commission/EACE/Eurydice. 2014. *Modernisation of Higher Education in Europe: Access, Retention and Employability 2014.* Luxembourg: Publications Office of the European Union. https://eurydice.org.pl/wp-content/uploads/2015/01/165EN.pdf.

Fenge, Lee-Ann. 2012. "Enhancing the Doctoral Journey: The Role of Group Supervision in Supporting Collaborative Learning and Creativity." *Studies in Higher Education* 37 (4): 401–414.

Finn, Michael G., and Leigh A. Pennington. 2018. *Stay Rates of Foreign Doctorate Recipients from U.S. Universities, 2013.* Oak Ridge, TN: Oak Ridge Institute for Science and Education.

Gibbs, Kenneth D., Jr., John McGready, and Kimberly Griffin. 2015. "Career Development among American Biomedical Postdocs." *CBE Life Science Education* 14, no. 4 (December): 44.

Hancock, Sally, and Elaine Walsh. 2014. "Beyond Knowledge and Skills: Rethinking the Development of Professional Identity during the STEM Doctorate." *Studies of Higher Education* 41 (1): 1–14.

Hillage, Jim, and Emma Pollard. 1998. *Employability: Developing a Framework for Policy Analysis.* London: Department for Education and Employment.

Hoh, Jin-Young. 2015. "What Predicts Whether Foreign Doctorate Recipients from U.S. Institutions Stay in the United States: Foreign Doctorate Recipients in Science and Engineering Fields from 2000 to 2010." *Higher Education* 70, no. 1 (July): 105–126.

Institute of International Education (IIE). 2018. *2018 Fact Sheet: China.* Washington, DC: IIE.

———. 2019. "International Students by Academic Level, 2016/17–2018/19." *Open Doors Report on International Exchange.* Washington, DC: IIE.

Johnson, E. Marcia, and L. Lynne Parmenter. 2017. "Transferable Skills for Global Employability in Ph.D. Curriculum Transformation." Presented at the conference of the Curriculum Transformation HERDSA Higher Education Research and Development Society of Australasia, Sydney, Australia. https://researchcommons.waikato.ac.nz/handle/10289/11745.

Kim, Dongbin, Jin-young Roh, and Erinn Taylor de Barroso. 2018. "To Stay or Not to Stay: A Decision to Make upon Completion of Doctoral Degrees among Asian International Doctorates in U.S. Higher Education Institutions." In *Understanding International Students from Asia in American Universities: Learning and Living Globalization,* edited by Yingyi Ma and Martha A. Garcia-Murillo, 215–239. Cham, Switzerland: Springer.

Knight, Peter, and Mantz Yorke. 2004. *Learning, Curriculum and Employability in Higher Education.* London: RoutledgeFalmer.

Le, Tam, and Susan K. Gardner. 2010. "Understanding the Doctoral Experience

of Asian International Students in STEM Fields: An Exploration of One Institutional Context." *Journal of College Student Development* 51, no. 3 (May–June): 252–264.
Lees, Dawn. 2002. *Graduate Employability – Literature Review*. York, UK: Learning and Teaching Support Network (LTSN) Generic Centre. http://qualityresearchinternational.com/esecttools/esectpubs/leeslitreview.pdf.
Li, Wendan, and Christopher S. Collins. 2014. "Chinese Doctoral Student Socialization in the United States: A Qualitative Study." *FIRE: Forum for International Research in Education* 1 (2): 32–57.
Li, Xiaowen, and Jianguo Xia. 2018. "Reflections on Curriculum Reform of Application-Oriented Undergraduate Universities." *Research in Higher Education of Engineering* 1:107–110.
Mok, Ka Ho, ed. 2017. *Managing International Connectivity, Diversity of Learning and Changing Labour Markets: East Asian Perspectives*. Singapore: Springer.
Molla, Tebeje, and Denise Cuthbert. 2015. "The Issue of Research Graduate Employability in Australia: An Analysis of the Policy Framing (1999–2013)." *Australian Educational Researcher* 42, no. 2 (April): 237–256.
Organization for Economic Co-operation and Development (OECD). 2019. *OECD Employment Outlook 2019: The Future of Work*. Paris: OECD.
Porter, Susan D., and Jennifer M. Phelps. 2014. "Beyond Skills: An Integrative Approach to Doctoral Student Preparation for Diverse Careers." *Canadian Journal of Higher Education* 44 (3): 54–67.
Qing, Shisong, and Yafang Liang. 2019. "An Analysis of Employment Diversity and Quality of Ph.D. Graduates." *Academic Degree and Graduate Education* 11:56–62.
Quality Assurance Agency for Higher Education. 2011. *The UK Doctorate: A Guide for Current and Prospective Doctoral Candidates*. Gloucester, UK: Quality Assurance Agency for Higher Education. http://www.qaa.ac.uk/en/Publications/Documents/Doctorate-guide.pdf.
Rogers, Sean E., Adrienne E. Eaton, and Paula B. Voos. 2014. "Effects of Unionization on Graduate Student Employees: Faculty-Student Relations, Academic Freedom, and Pay." *ILR Review* 66, no. 2 (April): 487–510.
Ugwu, Dorothy N., and Maria Adamuti-Trache. 2017. "Post-Graduation Plans of International Science and Engineering Doctoral Students Attending U.S. Universities." *Journal of International Student* 7 (1): 1–21.
US Department of Homeland Security. 2019. *SEVIS by the Number Data*. Washington, DC: US Department of Homeland Security. https://studyinthestates.dhs.gov/sevis-by-the-numbers/sevis-by-the-numbers-data.
Utley, A. 2003. "Industry Hits Out at Diluted Degree Trend." *Times Higher Education Supplement*, April 4, 2003.
Wu, Shiyou, Qi Wu, Xiaoijang Wei, Sarah E. Bledsoe, and David Ansong. 2020. "Exploring Factors for Achieving Successful Educational Attainment among Chinese Doctoral Students in the United States." *Journal of International Students* 10 (2): 244–264.
Yorke, Mantz. 2006. *Employability in Higher Education: What It Is–What It Is Not?* York, UK: Higher Education Academy. https://www.heacademy.ac.uk/knowledge-hub/employability-higher-education-what-it-what-it-not.

Zhang, Yi. 2016. "International Students in Transition: Voices of Chinese Doctoral Students in a U.S. Research University." *Journal of International Students* 6 (1): 175–194.

Zhao, Liying. 2013. *Demand for Effectiveness: Evolution of American Doctoral Education Assessment.* Beijing: China Science Publishing and Media.

Zhou, Ji. 2014. "Persistence Motivations of Chinese Doctoral Students in Science, Technology, Engineering, and Math." *Journal of Diversity of Higher Education* 7 (3): 177–193.

———. 2016. "International Students' Motivation to Pursue and Complete a Ph.D. in the U.S. Higher Education." *Higher Education* 69: 719–733.

PART IV

ORGANIZING LABOR

Interlude 10

Paying to Teach
A Profile of California State University System English Department Graduate Teaching Associate Programs

Martha Althea Webber

I worked as an assistant professor in the Department of English, Comparative Literature, and Linguistics at California State University at Fullerton (CSUF) for six years, from 2013 to 2019. My own educational pathway after high school, which included time at an occupational center and two community colleges before transferring to a university, connected me to the California State University (CSU) mission of educating first generation, nontraditional, and transfer students. Teaching master's-level classes and eventually mentoring graduate students as the CSUF Writing Center director meant that I was guiding many students who desired to become community college educators, much like the ones who inspired me over a decade before. To these students, being accepted into our department's teaching associate (TA) program was the clearest pathway for achieving their goals, even though many recognized their postgraduate reality would likely involve teaching as a part-time adjunct at multiple community colleges in the area. Eventually, I would be troubled to see the path forward was even more exploitative than that.

The one-year TA program had master's students teach one first-year composition class each semester as well as enroll in a three-unit pedagogy seminar in the fall and then a one-unit follow-up seminar in the spring. After being involved in my graduate employee labor union at the University of Illinois, Urbana-Champaign, including a successful 2009 labor strike over protecting existing tuition waivers for graduate employees (see Isaac, this volume, for a fuller discussion), I was surprised to learn that our TAs did not receive tuition waivers. I assumed we would offer them: I naively thought this was a common practice across graduate teaching assistantships. I knew that institutions that offered tuition waivers already benefited from underpaid graduate teaching labor. What did it mean to me to belong to an institution that provided teaching employment without a concomitant tuition waiver? Especially when the institution is the CSU, which professes a systemwide commitment to diversity and where more than one third of the students (about 160,000) in 2018 were first-generation? Without a tuition waiver, these teaching associates were paying the school for their job training: they paid more per semester in tuition than the TA stipend amount and their tuition went toward the pedagogy seminars required for the position.

In 2016 the CSU system was the largest producer of bachelor's degrees of any four-year public university system in the United States. The system prides itself on both its institutional origins as teachers colleges and its current practice of not only credentialing a near-majority of K-12 teachers in the state of California but also providing scholarship and funding programs to ensure the state attracts a diverse and dynamic workforce of teachers. However, a statistic it is likely far less proud of is its recent achievement of employing 51.2% of its teaching faculty on a part-time basis system-wide (CFA 2018). Among those part-time faculty are current master's students working as instructors-of-record for introductory courses, such as the first-year college composition course, a required course taught through departments of English in the CSU system.

Out of twenty-four CSU campuses total, twenty-one offer master of arts degrees in English and at least nineteen of these have a teaching associate program. In their online program descriptions, few of these programs refer to partial or full tuition waivers, with Humboldt State's Department of English highlighting in 2019 that these are only available to "select" TAs during "some" semesters, but that this funding is "contingent on the availability of funds and student eligibility (as determined by financial aid awards)." Now, the language on the website has shifted; as of this writing it vaguely tells applicants they "may receive a waiver" (Department of English 2022). In addition to the lack of tuition waivers, nearly all of these MA English programs require TAs to complete a graduate-level pedagogy course either prior to or concurrent to their appointment as a TA. In other words, the phenomenon I observed at my own campus seems to be true almost across the system: not only do TAs *not* receive a tuition waiver while they are teaching a stand-alone undergraduate course at the university, but part of the tuition they do pay goes towards their training and supervision as educators of undergraduates. In the fall 2018 semester at Cal State Fullerton, an MA English graduate student enrolled in seven or more units of coursework would owe $4,180.36 in tuition for the semester while earning roughly $3,000 after taxes teaching one stand-alone section of first-year college writing with an enrollment of twenty-five students.

In the fall of 2018, the graduate teaching assistants' union, the United Auto Workers (UAW) Local 4123, reached a tentative agreement with the CSU system administration that included new rights for student academic employees in terms of compensation for training. While they have yet to make inroads in bargaining for tuition waivers, the union secured new language in article 22 of the agreement that now stipulates "all required training and orientation undertaken during the term of the appointment shall be considered part of the workload for the term" except for "courses required of all students in a particular program, which does not include elective courses" (UAW/CSU 2018–2020). Moreover, the union bargained to protect its members from having to "pay additional tuition or fees as a result of enrolling in or repeating courses (including pedagogy courses) specifically related to training for their position" (UAW/CSU 2018–2021).

While this provision represents only a modest victory and establishes quite reasonable working conditions—that workers should not have to pay for their own training—the response on my campus at CSUF was for Human Resources and my department to suspend our TA program at the start of the spring 2019 semester. The TAs received less than two weeks' notice before the semester of this decision—well after they had submitted book orders, prepared their syllabi, and updated assignments and lesson plans for the spring. Already enrolled with students, the seven classes were reassigned by the department to its existing adjunct faculty, who number more than forty and are the primary teaching faculty for the university's first-year writing requirement (CSUF had 5,894 first year students in fall 2018).

When I learned about this during the first week of the semester, I also learned that I couldn't offer employment to the impacted TAs even if they had been previously employed by the writing center because of the timing of the cancellations. By the end of the term, my department readvertised the TA program for the next year, with their new plan redesigned to be technically in compliance with the TA's new contract while resulting in greater financial hardship on program participants. The department would now offer the pedagogy course in the fall as a seminar open to all graduate students; however, now it would serve as a prerequisite and "preferred qualification" for TA applicants, who would only teach (and earn money for) one first-year composition course in the spring semester instead of two as they had previously. Rather than finding (or at least advocating for) a solution that waived the pedagogy course tuition cost, their decision ultimately took critical opportunities for teaching experience and earnings away from graduate student workers.

Works Cited

California Faculty Association (CFA). 2019. Our Work. January. https://www.calfac.org/our-work/.

California State University Fullerton (CSUF). 2018. "Fall 2018 Fact Sheet." December. http://www.fullerton.edu/data/_resources/pdfs/ir/CSUF_Facts_Fall2018.pdf.

Department of English at Cal Poly Humboldt. 2019 and 2022. "Internships and Student Employment." January. https://english.humboldt.edu/graduate-program/student-employment.

United Auto Workers and California State University (UAW/CSU). 2018–2020. Unit 11 Collective Bargaining Agreement. https://www.calstate.edu/csu-system/faculty-staff/labor-and-employee-relations/Pages/unit11-uaw.aspx.

8 | "Fees Are Wage Theft"
Graduate Labor Unions Confronting the Neoliberal University

Jonathan Isaac

In 2000 administrators at some of the most elite universities in the United States were called to testify before the National Labor Relations Board (NLRB). At stake was an impending decision that, if upheld, would certify the first successful unionization campaign of graduate student workers at a private university, New York University.[1] Graduate workers, NYU's administrators argued, may indeed work for the university, but they are "predominately students" whose work is in service of their education (Truesdale 2000). Concealed by the administrators' claim was the reality that recognizing graduate student workers *as* workers (who are thus allowed to unionize) would have afforded them access to workplace protections, increased leverage in decision making, and collective bargaining at the expense of their employing university.

The NLRB ultimately determined graduate assistants were employees as defined in the National Labor Relations Act, though university administrators today continue to insist that graduate work falls outside of the employer-employee relationship in an attempt to obfuscate and undermine the cause of graduate labor organizing efforts. For example, in response to graduate workers voting to unionize at Columbia University in 2018, Provost John Coatsworth—who organized as a graduate worker in the late 1960s and early 1970s with the nascent teaching assistants' union at the University of Wisconsin–Madison—declared that "the relationship of graduate students to the faculty that instruct them must not be reduced to ordinary terms of employment" (qtd. in Kamath 2018). This "rhetorical sleight-of-hand" and the logics undergirding it are ubiquitous in today's higher education landscape (Brown, this volume).

The solidarity of the administrative class against graduate worker organizing has arisen in response to the restructuring of higher education over the last four decades under neoliberal logics that now overdetermine institutional decision making (see Fabricant and Brier 2016). Administrators have adopted corporate management practices and cut labor costs through, among other things, an increased reliance on graduate workers and adjunct faculty as a cheap and, ultimately, disposable source of labor. As I demonstrate in this chapter, universities likewise lean on their graduate workers as potential revenue streams through the imposition of mandatory student fees, one of several responses to federal and state divestment from higher education (see also Webber, this volume). These trends have deep and troubling implications for access to and equity in higher education for current and future students, not to mention for the future of graduate studies. As we are seeing at universities across the country, administrative imperatives to cut the costs associated with critically educating students apply downward pressure on institutions' precarious and underpaid labor force, disproportionately impacting students and workers at the margins of university life (see Billingsley; Rahman; Hollinger; this volume). Coupled with sustained attacks on non-revenue-generating programs, particularly in the humanities, universities are sacrificing their ability to critically educate students. The neoliberalization of the university comes at the expense of instructional faculty, students, and communities; graduate worker organizing can show solidarity with these other groups and foster material and ideological resistance.

While challenging the university's anti-worker logic requires sustained long-term organizing and political education, graduate worker-organizers are well-positioned to engage in this work. Especially in light of the COVID-19 pandemic, which has laid bare the profoundly asymmetrical power relations at colleges and universities across the country, graduate workers have started to recognize the university's reliance on their labor, as well as their capacity as workers to collectively challenge the governance models in higher education that have chipped away at tangible improvements to workplace conditions (see Cox, this volume). Since 2016, graduate workers have struck at American public and private schools alike—University of California-Santa Cruz, UC-Santa Barbara, Harvard University, Columbia University, University of Michigan, University of Illinois–Chicago, University of Illinois at Urbana-Champaign, and University of Chicago—over issues ranging from union recognition to international student fees. Notably, graduate workers at the University of Michigan struck at the beginning of the 2020–2021 school year over COVID and police abolition-related demands. Likewise, there have been increased organizing efforts at the University of Colorado–Boulder, Indiana University, Northwestern University, New York University, and Yale University. And yet, despite the organizing among graduate workers amid the continued assault on their working conditions, they are still faced with arguments that they are merely "privileged, histrionic, and demanding" students, aimed at undermining the grievances that they have as workers in the university system (Newman 1997). As organizing workers, graduate students have to face not only the uphill battle of organizing but the rhetorical struggle of naming their working conditions as such and developing a collective identification as workers.

In this chapter, I analyze the rhetoric around mandatory student fees for graduate students and the ways that my own union at UW–Madison, the Teaching Assistants' Association (TAA), developed its two-year campaign around the issue of fees between 2017 and 2019. I identify the ways that neoliberal logics worked their way into the union's campaign, complicating its messaging around fees as both a student and a worker issue. While the union was initially successful in reversing a decision around the fee payment deadline, the campaign stalled one year later after the union exhausted its avenues for "civil" protest and was unable to mobilize graduate workers to withhold their labor. In particular, I argue that the union's messaging curbed its capacity to educate graduate workers on the political valences of student fees as emerging from the uninterrupted flow of neoliberal rationality in the university. I suggest that this strategy may have been counterproductive to mobilizing TAA members in the long term to consider more disruptive tactics like striking, as members' organizing energy was dampened by administrators' continued refusal to act on financial relief. Ultimately, I advocate for graduate student union campaigns that suture the personal injustices felt by graduate student workers to a collective identification as workers laboring within neoliberal institutions. Only by moving past individuality to collectivism can graduate worker movements disrupt academic norms of civility, a necessity for successful organizing.

To that end, I begin with a brief history of twentieth-century educational funding as context for the role that student fees play in the contemporary higher education landscape, including at the University of Wisconsin. Then, I detail the prevailing rhetorical constructions of graduate workers and academic life that hinder labor organizing among the graduate labor force, before turning to a fuller case study of the tactics used by the TAA and UW administrators during the union's campaign around fee relief for graduate workers.[2] These fees represent an important tactic utilized by administrations nationwide to recoup finances lost through continued state disinvestment in higher education, and a study of the TAA's successes and setbacks affords graduate labor unions possibilities for more generalizable insights.

Austerity Budgets, New Revenue Streams, and Graduate Workers

In the middle of the twentieth century, federal funding was rising for education at all levels, expanding during World War II to account for research spending in service of the war effort. This funding continued after the war through the G.I. Bill, though this bill overwhelmingly excluded African American veterans (Humes 2006). In today's dollars, federal funds for education jumped from $5.6 billion in 1959–1960 to $29.5 billion by 1979–1980, largely to increase STEM education as the United States competed with the Soviet Union in the Cold War space race (NCES 1996). But over the ensuing forty years, governments and financial institutions across the globe facilitated a transfer of wealth in all sectors of the economy through the privatization of social services and the deregulation of corporate activity in what Thomas Edsall refers to as "one of the most remarkable campaigns in the pursuit of power in recent history" (qtd. in Harvey 2005, 54). This trend of divestment from robust midcentury public services is what we know as neoliberalism. As this process continued, severe austerity measures passed by state and federal legislatures monetized public goods like education through a process that David Harvey calls "accumulation by dispossession": rather than generating new wealth, neoliberalism has dispossessed people of access to formerly public goods that were won largely through grassroots movements (2005, 159). In so doing, neoliberalism creates new markets to which students and campus workers are beholden, such as the systems of debts and technology services now commonplace in universities. University administrations and governing boards now routinely propose austerity measures for their labor forces and non-revenue-generating academic endeavors, all while the size and cost of higher education's administrative class increases exponentially.

The state's austerity measures have compromised the status of American higher education as a public good through the continued decline in funding, and universities have responded by passing the costs of university operations onto students and their families. Wendy Brown identifies this transformation plainly: "Rising tuition rates, declining state support, the rise of for-profit and online education, the remaking of universities through corporate 'best practices,' and a growing business culture of 'competences' in place of 'certificates' have cast the ivory tower of just thirty years ago as anachronistic, expensive, and indulgent" (2015, 22–23). These changes have only accelerated since they began, and they have entrenched public education as a site of increasing corporatization, what Gary Rhoades and Sheila Slaughter define as the enactment and expression of "capitalism and heightened managerial control grounded in a neoconservative discourse" (1997, 33). Faced with such pressures, university administrators frequently further squeeze their casualized and exploited labor pool through implementing online instruction, replacing retiring faculty with contingent instructors, disempowering shared governance processes, and pushing increased workloads, larger class sizes, work speed-ups, and increased staff turnover as workers seek stability elsewhere—deepening the disruption austerity has wrought.

Beyond cutting labor costs, universities have begun imposing mandatory fees on their students as another way to balance budgets. The opaque naming conventions of these fees—"segregated fees" in the University of Wisconsin System, "special institutional fees" in the University System of Georgia, and "academic excellence fees" at Baruch College in New York (Marcus 2019)—obscure their actual import to the university's funding model. Even as university policies frequently state that these fees can only be used for activities related to the mission of the institution, infrastructural construction projects like state-of-the-art recreation centers and debt services are often funded through these "backdoor tuition hikes" (State 2010). In Fiscal Year 2020 at the University of Wisconsin–Madison, for example, $18 million of student fees were spent operating the campus student centers and funding their past-due construction costs (Associated 2019). This spending reflects a growing pressure on universities to provide not just an "education" but an "experience" for their students. As universities embrace a marketized understanding of their own missions—part of neoliberalism's cultural work—extracurricular facilities have become crucial selling points in students' decisions regarding which school to attend, and universities are compelled by competition for the limited market-share of student tuition dollars to market themselves within the frame of a consumer experience. We see this rationalization in a letter penned by UW administrators describing the fees: "Services and programs supported by segregated fees help make a UW–Madison education and experience highly attractive and enhance opportunities for success of all students" (Heller and Karpus 2019). This rhetorical posture illuminates the neoliberal economic paradigm, which justifies financial redistribution from state funding to individual payment for a public university even as it conflates necessary capital projects like building construction and maintenance with the consumer-oriented "attractive . . . opportunities for success of all students." Critical attention to administrative language foregrounds mandatory student fees, which can otherwise fade into the background of the student experience.

To some extent, it is unsurprising that graduate workers are rarely relieved of the financial burden of student fees. In the neoliberal milieu, the exhortation that everyone must pay their fair share is commonplace, and accepting austerity as a way of life has become more normalized (see Welch 2016). The decision to charge fees to graduate student employees is justified on the one hand by administrators' rhetorical insistence that graduate student workers are "predominately students" and is accepted as inevitable on the other hand by graduate workers, who recognize their precarity and relative powerlessness as individuals within the academic labor system. This produces a conflicting set of beliefs among graduate student workers about their role in the university system—are we students? workers? apprentices?—that makes labor solidarity and organizing particularly challenging. By insisting that graduate student workers are primarily students, universities can neglect their responsibility to provide certain workplace protections in order to protect their bottom line; as Marc Bousquet writes, "students are just one category of workers without rights—persons who work but who, in a growing web of law in service of exploitation, are construed as 'not workers' for purposes of the statutes that provide worker protections" (2008, 27). This rationalization only aids university administrators who are more and more on the hook for finding revenue sources for their operating costs in a neoliberal context that has mandated austerity measures for higher education institutions.

Beyond the pressures exerted by the university itself, depictions of graduate workers in the public sphere likewise sustain the university labor system by impeding graduate students' ability to see themselves, and thus organizing themselves, *as workers*. Kathy Newman, writing of the 1995 Yale grade strike, describes how the Yale union, GESO, was forced to counter the mainstream and interuniversity representations of graduate students as "privileged, histrionic, and demanding" (1997, 81). Newman identifies how depictions of graduate students in popular culture rarely depict them as part of a collectivity; more often than not, they are portrayed as lonely (*Marathon Man*), monstrous (*Candyman*), and oversexed (*Beverly Hills 90210*) (82). Though these depictions have matured over the last quarter century, internalized beliefs about the romantic nature of academic life persist. In his rhetorical analysis of the same Yale grade strike, Thomas Discenna argues that the premier obstacle to organizing graduate student workers was the inherited wisdom that unionization was incompatible with the nature of the academy and its supposed "life of the mind" (2010, 23). The pervasive figuring of academia as a life of the mind, adapted to by graduate students in order to survive graduate studies and perpetuated by university rhetorics, is exacerbated by the asymmetrical power wielded by universities to set the terms of the debate no matter the material reality (see Haley; Welsh; this volume). My case study on the TAA's campaign around mandatory fee relief for graduate student workers extends our ability to rhetorically reposition graduate student workers who are ideologically conditioned toward individualism in the neoliberal university.

Moreover, students themselves have largely internalized the false notion that student fees are controlled by students through student government structures, with one UW student writer characterizing the fees as "by students, for students" (Ben-Yitschak 2017). This language normalizes the unequal distribution of university decision-making controls; at UW and elsewhere, these fees can often be increased unilaterally by the governing boards of higher education institutions, shortcutting would-be shared governance systems. At Wisconsin, funds allocated by students represent just 3% of the collected fees, while the remaining 97% of the fees are spent at the discretion of the chancellor of the university, after mere "consultation with students" as mandated by UW Regent Policy (UW System 2017). The tiny fraction of expenditures over which UW students actually have meaningful control underscores that participation in decision making has been reduced largely to symbolic inclusion and has been divorced from actually having one's hands on the lever of institutional process and procedure (Brown 2015, 128). Students' invocations of fees as a vehicle for meaningful involvement in university decision making suggests a well-intentioned willingness to take shared financial responsibility in service of democratic ideals, as if to say that these fees are a way for students to be heard and involved in financial decision making. Yet, paradoxically, the rhetorical justification for segregated fees exposes the hollowing out of democratic processes consistent with the broader neoliberal paradigm's fear of democracy: the fees are themselves emblematic of the neoliberal restructuring of the university at the same time that they are rhetorically positioned as an egalitarian salve for the effects of such restructuring. Recognizing segregated fees as integral to neoliberal university governance practices allows us to recognize the complexity of these fees and their uses.

The normalization of fees as a necessary part of students' "college experience" masks the relentlessness with which universities like Wisconsin pursue this novel revenue stream and the fees' roots in logics of surveillance and value extraction. This is epitomized by the history of UW's International Student Fee, which as of this writing mandates payment of an additional $100 per semester for international students. This fee was first proposed by the university in 2003 to cover the costs of implementing the Student Exchange Visitors Information System (SEVIS), a program mandated by federal law following the September 11 attacks. The subsequent passage of the Patriot Act required universities to purchase and utilize this database to track the activity of international students (Woodworth 2003). Following intense pressure from the TAA and other campus organizations who claimed that this fee was discriminatory, then-chancellor John Wiley declared that the university would permanently absorb the administrative costs of SEVIS "as part of the necessary institutional costs of fulfilling [UW's] academic mission" (Dolbey 2003). However, in 2015, long after the 2003 decision, the university unilaterally announced it would be assessing international students $75 per semester "due to the cycle of repeated budget reductions to the Division of Student Life and the simultaneous increase in the number of international students" (International 2015). Currently, however, rather than funding the SEVIS program, the revenue from the fee fully funds the International Student Services (ISS) office—thus transferring the funding of this essential office from the university to international students themselves. When the TAA brought this history to light, the administration attempted to discredit the union by insinuating that the TAA's campaign would defund the ISS (Heller and Karpus 2019).

What is clear from the rhetoric surrounding student fees is that the balance of power in the modern American research university is sustained in part through regimes of language and norms that uphold neoliberal social relations and make meaningful change exceedingly difficult to enact. Yanira Rodríguez and Ben Kuebrich argue that the academy's "regime of civility," by which they mean an ambient presumption of reasoned and respectful dialogue, sustains its power relations and imposes constraints on those seeking deeper structural change (2018, 168). In their account of a successful eighteen-day sit-in at Syracuse University, Rodríguez and Kuebrich document how administrative rhetoric stressed civility via listening sessions in order to pressure students to "express themselves into passivity without any access to real decision-making power"; in opposition, organizers made visible the tactics of administrators in an effort to inoculate students against them (169). What Rodríguez and Kuebrich demonstrate is the necessity of acting strategically against institutional norms while simultaneously preparing participants to take actions one step further through education and critical awareness. Catherine Chaput similarly identifies how the academy's drive toward professionalization "locate[s], isolate[s], and neutralize[s]" potentially oppositional political possibilities in ways that "perpetually reconstitute" and sustain the university's functioning (2008, 10). Chaput places her hope in a theory of "working-class professionalism," which offers a vantage point from which academics can smuggle into the university a working-class politic. Together, these scholars point to the need to explicitly name the sorts of activities and knowledges that the rhetorical construction of the modern American research university makes possible, as well as what it attempts to hide or render illegible. The modern university is thus not a static entity or mere location but is rather constantly constructed and reconstructed through rhetorical processes through which it strives to sustain its truth regime. As I argue, the subject of the graduate worker is one subject among others that exposes these boundaries.

Refuting the regime of civility and circulating characterizations of the nature of academic life is an essential task for worker-organizers; even as graduate workers' actual working conditions reveal a different reality, there is an understandable seduction to these romantic ideals. But contesting these ideas allows worker-organizers to connect the affective dimensions of graduate worker life to the contemporary neoliberal conditions of graduate labor. Marc Bousquet insists we must disabuse ourselves of the idea that graduate student workers' instructional loads represent temporary subservience or the requisite apprenticeship for professors-in-training before landing tenure-track faculty jobs. Instead, Bousquet contends, we must identify graduate student workers as the "waste product" of a knowledge-producing system that relies on cheap labor to expand its productive capacity—"waste" because there is never capacity to eventually employ the volume of graduate degree holders produced (2008, 23). As Gordon Lafer puts it, "The real job market is for graduate student labor, not for Ph.D.s" (2003, 157). In the neoliberal university, the image of the graduate worker and the labor market into which they are entering are more and more divorced from a structural analysis of university operations, obscured behind administrative discourses of the value of an advanced degree and the assertion that graduate workers are "predominately students" or apprentices. To begin to accept one's position as the expendable "waste product" of higher education is to join the developing critical consciousness among graduate workers who recognize their working conditions as fundamentally political and who might be willing to disrupt the university's normalization and legitimization of its labor system.

Students, Workers, and Fees: The TAA's Campaign for Mandatory Fee Relief

In what follows, I analyze moments of the TAA's two-year campaign for mandatory fee relief that reflect how both the union and the university rhetorically constructed the relationship between graduate workers and the administration. I begin first with a rally held at the UW administrative building that was the culmination of nine months of organizing against a proposed payment deadline, identifying how the union relied on affective appeals to graduate students' sense of personal injury. Next, I analyze how the union followed up on its success with a pivot to an explicit recognition of student fees as a labor issue, employing the slogan "fees are wage theft" as its central message and hosting a "sit-in" at the administrative building to demand full financial relief from student fees for graduate workers. I also identify the ways that the UW administration sought to undermine or co-opt the union's messaging. I conclude by advocating for more direct tactics from the labor movement as the necessary addition to the deployment of rhetorical strategies in academic organizing.

TAA Campaign, Stage 1: A New Fee Payment Deadline and Students' Response

In the summer of 2017, without involving the TAA or other graduate student organizations, the UW–Madison administration announced that it would be moving the payment deadline of segregated fees for all graduate students from the third month of each semester to the week before the semester began. This meant that graduate student workers on a nine-month, academic year contract would be required to pay $641 each semester, on top of the $100 International Student Fee assessed to international graduate student workers, before receiving their first paycheck following winter and summer breaks. Following the announcement from UW administrators, TAA worker-organizers began a campaign that called for preserving the payment deadline to allow graduate students to save enough money to afford the fees. To initiate this campaign, TAA worker-organizers spent the first three months of the 2017–2018 school year soliciting testimonials from graduate students about the effect of mandatory student fees on their economic well-being; the union also circulated a petition demanding that the administration reverse its decision. The stories collected were made public at a March 2018 rally held in the UW administration building attended by around 150 TAA members, nonmember graduate workers, and allies. Attendees covered the central rotunda of the building in colored paper, on which were written the stories of graduate workers struggling to get by. From there, the demonstrators marched to the office of the vice chancellor for finance and administration, where lead organizers delivered the petition, signed by more than one thousand supporters. The group then marched across campus to the building

Figure 8.1, Posters attached to Bascom Hall, the UW–Madison administrative building, at the TAA's rally to protest the fee payment deadline change, spring 2018. Courtesy of the author.

that housed the Bursar's Office, where graduate student workers shared personal testimonies about the already-harmful impact of student fees and the added injustice of the new payment deadline. The day of action culminated in a closed-door meeting between selected graduate workers and upper-level administrators, where workers "share[d] their stories and call to action" (Wallner and Chechik 2018). Following these actions, and after nine months of organizing, administrators announced in a May 2018 email to all graduate students that they would honor the original fee payment deadline.

In their rhetoric, the TAA worker-organizers leading the campaign sought to emphasize personal testimony, implicitly relying on frames of individual economic hardship and the shameful behavior of administrators to elicit compassion and sympathy from university decision-makers. One testimony declared, "I am the lone provider of my younger sister after the passing of my father. I provide living, food, personal items and other things for her and myself. To pay such a large lump sum at once would make it nearly impossible to pay for rent and food for that month" (figure 8.1). Drawing upon personal financial circumstances, this testimony portrays segregated fees as a semiprivate injustice visited upon the individual and her family. Further, it implicitly seeks to shame its intended audience of university decision makers by demonstrating how their decision exacerbates her already challenging life circumstance. The framing of segregated fees as a moral injustice is likewise evident in the following testimony: "Rent rises every year! I pay $650/month for a 126 sq. ft. apartment *shared* with a roommate! SEG FEES ARE UNFAIR!" The speaker here expresses both indignation and an underlying sense of the administration's abdication of responsibility for the well-being of those it employs. By leaning on affective appeals, TAA worker-organizers correctly anticipated that administrators would listen empathetically to graduate workers' concerns.

Viewed cynically, the success of the campaign is owed in part to the union's recognition that its members' desired outcome—a delayed payment deadline—did not fundamentally threaten the main interests of the administrative class, that is, the fiscal health and funding model of the university. Reverting to the later payment deadline date would not jeopardize the money that the university would receive through student fees, but merely shift when the fees would be paid. Administrators may have determined that conceding on this small issue would quell a campaign that was appearing to gain traction. Further, the union's moderate demands can be better understood by considering local labor laws. Following conservative attacks to state labor law in 2011, the TAA had been operating for seven years without a legally enforceable contract, and it did not have avenues such as collective bargaining sessions through which to negotiate with administrators. As recollection of a legally binding contract receded further from public memory, the union found itself on uncertain footing with respect to its institutional legitimacy as a voice for graduate student workers. This reality necessitated that the union strike a balance between confrontation and collaboration. As such, I would argue that the campaign was a success in part because it did *not* require significant consciousness-raising or mobilization under the banner of graduate student workers *as workers*, which would have necessitated a much more extensive member education initiative. It did not require that the union question the imposition of the fees themselves as a politicized worker's rights issue; graduate assistants were not required to see themselves as part of the university workforce in order to recognize the effects of the student fee deadline on their lives. In this regard, the union demonstrated a kairotic awareness of the level of class consciousness of its membership and structured its members' participation through a framework of personal grievance that did not set up administrators as class antagonists, only personal foes.

At the same time, I would argue that this strategy came with downstream costs. The strategy of personal disclosure and injury risked divesting graduate workers of a sense of their own collective agency to change their working conditions by withholding their labor. Put another way, a strategy whose main aim is to invoke sympathy from administrative decision makers reinforces existing power dynamics rather than challenging them. While I am not saying that the campaign victory was immaterial to graduate student workers, this strategy did not ask them to take on what Thomas Discenna terms a "labor identity" that might have divested them of the constraints of civility and professionalism that frequently obstruct academic labor organizing efforts (2010, 25). Rather, the union's campaign actually reified graduate student workers' identities as aggrieved students, a decision that may have undermined the ensuing TAA actions, which were less successful. The TAA used the student fee deadline to rally graduate students around feelings of disrespect and injustice, a narrow tactic that successfully reverted the fee deadline while evading engagement with broader critiques of and resistance to the neoliberalization of the university and the administration's unilateral decision making. At the same time, this framing provided its administrative audience a way to demonstrate responsiveness to and compassion toward graduate student concerns without securing more meaningful concessions from them.

TAA Campaign, Stage 2: Exploited Graduate Workers Seek Full Fee Relief

One year later, in the 2018–2019 academic year, the TAA began demanding full fee relief from student fees for graduate workers. This time, a stronger demand needed revised tactics, which had perhaps been undermined by the previous campaign. The new campaign centered the language of employment in its public-facing materials, now refuting the notion that graduate student workers were "students first" or that their employment fell outside the typical employer-employee relationship. The union's campaign foregrounded the fact that graduate student workers at UW–Madison experience student fees in ways connected to their status as exploited laborers in the university system: as a form of wage theft. The campaign's official slogan was noted on one of the TAA's most popular buttons from the campaign: "Fees Are Wage Theft" (figure 8.2). By invoking the language of "wage theft," the union sought to position mandatory student fees within the employer-employee relationship, constitutive of the class dynamic between graduate workers and the university. The straightforward slogan made visceral the reality that after the university handed its workers their (meager) paychecks, these workers had to hand a portion of it right back. Moreover, union worker-organizers used this

Figure 8.2, The primary button used in the TAA's campaign for full fee relief, spring 2019. Courtesy of the author.

language to expose as hollow the frequent assertion that graduate student workers are students, not workers. By challenging this logic through the invocation of "wage theft," the TAA shifted to embrace the language of employment, exploitation, and labor concerning graduate student workers.

Even with their new recognition of fees as a workplace issue, the union's messaging at times reinforced neoliberal logics. In one of the more widely distributed posters during the campaign, the TAA compared Wisconsin's failure to cover student fees with peer institutions that covered between 70 and 100% for graduate students (figure 8.3). The poster is divided into two columns that display the logos of UW's peer institutions—the Universities of Illinois, California, North Carolina, and more—alongside the percentage of fee coverage the schools offered their graduate workers, in each case between 70 and 100% fee remission. Above these columns are the words "ALL THESE SCHOOLS PROVIDE FEE RELIEF FOR GRAD WORKERS." At the bottom of the poster sits the University of Wisconsin's logo, encircled by a red box next to the number "0%" and the question, "WHY NOT UW–MADISON?" As with the previous year's campaign, this poster implicitly relied on fostering a sense of injustice over the situation of graduate student workers at UW; unlike the previous year's campaign, however, it did so using the framework of market competition. As neoliberal austerity budgets necessitate that universities "compete" with peer

ALL THESE SCHOOLS PROVIDE FEE RELIEF FOR GRAD WORKERS:

I 71% — UNIVERSITY OF ILLINOIS URBANA-CHAMPAIGN

UCLA 72% — UNIVERSITY OF CALIFORNIA, LOS ANGELES

P 87% — PURDUE UNIVERSITY

IU 90% — INDIANA UNIVERSITY BLOOMINGTON

Cal 96% — UNIVERSITY OF CALIFORNIA, BERKELEY

MSU 100% — MICHIGAN STATE UNIVERSITY

PSU 100% — PENNSYLVANIA STATE UNIVERSITY

NC 100% — UNIV. OF NORTH CAROLINA AT CHAPEL HILL

WHY NOT UW–MADISON? **0%**

TAA — @TAA.MADISON / @TAA_MADISON / WWW.TAA-MADISON.ORG

% OF GRAD WORKERS' MANDATORY FEES REMITTED. DATA COMPILED 2018–2019 BY TAA MEMBERS.

Figure 8.3, A poster disseminated by the TAA during its fee relief campaign, spring 2019. Courtesy of Ethan Beihl.

institutions for graduate student labor, the TAA's strategy to evidence the ways that UW–Madison lagged behind poses a question to which there is a market-based solution: cover the fees in order to compete with other schools.

Here, the union doubled down on the neoliberal maxim of market competition and aligned itself with administrators' interest in remaining competitive in the market for top-tier graduate students. In so doing, however, the TAA's framing compromised its analysis of student fees in the landscape of the neoliberal university, choosing not to educate its members on the broader neoliberal logics that displace the costs of public education onto students through unilateral decision making by a managerial university administrator class. In my reading, this tactic undermines the ability of union members to fight for anti-neoliberal reforms in the university by allowing the logics of extraction that undergird student fees to remain concealed.

Further, the statistics from the poster were never addressed or referred to by UW administrators, perhaps because they were at odds with the university's national and international rankings. Despite the fact that University of Wisconsin–Madison does not provide fee relief for graduate workers, many of its graduate programs are ranked among the best in the world and it had been recently ranked the thirteenth-best public college or university by *U.S. News and World Report* (Meyerhofer 2019b). This analysis corroborates Phillip Goodwin, Katrina Miller, and Catherine Chaput's assertion that the statistical health of the neoliberal university outweighs personal or even collective grievance, and it calls into question the efficacy of appeals to employers and administrators in the idiom of the market (2017). Whereas Goodwin et al. contend that academic unions should strategically use the language of neoliberalism in their appeals to administrative audiences, the ultimate failure of the TAA's campaign to secure full fee relief suggests the need for broader and continuous political education for union members themselves.

Near the end of the school year, the TAA brought its demand for full fee relief to Bascom Hall, the home of the UW administration, with a multihour action of over four hundred participants. The action was called "Sit In at Bascom Hall," summoning images of the longstanding protest strategy of occupying a building until certain demands are met; in the labor tradition, "sit-in" or "sit-down" strikes were popularized by the successful Flint sit-down strike of 1936–1937, in which unionized workers at the General Motors plant in Flint, Michigan, physically occupied the plant and refused to leave, thus preventing automobile production from continuing uninterrupted (Paul 2020). The TAA's sit-in was not an indefinite strike at a centralized place of production like a factory or office; rather, it was a timebound action at a symbolic location that aimed to unify a public around their shared status as workers and put pressure on administrators to act. Even as it did not go as far as other labor sit-ins, the event sought to, in the idiom of labor organizers, "escalate" the confrontation with the administration, instilling the sense among graduate student workers that more adversarial action might soon be required.

Finally, this action invoked the language of confrontational labor organizing predicated on the identity of "worker." In one hallway there hung a large piece of blank paper where attendees could write notes of solidarity to graduate student workers at the University of Illinois–Chicago, who were at that moment on strike over the very same fee issue as the TAA. In another hallway, worker-organizers hung a banner where attendees could write their responses to the question, "If our admin do not listen, what do we do next? How do we win?" Many of the responses, as noted by a *Wisconsin State Journal* article covering the event, "represent clear escalations from the non-confrontational style on display" (Meyerhofer 2019a), reflecting an untapped radicalism among TAA members that the union failed to deploy. The sit-in also prominently featured the voices of international graduate student workers, who connected the International Student Fee's sanctioning of surveillance to the material constraints placed upon them by their F-1 visa status. The deployment of the rhetoric of labor and work in this action was meant to bind graduate workers together around shared grievances. Further, the TAA sought to situate graduate student workers within a national graduate labor movement and international politics. In doing so, it did not shy away from the depiction of graduate students as "demanding," though their appeals were limited.

Even with language that foregrounded the labor conditions of graduate student workers, the event was largely seen from the outside as "non-confrontational" (Meyerhofer 2019a), underscoring the uneven tactics behind the event. Chanting took place inside the halls and the four hundred attendees filled the space in a way that the previous rally did not, but workers did not interact with decision makers. Whereas the 2018 rally delivered a petition directly to upper-level administrators, this event was contained to the front half of the building, allowing administrative work to continue unimpeded in the back half. Indeed, the echoes of the chanting hardly made it to the offices near the back of the building. Thus, the potential unruliness of this action was still limited by an air of respect for the work being done in UW's administrative seat. The protestors pursued no face-to-face confrontation with the university decision makers and did not prepare for disrupting "business as usual," a requirement for more materially coercive coordinated labor action. Read in this way, the event suggests an uneven attempt to raise graduate workers' threshold for taking action—what labor organizers would call a "structure test." But this action was not followed up with more confrontational actions—it displayed trappings of radical action but did not follow through on them. The sit-in did not raise awareness about the administration's strategies in disempowering the union and its members—stalling, closed-door meetings, empty overtures to dialogue—to foster a consciously confrontational stance with administrators. Graduate student workers at this rally were not prepared to confront administrators' expected response to the union's demands nor their many efforts to undermine the legitimacy of the union and its members' grievances. Without these intentional and difficult efforts to prepare a greater number of graduate workers to take more disruptive action, the fee campaign stalled following the sit-in.

Despite the strong turnout at the event and its framing of fees as a workplace issue, the union's attempt to solidify the status of "workers" for its constituency was deflected by administrators, who took two weeks to respond to the union's demands. In their written response to TAA co-presidents, UW administrators wrote, "Philosophically, we believe all students—graduate and undergraduate alike—must pay segregated fees to support high-quality services . . . In our view, allowing certain populations exceptions or opt-outs could lead to others asking to be similarly exempted and ultimately undermine the funding model that provides valuable services to all students" (Heller and Karpus 2019). Here, administrators disregarded the union's claims on the grounds of their employment status, reasserting the logic that all *students* pay the fees. By framing the union's grievance as one being made by "certain populations," they ignored the specific class nature of the TAA's argument of fees as a workplace issue, misrepresenting the union's claims as an assertion of special privilege for graduate students rather than exploitation of graduate student *workers*. There is a knowing double-speak at play here—but administrators have broad latitude in setting the terms of debate, and in this case, they were able to naturalize the material hardship incurred by rising student fees and unilaterally define to whom those fees are assessed. This reality makes it harder, but arguably more necessary, for the campaigns of graduate labor unions to identify and expose administrative discursive tactics for what they are and win members to collective action as exploited workers, not unhappy students.

The following semester, in fall 2019, the TAA was confronted with the case of a high-profile abusive professor that stalled its organizing around student fees. And after that came the COVID-19 pandemic, which immediately reorganized the TAA's priorities. The union organized around the university's reopening plans and established a Mutual Aid Fund that distributed over $30,000 to graduate students facing financial uncertainty. The pandemic brought into even starker relief the labor conditions of graduate workers, as teaching assistants invested significant time to convert their courses to online instruction with no financial remuneration for their labor (see Shapiro, this volume). Further, it exemplified the consolidation of decision-making powers by the administrative class at the university, as neither the TAA nor the faculty union were consulted in the university's reopening plans. While this is not unique to the University of

Wisconsin, it suggests that academic labor unions are at a pivotal point in their ongoing struggle not just for material redress but for meaningful workplace decision-making controls.

As campus organizing moves forward to confront administrators' exploitation of their workers and disregard for all community members' safety on campus, the TAA will once again need to expand its analysis of the university to communicate feelings not just of personal injury associated with graduate workers' status as exploited workers but of their condition as workers in a neoliberal totality whose funding model spells the ruin of public higher education's mission and responsibility. The union will also need to contend with the reality that striking and otherwise withholding labor may be the one incontrovertible tactic that can challenge neoliberal funding models. Following growing examples of educators "bargaining for the common good" (Thomhave and Sehrsweeney, 2021), future campaigns might broaden their messaging, positioning graduate student workers as defenders of a university for which administrators are fundamentally unwilling to fight. This necessitates a pivot in the messaging, from "Fees Are Wage Theft" to something approaching "Fees Are Wage Theft That Undermine the Education of Wisconsin Students," or perhaps, taking inspiration from the Chicago Teachers Union's famous slogan, "The TAA is Fighting for the University that Wisconsin Deserves." By connecting the dots between the ongoing financialization of higher education, the material conditions of graduate workers, and the learning conditions of enrolled students, the TAA can cohere a collective identity centered on something that it is fighting for, rather than something it is fighting against. Making this connection will be one necessary part of a larger campaign strategy on the road to reforming university governance and policy.

Conclusion

Graduate labor organizing faces an uphill battle, especially as the landscape stabilizes following the COVID-19 pandemic, but it is apparent that labor organizing in other sectors is heating up. Graduate labor unions have the opportunity to tap into not just contemporary social movements, but also the growing support for public- and private-sector workers who have gone on strike during the pandemic. When graduate workers at the University of Michigan went on strike in September 2020 to protest the university's COVID reopening plans, they promoted anti-police demands that emerged from the Black Lives Matter uprising of that summer, in solidarity with Black members of the university community affected by overpolicing. They also coordinated with a strike of student dining services employees, an additional example of cross-movement solidarity in a single community (Thomhave and Sehrsweeney 2021). These movements reflect a growing recognition that collective workplace actions have the potential to transform institutions, much more so than purely rhetorical actions, such as letter-writing campaigns, which appeal to the moral decency of institutional actors. Graduate labor unions must do the hard work of organizing, showing solidarity with communities in and outside the university, and escalating their members' capacity to act disruptively when needed. And they must pair this work with a clear-eyed understanding of the material and discursive tactics that universities will use against them, tactics that emerge from the neoliberal assault on public education. Unions cannot rely solely on institutions like the National Labor Relations Board or the noblesse oblige of liberal-leaning college presidents; it is only by pairing argumentation with on-the-ground tactics that the neoliberalizing university's policies can be effectively challenged.

The rhetorics of neoliberalism are everywhere and nowhere. When administrators can plainly outline their justifications for saddling students with more and more of the costs of the university, we can safely conclude that neoliberal logics have been thoroughly absorbed in higher education. This isn't to say that countering arguments at the discursive level is ineffectual, but rather to say that it is insufficient on its own. My analysis of the TAA's campaign for full financial relief from mandatory student fees offers a starting point for mobilizing graduate student workers in opposition to the neoliberal funding model of the university, by weaving together the deeply-felt injury of graduate students at the mercy of their universities with a collective identity as exploited laborers. As scholars, but also as workers and organizers, we must supplement our rhetorical analyses with the attention to tactics that is second-nature to labor organizers: escalating campaigns, time frames, mobilization, and mapping power in workplaces. We need material and discursive strategies and tactics—using market and nonmarket framings—that expose the logics of the university and imagine alternative possibilities. As scholars committed to equity and dignity in our workplaces, we need to expand our notions of the tactics that work, recognizing and theorizing anew when challenges to the neoliberal university are confronted by the limits of the dominant discourse.

Here, we might look to the analyses of scholars working at the intersection of labor and rhetoric, like Dana Cloud, who demanded almost fifteen years ago that we "fight the temptation to make a virtue out of the meager symbolic substitutes for redress offered by employers. Nor should we assume that agency and change happen only in the discursive realm" (2005, 535). Indeed, one of the most famous and evocative demands for labor stoppage came from university organizer and Berkeley Free Speech Movement leader Mario Savio, who declared on the steps of Sproul Hall at the University of California–Berkeley in 1964, "You've got to put your bodies upon the gears and upon the wheels . . . upon the levers, upon all the apparatus, and you've got to make it stop! And you've got to indicate to the people who run it, to the people who own it, that unless you're free, the machine will be prevented from working at all!" (1964). Integrating our knowledges as scholars and organizing workers is the challenge in the semesters ahead for graduate worker-organizers.

Notes

1. In this chapter, I use "graduate assistants," "graduate student workers," "graduate student employees," and "graduate workers" interchangeably.
2. In full disclosure, I was the treasurer of the TAA and one of the lead organizers of this campaign during the 2018–2019 academic year.

Works Cited

Associated Students of Madison. 2019. "Segregated Fees: FY20 Breakdown." https://www.asm.wisc.edu/branches/ssfc/.
Ben-Yitschak, Yogev. 2017. "Students Must Maintain Involvement in Fight to Protect Segregated Fees." *Badger Herald*, September 13, 2017.
Bousquet, Marc. 2008. *How the University Works: Higher Education and the Low-Wage Nation*. New York: NYU Press.
Brown, Wendy. 2015. *Undoing the Demos: Neoliberalism's Stealth Revolution*. Cambridge, MA: Zone Books.
Chaput, Catherine. 2008. *Inside the Teaching Machine: Rhetoric and the Globalization of the U.S. Public Research University*. Tuscaloosa: University of Alabama Press.
Cloud, Dana. 2005. "Fighting Words: Labor and the Limits of Communication at Staley, 1993 to 1996." *Management Communication Quarterly* 18 (4): 509–542.
Discenna, Thomas. 2010. "The Rhetoric of Graduate Employee Unionization: Critical Rhetoric and the Yale Grade Strike." *Communication Quarterly* 58 (1): 19–35.
Dolbey, Matthew. 2003. "Chancellor Rules on SEVIS fee." *Badger Herald*, August 29.
Fabricant, Michael and Stephen Brier. 2016. *Austerity Blues: Fighting for the Soul of Public Higher Education*. Baltimore: Johns Hopkins University Press.
Goodwin, Phillip, Katrina Miller, and Catherine Chaput. 2017. "Accountable to Whom? The Rhetorical Circulation of Neoliberal Discourse and Its Ambient Effects on Higher Education." In *Rhetoric in Neoliberalism*, edited by Kim Hong Nguyen, 15–37. London: Palgrave Macmillan.

Harvey, David. 2005. *A Brief History of Neoliberalism*. Oxford: Oxford University Press.
Heller, Laurent, and William Karpus. 2019. Letter to TAA co-presidents. April 18. http://taa-madison.org/administration-response-to-graduate-workers-found-inadequate-and-misleading/.
Humes, Edward. 2006. "How the GI Bill Shunted Blacks into Vocational Training." *Journal of Blacks in Higher Education* 53 (August): 92–104.
International Student Services. 2015. "International Student Fees." November 20. https://web.archive.org/web/20151208095725/http://iss.wisc.edu/announcements/2015/international-student-fees.
Kamath, Rahil. 2018. "Columbia Refuses to Bargain with Graduate Student Union, Moves to Challenge Labor Board Decision in Federal Court." *Columbia Spectator*, January 30, 2018.
Lafer, Gordon. 2003. "Graduate Student Unions: Organizing in a Changed Academic Economy." *Works and Days* 21 (1–2): 153–168.
Marcus, Jon. 2019. "Graduate Students Are Mounting Degrees of Protest over 'Hidden Fees.'" *Washington Post*, August 2, 2019.
Meyerhofer, Kelly. 2019a. "UW-Madison Graduate Students Stage Sit-in Seeking Fee Waivers, Better Working Conditions." *Wisconsin State Journal*, April 6, 2019.
———. 2019b. "UW-Madison Rank Rises to 13th Best Public College in America, Report Says." *Wisconsin State Journal*, September 9, 2019.
NCES. 1996. "Estimated Total Expenditures of Educational Institutions, by Level, Control of Institution, and Source of Funds: 1979–80 to 1993–94." https://nces.ed.gov/programs/digest/d96/d96t032.asp.
Newman, Kathy. 1997. "Poor, Hungry, and Desperate? or, Privileged, Histrionic, and Demanding? In Search of the True Meaning of 'Ph.D.'" In *Will Teach for Food: Academic Labor in Crisis*, edited by Cary Nelson, 81–123. Minneapolis: University of Minnesota Press.
Paul, Catherine A. 2020. "Flint Sit-Down Strike (1936–1937)." Social Welfare History Project. May 12, 2020. https://socialwelfare.library.vcu.edu/eras/great-depression/flint-sit-strike-1936-1937/.
Rhoades, Gary, and Sheila Slaughter. 1997. "Academic Capitalism, Managed Professionals and Supply-Side Higher Education." *Social Text* 15, no. 2 (Summer): 9–38.
Rodríguez, Yanira, and Ben Kuebrich. 2018. "The Tone It Takes: An Eighteen-Day Sit-In at Syracuse University." In *Unruly Rhetorics: Protest, Persuasion, and Publics*, edited by Jonathan Alexander and Susan C. Jarratt, 162–182. University of Pittsburgh Press.
Savio, Mario. 1964. "Sit-in Address on the Steps of Sproul Hall." December 2. americanrhetoric.com/speeches/mariosaviosproulhallsitin.htm.
State Journal staff. 2010. "UW Students Vote Down Natatorium Renovation Funding." *Wisconsin State Journal*, April 15, 2010.
Thomhave, Kalena, and Matt Sehrsweeney. 2021. "University of Michigan Strike Showed the Power of Student Organizing." PopularResistance.org, January 7.
Truesdale, John. 2000. *New York University and International Union, United Automobile, Aerospace and Agricultural Implement Workers of America, AFL–CIO, Petitioner*. October 31. Washington, DC: National Labor Relations Board. https://www.managementmemo.com/files/2015/08/New-York-University.pdf.

UW System Administrative Policies. 2017. "Administrative Policy 820: Segregated University Fees." November 9. https://www.wisconsin.edu/uw-policies/uw-system-administrative-policies/segregated-university-fees/.

Wallner, Grace, and Sonya Chechik. 2018. "Graduate Students Fill Bascom Hall, Demand Flexible Seg-Fee Payment Plan." *Daily Cardinal*, March 22, 2018.

Welch, Nancy. 2016. "First-Year Writing and the Angels of Austerity: A Re-Domesticated Drama." In *Composition in the Age of Austerity*, edited by Nancy Welch and Tony Scott, 132–145. Louisville: University Press of Colorado for Utah State University Press.

Woodworth, Nikki. 2003. "Council Takes Stand against SEVIS." *Badger Herald*, May 7, 2003.

Interlude 11

A How-To Guide for Combating the Invisibility of Graduate Student Parents

Alex Hanson

1. Go from being a mother in academia to a single mother in academia. A semester into a doctoral program, navigate the academic world with a young daughter and without support from a partner.
2. Learn how to maximize fifteen-minute intervals to write seminar papers, compose emails to faculty and colleagues asking for extensions on assignments and incompletes, reschedule meetings, explain class absences due to a sick child, and maneuver on an uphill campus with a stroller and a toddler when daycare is closed.
3. Respond to social event invitations with "I can come if it's okay to bring my daughter."
4. Discover strategies for getting work done: screen time is sometimes a means of academic survival; heavy theory makes good bedtime stories for a child resisting sleep.
5. Discover that there is little support and fewer policies for graduate student parents at the private R1 university you attend. Explore how this situation can be changed.
6. Complete hours of research. Learn about what other colleges and universities offer. See how places like UC Berkeley and the University of Pennsylvania offer graduate student parents up to $10,000 worth of financial support for childcare, offer paid parental leave, allow students to remain enrolled full-time while on that leave, and provide emergency back-up child care ("Family Resource Center" 2018 and "Student Parent Center: Resources" 2021). Begin searching your own university website to see what policies and support are in place for graduate student parents. Learn that they offer a $1,000 childcare grant until your child turns six, that the parental leave policies

Guide for Combating the Invisibility of Graduate Student Parents | 265

operate on a case-by-case model where departments and graduate students determine what is best, that there is a childcare subcommittee through the Graduate Student Organization (GSO), and that there is childcare on campus, but it has at least a two-year wait list.

7. Use your frustration with the lack of support as a resource to resolve the lack of support for graduate student parents.
8. Meet with members of the GSO executive committee. Learn that none of the committee members have children and suddenly understand better why their meetings are at 5:30 on weekdays. Listen to one refer to lactation rooms as "milking stations," and another say that your concerns are valid, but they had "not considered them before" because they have no children. Feel hopeful when they say that you should contact someone in the graduate school but then feel frustrated when they fail to direct you toward a specific person, and then decide to approach a graduate admissions administrator.
9. Meet with the graduate admissions administrator, who eagerly nods her head when you express interest in creating a collection of resources for graduate student parents. Feel defeated when you ask her for support and she responds with, "I could connect you with a mother's group in a nearby area, but they're mostly affluent, married mothers, so I'm not sure how helpful that would be to you."
10. Connect with the chair of the GSO Childcare Subcommittee and feel hopeful about the possibility of change. Help organize a picnic for graduate families and learn at the picnic that childcare and housing are central challenges. Realize there are other graduate students like you. Feel less alone.
11. Reach out to your program chair and work on developing language for family-friendly syllabus policies; take small steps to combat the invisibility of students with children.
12. Discover there are no images or details about the lactation rooms on campus. Create a Google Map with pictures and videos you take of the spaces; include descriptions of your experiences accessing these spaces. Share the map with a neighboring SUNY Women's Caucus and post it to the Childcare Subcommittee website.
13. Email Human Resources because the lactation rooms don't have what they say they do on the university website. Try not to think about why someone else isn't monitoring the supplies.
14. Research where funding for graduate student parents comes from at other institutions. Learn that it can come from the student activities fee; think about how the $50 you pay a semester for the Oktoberfest you've never attended and the Trivia Night you can never

go to could instead help increase the childcare grant you receive or get more changing tables on campus.
15. Prepare arguments for how support for graduate student parents helps increase retention. Read about how graduate student mothers are at a high risk of attrition (Ellis and Graybill 2015, 153). Read about how the majority of student parents are students of color, and many are also single parents. Ignore the pit in your stomach when you realize that this is another instance where students who are the most marginalized are ignored by your institution.
16. Reflect on your own history and privilege as a cisgender, white, able-bodied woman and realize the experiences you have had, and the ones you did not have to have, because of your positionality.
17. Meet with an associate dean. Feel comforted that someone seems to understand. Feel hopeful as you sit in her office while she drafts emails to administrators in the Title IX Office and Disability Services Office because she knows what you mean when you say, "I have emailed people, but I have no power."
18. Steel yourself for all of this "maternal labor [to be] made invisible" (Villanueva, this volume). Keep in mind that it is this same labor that maintains the very institution you are trying to change (Hanson 2021, 85).
19. Send thank you emails and cards to the single mothers who offered you guidance throughout this process. Be grateful that you are not doing this work alone; collective action done with a network of people will change academic institutions to be more inclusive of single moms (Haley, this volume).
20. Remember:
    - "Graduate student mothers are at a higher risk of attrition than almost any other group in American Universities" (Ellis and Graybill 2015, 153).
    - "Students of color are especially likely to be parents" (Schumacher 2015, 1).
    - "Many student parents are single" (Mercado-López 2018, 1).

Works Cited

Ellis, Erin Graybill, and Jessica Smartt Gullion. 2015. "'You Must be Superwoman!' How Graduate Student Mothers Negotiate Conflicting Roles." In *Teacher, Scholar, Mother: Re-Envisioning Motherhood in the Academy*, edited by Anna M. Young, 151–165. Lanham, MD: Lexington Books.

"Family Resource Center." 2018. Family Resource Center, University of Pennsylvania, www.familycenter.upenn.edu/.
Hanson, Alexandria. 2021. "Maintaining the Institution: Understanding the Invisible Labor of Single Moms." *Journal of Multimodal Rhetorics* 4, 2 (Winter): 85–92.
Mercado-López, Marissa M. 2018. "How Faculty Can Help Student Parents Succeed." *Inside Higher Ed*, November 30, 2018. https://www.insidehighered.com/advice/2018/11/30/advice-supporting-student-parents-and-other-caregivers-opinion.
Schumacher, Rachel. 2015. "Prepping Colleges for Parents: Strategies for Supporting Student Parent Success in Postsecondary Education." https://iwpr.org/wp-content/uploads/2020/11/Support-for-Student-Parents-Paper_MAIN_6-17-15-clean.pdf.
"Student Parent Center: Resources." 2021. Student Parent Center, UC Berkeley. studentparents.berkeley.edu/new-and-expecting-parents.

9 | "We'll Be Taking This with Us"
Relationality and Idealism in Three Graduate Union Locals

Anicca Cox

Graduate student laborers occupy a unique and important place in higher education: while they produce significant amounts of research and conduct large portions of undergraduate teaching, their highly skilled, yet low wage and temporary work also protects the financial interests of institutions (Bousquet 2003). However, where once the promise of future gainful employment accompanied their endeavors, job prospects for graduate students are increasingly less certain (Jaschik 2018; National Science Foundation 2018). In the face of both such future precarity and their immediate working conditions, graduate students have sometimes turned to organizing their own labor (Isaacs 2018). In academic spaces more generally, a return to strike tactics (Mantler and Riedner 2018) and to more general principles of politically focused organized labor is emerging as a way of preserving the integrity of our higher education institutions (McIlvena 2019). As universities struggle under the exploitative systems of late-stage capitalism, graduate student unions can offer insights into necessary changes to be made in academe. In this study of three graduate student union presidents in one midwestern state, I argue that graduate student unions are reliant on cooperative, relational organizing models that are grounded in political idealism. Graduate unions' political orientations are aimed at preserving institutions' democratic visions, improving working conditions, and increasing social justice, thereby providing valuable models for change in the landscape of labor organizing in higher education and potentially across public spheres as well.

These approaches to organizing and leadership, which graduate labor unions (hereafter "grad locals") frequently take, are particularly valuable to labor organizing in the current landscape of higher education because they are socially inclusive and harken a return to a solidarity model, an approach based in mutual aid and inclusion across working units (Lynd and Konopacki 2015). Members of grad locals work together across disciplines and departments, tend to organize beyond just economic issues (known to organizers as "bread and butter"), and often aim their sights at workplace protections based on a broad set of social justice and political concerns—increasingly so under pandemic conditions. Grad locals do so with a measure of some audacity due to the very precarity or "nonpermanence" they face as workers employed by their graduate schools. In the interviews collected for this study, graduate students' temporary status as university workers emerged as both a source of strength—allowing these grad locals to take risks other campus unions wouldn't—and as motivation, to do work with and *for each other*, including for the future graduate student workers who would succeed them. The work they take up proceeds in collective configurations with shared and networked understandings of activity and success (Gilbert 2013; Isler 1999), and they are frequently political, activist, and oriented toward social as well as economic concerns (Rhoades and Rhoads 2005). Finally, in this study, research subjects reported that the work they do as graduate union members is valuable to them in the future in their careers. For example, one participant took work later as professional labor organizer while the others simply reported that a focus on labor and social justice and on the political nature of workplaces were tools they took forward into their academic and public-sector careers.

Scholarship on Graduate Labor: Historic and Contemporary Landscapes

The history of organized graduate labor is usually traced to two trends in American culture. The first is the political student movements of the 1960s and '70s, at institutions like UC Berkeley. Out of this activism, the first recognized graduate union was formed at the University of Wisconsin in 1970 (Gilbert 2013; Parbudyal Singh, Zinni, and MacLennan 2006). The second trend intertwines the rise of grad locals with other academic labor formations like faculty bargaining units (Bousquet 2003). However, in their case studies on graduate employee unions, Rhoades and Rhoads (2003) refute the claim that grad locals work in close relationship with other academic units, detailing the frequent separation, tension, and even occasional antagonism between the two (182). Regardless, both genesis stories happened during a time of general increases in unionization across college campuses, which led to a measure of union density in institutions nationwide. Estimates from the 2000s account for around forty universities with recognized graduate unions (Parbudyal Singh, Zinni, and MacLennan 2006). However, a more recent independently gathered listing from 2016 shows a drop to thirty-three recognized grad locals in the United States (Coalition 2016).[1] This decline is important to note as it coincides with widespread anti-union right-to-work legislation (RTW).[2]

Unlike their faculty union counterparts, graduate organizations continue to struggle both at the national and institutional level over their very right to form unions. As Jonathan Isaac notes in this volume, they also frequently struggle to maintain union status in the context of national policies. As Isaac discusses, antagonism toward grad locals can be seen as a direct result of the tension they face in terms of their perceived validity, which exists along a divide between them being viewed as either employees or student-apprentices (Anonymous 2004; Holden 1996; "Yes, We Are Students" 2006; Rogers, Eaton, and Voos 2013). Universities typically maintain that graduate students are first and foremost *students*, espousing an apprenticeship model that frames its resistance to unionization as an emotional concern for the negative impacts of such unionization on the faculty/student relationship. Bollinger (2001) offers a quote from a university administrator that well sums up this position: "What I would emphasize here is the lack of fit between what a union does and the character of an educational community we should aspire to achieve" (n.p.). Using the apprentice model, universities consistently express distrust of unionized graduate students attempting to work and negotiate *as workers* rather than merely as students. As Isaac also correctly notes, countering this paradigm is one of the most challenging obstacles graduate student workers face as they seek labor protections.

This attempt at restricting unionization is mirrored at the national level, especially in those cases involving private institutions where the National Labor Relations Board (NLRB) has supported a divide between work and education by using a "'primary purpose'" test that decides the validity of a bargaining unit. If the primary purpose of a requesting unit is deemed economic, only then can it acquire collective bargaining rights (Gartland 2002; Rohrbacher 2000). Using this test, the NLRB has repeatedly ruled that the work graduate students perform in their "apprenticeship" as TAs and researchers at private colleges and universities is primarily for the purposes of their own training and education, rather than essentially salaried work. This restrictive view is disempowering even for grad locals who *have* successfully gained recognition at both private and public institutions because it allows a university to deem issues like harassment or academic freedom as "academic" issues, unrelated to employment, thereby limiting union capacity to advocate for protections on behalf of its membership. Such issues are further complicated by Title IX and FERPA guidelines (which govern gender-based discrimination and student privacy, respectively) and a rising spate of sexual abuse and harassment suits in large universities. The institutional impulse is often to take up "accountability" models, based in carceral logics of policing in order to comply with federal mandates, rather than relying on localized and contextualized models like survivor-centered, transformative, or restorative justice models. Examples include policies that make graduate teaching assistants (GTAs) "mandatory reporters" who are required to report instances of sexual misconduct or trauma of their undergraduate students to both police and institutional bodies with little training on how to do so effectively and without the consent of the student. These policies, which are set at the state or federal level but adopted by universities, frequently leave already precarious graduate workers and the unions they are a part of with little say in some of the concerns of their employment. As others in this collection note (Billingsley; Gacke-Reed; Hanson; Villanueva; Hollinger; Wang, Xiong, and Ye), graduate students who experience multiple marginalizations or histories of exclusion and oppression often are subject to increased layers of difficulty and complexity in the face of university policies that affect their employment.

Student vs. worker dynamics are promoted by what some of us in the academy see as the rise of neoliberalism and the corporatization of the academy, which rely on cheap, contract labor to maximize profit while also shifting the costs of this inequity onto the recipients of these very low wages themselves (Chomsky 1999; Kotz 2002; Scholte 2005). A typical response to this problem is to blame departments and programs for overproducing PhDs past what the market demands and to push for smaller enrollments as an ethical solution within a market logic paradigm of boom and bust. Bousquet's essay on academic labor and production (2003) rightly rejects this logic and argues instead that the phenomenon is not by accident and that in fact the neoliberal corporate university is built on this very type of unstable, shifting workforce. He explains that "the system will continue to require 'just enough' of these [other] term workers" (209), while pointing to the increasing casualization of labor in general and the positioning of graduate students (as well as others) as "flex labor" (210) as a fiscal strategy for the university. Within such a system, organized labor grows ever more important as a response. Indeed, the work of this collection denotes the value of collective organizing as well as the value of research, theorizing, and direct action for this class of worker.

However, with the expansion of RTW legislation and conservative representation on the NLRB, some grad locals have been decertified, including those at NYU, Yale, Brown, and other private universities (Rogers,

Eaton, and Voos 2013). RTW laws are aimed at a reduction of union density, thereby weakening bargaining power and leading to further exploitation of graduate student, and all, labor. Yet, as Rogers, Eaton, and Voos's (2013) empirical study of graduate students demonstrates, lack of union representation results in documented lower levels of job satisfaction, pay, and protection for workers. Taking a quantitative approach, the study effectively disproves anti-union arguments by showing that unionization has positive outcomes for pay and protection as well as academic freedom and the ability of graduate students to complete their degrees.

In the face of such resistance to their efforts, graduate locals assert that their members' labor is, in fact, that of employees *in addition to* that of students. In a brief interview titled "Yes, We Are Students, But We Are Also Workers" (2006), four NYU graduate students assert the need for union representation. Despite the "corporate-minded administrators [who] speak in exalted terms about the academic mission . . . activist and largely idealistic graduate students find ourselves talking about bread and butter issues" (n.p.). Abram (2000) further examines bargaining models in grad locals and similarly argues against the "student/teacher" distinction, arguing that graduate students are *both*—"just as faculty members are both teachers seeking to enlarge knowledge and wage earners seeking to put bread on the table" (1190). If this dual role is recognized, Abram argues, "the debate over the proper role of collective bargaining for graduate student assistants can be more productive" (1190). Thus, collective bargaining expands graduate student worker protections to more closely match those of unionized faculty who are able to address a wider range of concerns associated with their employment than simply pay and benefits.

As the literature demonstrates, graduate unions seek to create or maintain a union presence in those organizational models based in a broad range of concerns from economic to political. The results of the case study offered here confirm previous arguments and add to an understanding of the motivations and relational practices grad locals employ to achieve their goals. Specifically, the union leaders I interviewed have adopted organizational structures to match their ideological stances and institutional positionings, signaling an articulation of unionism that values democratic models over hierarchical, managerial ones. Particularly, they take up stances of intersectional solidarity and justice.

Benderly (2016) notes that grad locals have also shifted organizing models by moving away from other academic union models based on "craft" unionism, "like the historic craft guilds of Europe, [which] protect[ed] the interests and incomes of highly skilled workers by controlling access to occupations." Instead, grad locals have modeled themselves on industrial unions "which seek to unite the employees in a given workplace to use their collective leverage to bargain for improved wages and working conditions." Benderly argues that this is a natural response to graduate workers' conditions, having "gone from protégés slated to join their professors as colleagues in the ranks of the academic guild to low-paid staffers carrying out tasks for their employers' benefit with little realistic chance of ever becoming professors" (n.p.). However, it is important to note that grad locals present an example of labor work at the *intersections* of worker and professional identities, where continued notions of professionalism-will-save-us-all sometimes persist (Tillet-Saks 2017) and threaten to reproduce existing power dynamics rather than to supplant them. When reliant only on their "future professional" identity, graduate locals run the risk of complicity in the very neoliberal practices from which they seek to protect their members.

Nonetheless, graduate union structures, while not entirely communal, have made moves towards dispersed models of power. For example, in the locals in this study, decisions are frequently made by council, members are active and in leadership, new members are organized and trained by other rank and file leaders, projects are worked on in collective groups who plan direct actions together and put pressure directly on the university power structure, and contract negotiations are designed and carried out by a large, shifting group of member-leaders. These organizational and structural models serve grad locals in ways that maintain continuity and engagement across an ever-shifting workforce.

In addition, at the time of writing, the country has been gripped by the COVID-19 pandemic for nearly two years. While this study was conducted before the pandemic, the unions studied here continued using their working practices to address the intersecting concerns of health, labor, and social justice that arose in the face of the pandemic and the racial uprisings of 2020. For example, the graduate union at my former institution took a series of regular, proactive, visible steps in the form of open meetings online and regular communiques to inform members on their rights and protections. They also offered political training, like a workshop on abolitionist unionism, in response to the growing national awareness of racial injustice. They used the university response to COVID to push for greater flexibility, transparency, and care-informed responses to labor demands, with intersecting concerns for worker safety and social justice at the forefront. This response on the part of union leadership illustrates well what the larger study demonstrates: the power of graduate student labor organizing around a set of ideological principles aimed at protecting one another and future generations of grad workers as well as building solidarity with all workers.

Inquiry, Methods, and Sampling

This study sought to understand how grad local organizational and leadership structures function and, further, what has motivated leadership to make what might be considered more radical, courageous, or innovative decisions in terms of those structures. In particular, I focused on contract negotiations and advocacy work. I wanted to know what about grad locals' work might stand out against more traditional trade or academic union models. For example, many unions have salaried "business agents" or "presidents" whose job it is to manage much of the organizing and day-to-day operations of the union, including recruiting new members. In comparison, graduate unions usually have smaller budgets, and much of the recruitment work, design, and planning falls to relatively inexperienced graduate student volunteers. What values then motivate individual participation in grad locals where work is part-time, volunteer, and autonomous? Most importantly, what do grad local members do, believe, and contend with as unionized academic workers that might come to bear on their positioning, tactics, and ideologies?

The research described herein comes from a small-sample case study of three grad locals (local chapters of a larger union) in one midwestern state. The case study relied on a convenience sample based on existing contacts in my professional network. The aim of this work was to take a preliminary step toward more fully understanding the landscape of graduate student organized labor, particularly their leadership and organizing strategies. I did so by broadly inquiring into the participants' understanding of their own leadership, success, and expertise in their organizing work.

To assemble the cases, I conducted interviews with three grad local union presidents from three large, midwestern universities in a single RTW state. These presidents were all women, under the age of thirty, and graduate students from fields within the humanities who had participated in their own grad locals for more than two years. The three participants all worked under the same liaison to a parent union via a state chapter of the American Federation of Teachers (AFT). In designing and conducting the interviews I used insights from my own two-year experience in leadership within one of the locals, which also helped me contextualize and make sense of the interview data, including in the discussion section. Beginning qualitatively and subjectively from a grounded theory approach (Saldaña 2009; Charmaz 2014), I used holistic coding methods in two open coding cycles to discover themes in the interview transcripts. A selection of themes and categories from both cycles can be seen in the results section in table 9.1.

Results

The coding process revealed the two central themes of this chapter: relationality and idealism/ideology.[3] The data was descriptive of the roles graduate unions play in institutional labor conversations and foregrounded how graduate labor union structures might in fact speak back more broadly to the academic and wider labor landscape. I discovered that the discursive and epistemological structures that support the work of grad locals both relationally and ideologically are intimately related to their positioning as worker-students and as a dynamic labor force.

Relational strategies from this study (theme 1) encompassed building relationships in three spaces: (1) intra-membership, (2) with a parent union, in this case a state-level chapter of the AFT, and (3) with the university. In the discussion of these themes, I consider whether these relational structures in grad locals mark a move away from service union models and into more democratic and cooperative structures.[4] This first theme of relationality is then interposed with the second which I refer to most frequently as "ideology." What I name as "ideology" covers an array of belief structures which surfaced in interview participants' comments around notions of activism, progressive political leanings and values around mutual aid and defense. While this ideology appeared as nonspecific, unlike, say, liberalism or conservatism, and while I do not tie it in this study to a specific theoretical framing in a disciplinary sense, I use it to speak to motives described by grad local leadership that went beyond "bread and butter" issues in labor work like pay and worker safety. In general, this ideology manifested in what we might call an intersectional solidarity, often specifically related to social justice. Because the participants all argued that their ethical locations guided their organizing work, I sought to discover how those less materially bound values supported work in grad locals as union members saw themselves in political terms and as they worked to foster continuity across a transient leadership and membership structure.

Table 9.1 below describes some of the initial codes and themes from the raw interview data and highlights some of how principles of leadership manifested in organizational relationships for specific purposes.

Table 9.1. Sample of Items from Coding

First Cycle	Second Cycle
"recruitment experience"	"leadership models: team, collective, democratic"
"reluctant leader"	"changing the university: helping"
"organizing stewards"	"political goals"
"institutional memory (lack of)"	"organizing goals"
"living up to goals of university"	"organizational structure: decision making/ distribution of work"
"direct engagement"	"connection to labor landscape"
"AFT"	"long-term benefits of membership"
"institutional character"	"nonstatic/nonpermanent"
"labor movement"	"history of: labor, grad locals, institutions"
"shared leadership"	"member relationships/member driven"
"staff models/member driven models"	"social justice"
"facilitation, pedagogy"	
"nonpermanent"	
"collaboration"	
"relationship to the university"	
"RTW"	
"shifting membership"	
"problem solving with university"	
"union bodies"	
"affinity"	
"misconceptions about unions"	
"gender discrimination"	
"solidarity"	

Discussion

Theme 1: Three Types of Relational Structures in Grad Local Organizing

My findings indicate that, as a result of members' nonpermanent status, graduate union leadership is typically enmeshed in a complex series of relationship stances and negotiations. These require an often-unavailable sense of continuity and institutional memory as well as the relational skills to mobilize groups of fellow graduate students who work on a volunteer basis. Interview participants identified this work, unpaid and often undirected, as arising out of a preliminary general interest in union work that was grounded in left-leaning political stances so far as they aligned with ideological values of mutual aid, improved working conditions, and worker protections. Each of the participants had other, initial roles in their school's graduate union, which they moved through over the course of several years before stepping into leadership. They worked variously on "stewards' councils,"[5] grievance committees,[6] or on contract negotiations.[7] Further, they all expressed what one called a "reluctant leader" identity. Rather than being guided by a desire to learn leadership skills, they were instead motivated by their willingness to work for others. One laughed and remarked, "He [fellow union member] was like, 'do you want a leadership position?' and I was like 'not really.'" Another explained, "I am very much a reluctant leader. I very much didn't want to be president." The third explained, "I think I just got in that role because I had the experience and I was willing to do it. That's often the reality of a grad local. It's that, somebody has to be willing to do the work."

Member Relationships

Three levels of relational activity appeared in interviews and observations. The first was intra-member relationships. Tied closely to ideology/political stance, discussed in the next section, each of the presidents worked in collaboration and cooperation with the member constituents they represented. Their shared stance on the importance of membership participation, and increasing democratization and shared labor over a single leader's authority, was unanimous. Their relational stances on this work differed somewhat, but consistent themes emerged in our discussions, primarily that of fraternity with other members as a model for organizational power. One noted, "Increasingly [for me] it's just a sense of duty to the other grad students and peers. Relational ties that you have in grad locals are one of the things that people don't always realize unless they're in it, like how much of what you do, you actually do for the people you're working with." Another, while expressing less of a sense of "duty" in this way, highlighted how relationship building was central to the skillset necessary for her work: "At my union you have to be able to remember people's names, their countries, their degrees, their children, you have to be able to know people." She continued, "unions are *only* the solution if people show up to *be* the solution. We try to do it together and do it perfectly and it's better than no movement at all." Another described the relational aspects of her work in the nature of democratic unity within her membership: "The long-term health of the organization should be everyone's priority and so that means that you don't step into leadership and sometimes it means that you do. It feels very much like a long relay race and you just sort of carry the baton."

For one union, this sense of democratization directly informed the new bargaining models being used, as negotiators moved away from the leadership of paid organizers and a discrete, dedicated "bargaining team" toward a model wherein existing parties (including multiple committees and stewards) and those with an affinity for particular bargaining "planks" would then take lead on the tactics employed for upcoming negotiations with the university. This same affinity-based engagement model was used by another union in the study where, while not in a contract year, the president of the grad union selected members with affinity toward a given issue to work on relevant projects like childcare, housing, and organization of international students. This approach facilitated broad, ongoing engagement from general membership, not just union leaders in elected positions.

Union Relationships

Interviews surfaced a second set of relational practices among grad local presidents' learning and leadership, encapsulated in their interactions with their parent union. The parent union provided support to these local presidents in a number of capacities including tangible, material support via paid staff to work with graduate students and in AFT consultants who advised staff and membership. In essence, AFT carried the role of "sponsor" rather than controlling body in the way it trained, discussed, and modeled educational/academic union work for novice organizers/graduate students. In turn, these grad locals paid annual membership dues to the larger federation. Additionally, this association provided leaders access to off-site training and offered connections with the larger state and national work of academic and educational labor organizing.

The presidents interviewed here had varying levels of proximity as well as varying responses to their associations with AFT. Their reluctance to wholeheartedly embrace their association with AFT primarily stemmed from a sense of AFT structures not being "made for us" based on the AFT's historical and present focus on K-12 teachers, which impacted dues structures and training models. This became further evident as the participants noted their nonpermanent status as graduate student workers. Whereas "being in a federation makes a lot of sense for people who are career employees" (especially since AFT protects and manages their pensions), one participant noted that for grad locals, members' concerns focused on effective contract bargaining for increased pay and protections. She explained that grad locals gain their sense of continuity in what they can secure for future generations of graduate students, rather than through members' individual gains.

However, participants unanimously acknowledged the real importance of their association with AFT: the support and expertise given by a dedicated consultant as well as a connection to larger political landscapes. Participants noted an appreciation of the power that comes with being part of a labor federation over "going it alone" as a local. One noted:

> We do get a lot of benefit from just being a part of this larger labor network in that we can talk to other locals that we know who are bargaining similar contracts to us and say, kind of look how are things going and what are they doing. And then the other bit of it is the political work. And that's the part of labor that I think people are more hesitant to talk about but considering all of the attacks [in the state] on education one of the only things that's held that back is labor lobbying.

This frank comment illustrates that graduate student organizing cannot be understood apart from the wider political context. In the RTW state where this study took place, this participant understood the AFT's political lobbying for labor unionism as an essential part of the value the association conveyed. Nevertheless, in terms of relational actions, it was clear to some that the AFT's direct involvement in membership relationships was not always useful and that much work was better left to the grad local members as they understood their membership more fully. These presidents were careful to maintain boundaries with the parent union, in order to maintain their own models of membership, organizing, and action.

University Relationships

Perhaps one of the most complex sites of relational structures for grad union presidents and grad locals was the nature of the relationships they entered into with the university. While many assume that union work by nature puts workers in tension with "bosses," this interview sample revealed that this tension was a dynamic one, at times adversarial and at others productive. Through collaborative work between union leadership and the university, grad locals were able to improve a number of structures for grad students from tuition and fees to TA training and initiatives for healthcare, childcare, and housing. This relationship was not an altogether easy one, as each president unequivocally noted that the university often enacted policies or maneuvers that harmed graduate students or failed to protect them. Nonetheless, they were all engaged in some form of cooperative project and issue-based negotiations with the university rather than solely positioned against it. Because these leaders were often working with their own advisors, deans, or department heads, the need for a level of cooperation and mutual problem-solving involved a nuanced set of relational practices from them that were tactical as well as personal.

Rather than viewing the institution as the "other," the grad local presidents in the study saw their work as offering effective "checks and balances" to the university. As one put it so succinctly, "Well, the university would be a disaster without us because their instinct is always to screw grad students . . . I went into universities only because I think they're so broken that people should do something to make them better." Accordingly, this participant saw one of the effective roles of unions as "sav[ing] the university from itself," noting, "that's an emotional process." Another said that her union's relationship with the university was very intentionally "not antagonistic" and further that "we really make things easier for the functioning of the entire university, occasionally we're annoying, but for the most part we're doing a lot of work for them." As examples, she cited instances when the union solved payroll problems the university hadn't caught. The third president referred to the grad local as acting in a human resources capacity: "The university needs unions because we are their HR, the university would be swimming in lawsuits if it wasn't for the union checking and saying, 'Are you sure you want to do it this way? You could just pay them the thousand dollars you owe them [a graduate student] and they won't have to take this to court.'" Examples of unions and universities partnering that emerged from this study included one union successfully negotiating for the removal of a costly fee charged to engineering graduate students every semester, and another negotiating on behalf of international students to protect them from unfair dismissals over absences related to issues with their visas and presence in the country. The third was working through their steward's council, and with the university, to redesign course loads for a required undergraduate course taught heavily by graduate TAs. Despite the need for grad locals to push back against regressive or exploitative university policies, much of that work happened through relationship building with departments, faculty, or administration via positive partnerships. Yet each of these positive partnerships emerged from a moment when grad locals had to push back against regressive or exploitative university policies.

However, much about these relationships with the university was characterized as tenuous. There were many instances the participants described when departments failed to support their graduate students or were outright harassing and harming graduate students in ways that the union was not able to intervene in. One president related:

> The biggest thing the union is dealing with right now is people who are experiencing discrimination and harassment and are teaching assistants but we have been told, when we go to talk about discrimination and harassment as representatives of them, as teaching assistants, is that their discrimination and harassment isn't about teaching, it's an academic issue and we don't have standing to talk about academic issues and so this is the university's way of basically saying that we are not allowed to protect people.

The university's strategic division between issues affecting graduate students as students—"academic" issues—and as workers—here, "teaching" issues—echoes much of the extant literature surrounding the struggles grad locals face in this country. As Jonathan Isaac also discusses in this volume, this tension is at the heart of what makes grad locals different from other academic bargaining units and presents a central challenge for successful organizing work on their part. For interview participants, the divide between graduate students being seen by their intuition as workers versus as students limited holistic responses to labor infringements for grad workers, preventing grad locals from intervening in serious matters when they were deemed "academic" by the university. Further, the distinction between TAs and RAs (teaching vs. research roles) or "teaching exempt" categories of graduate workers present in many state labor laws limits bargaining rights and inclusion for graduate student employees. Issues of childcare, anti-harassment and discrimination, fair housing, and other general protections are significant to grad locals, yet they are often limited by being able to only negotiate over economic issues or by not being able to represent all graduate workers on their campuses. Thus, graduate student organizers must remain on functional and even intimate relational terms with universities who strategically manage their identities to limit the protections available to them.

Theme 2: Ideology and Politics

While graduate unions are well concerned with "bread and butter" issues like pay and health benefits, the interview subjects for this project overwhelmingly saw their projects as more broadly political and ideological. Participants saw grad locals as uniquely important in larger conversations about labor and justice inside and outside of the academy. In fact, participants' political and radical stances were one of the things they cited as transferrable over time. Members are only temporarily in grad locals, but their evolved attitudes about fairness, working conditions, and justice move forward with members as they progress into other professional or academic spaces. Of special importance for this sample was the very nature of the intersection of these complex realities. The presidents in this study, as well as their general membership, represented a nonpermanent workforce that, rather than being guided solely by material gains, was guided by notions of fairness, protection, collectivism, activism, and idealism around the potential of institutions of higher learning to "make the world a better place."

Solidarity

One president saw the political ideology of her union at work in a solidarity/alliance capacity for other causes and groups. She explained, "We have a Stop Spencer organization, we've had some DACA related activism. We're supporting something called the inclusive teaching network right now which is an attempt to form long-term teaching support circles for people who are trying to make their classrooms more inclusive." She added that the grad local provided meeting spaces for other groups, printed fliers for events for them, and showed up in solidarity for events and actions. Later she reflected that, beyond the basic quality of living improvements a union can negotiate for, what lasts for her membership are the skills from and new orientations toward collaboration and consensus building: "That kind of radicalization process, combined with the genuine collaborative work of being in a union, that, I think, is the real benefit to the membership." She further noted that there is real value to a union experience, as members learn that "success comes from people lifting their heads up and working together . . . [It's] unlike any other experience I've had as a grad student and that is, I think, the real gift of the membership."

Power and Precarity

One president-participant explained in our interview together that "[grad] unions are very exciting and for me, as a person who firmly believes in the diffusion of power, is that grad locals actually live that. They're not just a bunch of people trying to kind of hold onto power because it doesn't make any sense, right? You know you're going to be gone." She continued, "that's the one upside of organizing a non-permanent working group. There's a lot of movement, that's exciting." She cited "good relationships" with one another as integral to the success and power of the bargaining unit and continued by describing some of what she feels the grad local model has to offer to labor movements:

> that move to have a more just world, I think actually *that* idealism is in grad locals. So many locals have just become cynical and I think that's the business unionism, it's a very cynical thing. The growth of the union movement is coming from young people . . . and they're doing stuff that grad locals have been doing. There's a lot that the larger labor movement can learn from grad locals.

Further, she explained that grad locals resemble nonpermanent working groups of hotel, healthcare, and fast-food workers, who have recently been unionizing:

> They're undervalued, they're underpaid and they're temporary. You know, I think that there's a social prestige that's different for grad students. [But] looking at what grad students to do successfully unionize and realizing that it's not about like long term economic stuff, it's about social justice and I think that really is the thing that people who are trying to organize workplaces, they need to look to more broadly.

In the contract negotiations I was a part of in one of the grad locals in this study, we did indeed lead with this political-ideological set of concerns, where much of our negotiating work directly centered concerns of social justice. Through those efforts, in fact, we were able to secure a place at the table in university-wide conversations about relationship violence and sexual misconduct as well as anti-harassment and anti-discrimination policies. We further bargained for equity in language assessment practices for international graduate TAs as well as protections for undocumented graduate students, and we secured financial support for additional training for TAs from marginalized identities. While much of this does not fall under typical union activity around wages, healthcare, and workplace protections, and while we were in many ways constrained by the permissive nature of our noneconomic concerns,[8] our union, and all those in this study espoused such concerns as central to their work. This approach speaks to a boldness in grad locals, who are willing to fight for the broadest possible range of concerns related to their work, moving beyond economic issues into holistic notions of the teacher-researcher-worker role that graduate students play.

Graduate locals, like other unions, do seek power. But it is important to examine the ways in which they do so and for what purposes. One interview participant acknowledged what she sees as an inherent courage and radicalism in grad locals: "You have a tendency to find the most radical portions in grad school, right? You have people who are the closest to some of those radical readings about capitalism and socialism and collective bargaining, to collectivism." Noting the unique character of grad locals, she parsed distinctions from other forms of unionism. In grad locals,

> there's no institutional memory to give membership folks a sense of identity the way that like steelworkers were union members all their lives. Grad locals aren't like that, to say your identity is with your union. Their identity is as graduates, as students and as teachers . . . and union teachers protect other teachers. We have the tendency to be more aggressive; we'll make demands that people are like, "You should not be making demands for that." And we're like, "Why not?"

Additionally, social justice consciousness was something this participant noted as being built into the organizational structure of her union, where international students and people of color have strong representation and leadership roles. Along with graduate unions' refusal to support police unions in response to police brutality and in solidarity with #BlackLivesMatter, she saw a social justice consciousness as being valuable to the larger labor landscape and directly to her state AFT chapter. Relating a meeting she had with AFT, when asked by them "how do you get people of color [to work with you]?" she responded, "Have any of you considered hiring a Black organizer and putting your money where your mouth is? Have you ever considered putting people of color in positions of leadership, not just giving them lip service?" Given what she acknowledged as trade unionism's long history of racism and exclusion, her story is a particularly salient one when considering the value of grad local models as ones of changed practices in organized labor.

Conclusion: Grad Locals as Models

Grad locals are arguably inherently political, in that they organize for improved working conditions for all, a political act. A strength of the grad locals in this study, in the context of their politics, was their awareness of the changing nature of the workforce broadly in the United States. They understood that addressing the concerns of their most marginalized members was imperative to their functioning. At one local, for example, international students comprised the majority of membership—so costly fees, housing protections, and language discrimination became central to their work. Another local sought protections for students with DACA status, victims of sexual assault, and healthcare for families as well as anti-oppression training for member leaders. The third pursued healthcare services for transgender students. These were all ways that grad locals in this study put their ideals of intersectional solidarity and social justice into practice.

In addition, participants' ideology was shaped by working within the particular constraints of the corporatizing university. Rhoads and Rhoades (2003) also noted this context in their study sample: "The majority of graduate union organizers disparaged the exploitation of the workforce and the use of part-time labor, relating these patterns to a devaluing of undergraduate education at research universities" (258). Rhoads and Rhoades cite an extended critique of corporatization in the academy in the way that it exploits labor for profit, and contend that in the context of graduate employee unions the "movement has a political quality to it—that is, the movement seeks to alter the distribution of power within the academy through collective bargaining" (243). Similarly, this study demonstrated that grad locals saw their work as improving the institutional structures they work inside of, which they viewed as inherently troubled.

Added to recent public writing on grad locals (Moattar 2018; Benderly 2018), my case study suggests that many of the central, critical issues raised around graduate labor are ongoing—the need for protections as workers *and* students, the positive impact unionized labor has on working conditions and pay as well as graduate students' sense of well-being. Given the historical precedents that graduate unions have faced as barriers to their successes and interests—conservative politics, anti-union sentiment, RTW legislation, university resistance, and corporatizing universities—this study suggests that graduate unions are nonetheless able to succeed because of their approaches to organization, leadership, and action. The work of grad locals is ever more important as we have seen the radical disintegration of our working lives under COVID-19 and the increasing grip that capitalism seeks to gain. The pandemic has, in fact, highlighted worker power in new ways. Grad unions are well-poised to contribute to that conversation in meaningful ways as well as to learn from our union siblings across sectors.

The grad locals in this study demonstrated how they ask for a lot in contract negotiations, and because they ask, organize, and push hard, they do, in fact, often get what they ask for. The protections and benefits they receive from this work position them as being able to protect their members, bring visibility to their labor and create intersectional, decentered, collectivist union models. We might argue that their successes come in through the way grad locals do not seek power in individual leadership, in permanency, or in making nice with the university over the long-term, *and* because they are both critical of and willing to cooperate to their advantage with the institution for better working conditions. In this way, grad locals and their approaches to gaining worker power can potentially make excellent models for other organized labor.

Their subject positions, often described as being those of *future* professionals rather than long-term workers (Isler 1999; Gilbert 2013), make them unique—whether that future work is inside or outside the academy, in teaching institutions or research ones, or whether they are working toward two-year master's degrees or lengthier doctoral degrees. This fact shapes their motivations, which emerged from this study as both material *and* ideological. In this context, Isler (1999) rightly argues for the value of grad locals as models for multiple work forces:

> The singular case of graduate student employees demonstrates that not only working organizations, but other social movements must develop strategies to deal with memberships that are in flux or transition. Any social movement that assumes its membership is in stasis when it is in fact an ever-changing body will learn quickly that strategies for organization must be adapted to better for the more dynamic setting" (n.p.).

Better workplace protections, wage equity, academic freedom, and the ability to address grievances are directly related to the living and working conditions of university employees even if they are employees who also act in student capacities. The rise of the neoliberal university, with its reliance on individualistic ideologies as well as a precarious, temporary, unorganized labor force that undermines its own democratic ideals, is a conflict that grad locals are on the front lines of, a conflict they are engaged in through attempts at collectivist, democratic, and intersectional-solidarity models of organization and action.

This study presents a view of grad local work that can operate in tandem with the university and in fact, hold it to a higher standard. As one participant noted, this kind of unionism "is very much in line with its [the university's] loftiest principles of teaching and research." These models of healthy relationality to a frequently deeply dysfunctional and harmful system are important ones and speak to the potential of faculty, administrators, and students working together to correct some of the most egregious infringements visited upon workers in academic spaces. The union leadership participants in this study suggest the reorientation of union models from service to democratic, in which participants group themselves based on affinity, interests, and skills in nonhierarchical structures to work collectively via direct action. In this way they are empowered to advocate for change based in shared values and political stances.

Though this sample only begins to examine the complexities of grad locals, I close by affirming the unique position they occupy as valuable sites for investigating resistance to ever-corporatizing universities that seek to employ teachers and researchers at the lowest possible cost. The participants in this study all acknowledged some version of the sentiment that what grad locals have dealt with resembles in many ways what one participant referred to as "what work looks like now." This is both concerning and important. As the rise of the contract worker and simultaneous loss of long-term industrial unionism continue, grad locals may very well exist in an interstitial space that is a useful model for all organized labor. We are workers, teachers, learners, nonpermanent and nonstatic and yet organized and collectivist—and have been for nearly fifty years. Beyond their organizing successes on campuses, participants in grad locals also take what they have learned and bring that labor consciousness to future endeavors, thereby potentially reshaping the academy and public sphere in their later careers. Perhaps their strategies could provide us with a way to consider more broadly, as other nonpermanent workforce coalitions do, a labor landscape that works beyond simply the closed circuit of employment issues, ultimately engaging political and social spaces where power can come from the grass roots upward.

Notes

1. Potential causes for this drop are the rise of right-to-work legislation as well as neoliberal, corporatizing institutional structures in the university.

2. Right-to-work legislation began with Truman's 1947 Taft-Hartley act, an amendment to the National Labor Relations Act. Taft-Hartley barred laws that supported compulsory union membership, restrictions on strikes, etc., in unionized workplaces. Currently approximately twenty-seven states have adopted RTW laws.

3. For interview questions, see appendix A.

4. Service model unions are typified by a paid leadership structure, where membership primarily pays dues and can be somewhat minimally involved in the day-to-day operations of the union. Paid leadership is tasked then with resolving grievances and contract issues as opposed to grass roots organizing by dues-paying members.

5. Groups of members working as individual representatives in departments and liaising with the union on a council.

6. Committees whose job it is to oversee complaints and filing of grievances on behalf of students with the university.

7. Refers to collective bargaining efforts whereby unions negotiate a contract with the university for pay, benefits, etc.

8. In contract negotiations, items are negotiated in two categories: permissible and mandatory. Permissible subjects are those that either party can deem not wor-

thy of negotiation and which can be dismissed without consequence. They include most social issues related to graduate labor. Mandatory subjects include pay and benefits, primarily.

Works Cited

Abram, Michael E. 2000. "Graduate Student Assistants and Collective Bargaining: What Model?" *PMLA* 115, no. 5 (October): 1188–1191.
Anonymous. 2004. "Academic Unions." *Radical Teacher* 71:40
Benderly, Beryl Lief. 2016. "The Implications of Graduate Student Unionization." *Science Magazine*, September 2, 2016.
———. 2018. "The Push for Graduate Student Unions Signals a Deep Structural Shift in Academia." *Science Magazine,* June 6, 2016.
Bollinger, Lee C. 2002. "Letter to the Columbia University Community." March 7, 2002.
Bousquet, Marc. (2003). "The Rhetoric of 'Job Market' and the Reality of the Academic Labor System." *College English* 66, no. 2 (November): 207–228.
Charmaz, Kathy. 2014. *Constructing Grounded Theory.* London: Sage.
Chomsky, Noam. 1999. *Profit over People.* New York: Seven Stories Press.
Coalition of Graduate Employee Unions. 2016. "List of Graduate Employee Unions, US." http://www.thecgeu.org/wiki/United_States.
Gartland, Gregory. 2002. "Of Ducks and Dissertations: A Call for a Return to the National Labor Relations Board's 'Primary Purpose Test' in Determining the Status of Graduate Assistants Under the National Labor Relations Act." *Journal of Labor and Employment Law* 4 (Spring): 624–640.
Gilbert, Daniel A. 2013. "The Generation of Public Intellectuals: Corporate Universities, Graduate Employees and the Academic Labor Movement." *Labor Studies Journal* 38, no. 1 (March): 32–45.
Holden, Constance. 1996. "Grad Students Press for Right to Strike." *Science* 274, 5292: 1461.
Isaacs, Deanna. 2018. "The University of Chicago Grad Student Union Demands Recognition, Even without Government Certification." The Chicago Reader, October 23, 2018. http://www.chicagoreader.com.
Isler, Jonathan. 1999. "Labor Organizing in a Nonstatic Workforce." *Nature, Society, and Thought* 12 (1): 71.
Jaschik, Scott. 2018. "The 2018 Surveys of Admissions Leaders: The Pressure Grows." *Inside Higher Ed*, September 24, 2018. https://www.insidehighered.com/news/survey/2018-surveys-admissions-leaders-pressure-grows.
Kotz, David M. 2002. "Globalization and Neoliberalism." *Rethinking Marxism* 12, no. 2 (Summer): 64–79.
Lynd, Stoughton, and Mike Konopacki. 2015. *Solidarity Unionism: Rebuilding the Labor Movement from Below.* 2nd edition. Chicago: Charles H. Kerr.
Mantler, Gordon, and Rachel Riedner. 2018. "Neoliberal Higher Education: Background of the Pennsylvania State College and University Faculty Strike of 2016." *Academic Labor: Research and Artistry* 2 (14): 147–163.

McIlvena, Noeleen. 2019. "There Has to Be a Place in Society Where It Doesn't Matter Who Your Daddy Is." *Jacobin Magazine*, February 18, 2019. https://www.jacobinmag.com/2019/02/wright-state-university-strike-noeleen-mcilvenna.

Moattar, Daniel. 2018. "How Graduate Unions Are Winning—and Scaring the Hell Out of Bosses—in the Trump era." *Salon*, December 2, 2002. https://www.salon.com/2018/12/02/how-graduate-unions-are-winning-and-scaring-the-hell-out-of-bosses-in-the-trump-era_partner/.

National Science Foundation, National Center for Science and Engineering Statistics (2018). *Doctorate Recipients from U.S. Universities: 2016*. Special Report NSF: 18–304. Alexandria, VA. https://www.nsf.gov/statistics/2018/nsf18304/.

Rhoades, Gary, and Robert A. Rhoads. 2003. "The Public Discourse of U.S. Graduate Employee Unions: Social Movement Identities, Ideologies and Strategies." *Review of Higher Education* 26, no. 3 (Winter): 163–185.

———. 2005. "Graduate Employee Unionization as Symbol of and Challenge to the Corporatization of U.S. Research Universities." *Journal of Higher Education* 76, no. 3 (May–June): 243–275.

Rogers, Sean E., Adrienne E. Eaton, and Paula B. Voos. 2013. "Effects of Unionization on Graduate Student Employees: Faculty-Student Relations, Academic Freedom and Pay." *ILR Review* 66, no. 2 (April): 487–510.

Rohrbacher, Bernhard Wolfgang. 2000. "After Boston Medical Center: Why Teaching Assistants Should Have the Right to Bargain Collectively." *Loyola Law Review* 33: 1850–1916.

Saldaña, Johnny. 2009. *The Coding Manual for Qualitative Researchers*. London: Sage.

Scholte, Jan Aart. 2005. "The Sources of Neoliberal Globalization." United Nations Research Institute for Social Development, Overarching Concerns Programme, paper no. 8.

Parbudyal Singh, Deborah M. Zinni, and Anne F. MacLennan. 2006. "Graduate Student Unions in the United States." *Journal of Labor Research* 27, no. 1 (March): 55–73.

Tillet-Saks, Andrew. 2017. "Labor's Last Chance for Solidarity." *Jacobin Magazine*, July 7, 2017. https://www.jacobinmag.com/2017/07/trump-unions-patco-right-to-work-labor.

"Yes, We Are Students, but We Are Also Workers." (2006). *Cinema Journal* 45, no. 4 (Summer): 85.

Appendix A

Interview Questions

1. Can you tell some of the story of how and why you entered your current position in the union? (What made you want to do the work, when and how did you get your start, how did you learn your job, etc.)?
2. What are the challenges you face in your intermediary and/or

leadership role between the university structure, union structure, and the AFT?
3. What skills are needed to do your work and how did you learn those skills?
4. How do you measure your successes in your current role?
5. How do you see the work of the union benefit its constituents, the larger union landscape, or the university?

Afterword
Striking for a Safer Campus Community
Kalena Thomhave and Matt Sehrsweeney

This volume describes the many forms of labor performed by graduate students. Throughout the summer of 2020, we in the graduate student union at the University of Michigan (UM) took up the labor of organizing for our community's safety, rejecting the university's plan to bring tens of thousands of students to campus in the midst of a global pandemic. As the Graduate Employees Organization (GEO), Local 3550 of the American Federation of Teachers, saw it, UM was making a shameless tuition grab that threatened lives across the region—as so many universities were.

Compounding the dangers of their plan—and coming immediately after the summer's calls for justice against police violence that erupted after the police murder of George Floyd—the university's COVID compliance plan involved using armed campus police to monitor student behavior. Our membership found the university's blueprints dangerous and unacceptable.

Instead, GEO called for a more robust testing program, an option for graduate students to work remotely, childcare subsidies for caregivers, and better resources for international students. In a further call for safety on campus, we also demanded radical changes to university policing, including demilitarizing and defunding campus police. The university, however, was intransigent and uncompromising.

As a result, in what was both a breach of our newly signed contract and a breach of state law, GEO members voted to strike. After a whirlwind nine-day campaign, with undergraduate resident advisors also walking off the job, dining hall workers instituting a work slowdown, and thousands supporting our effort both in the Ann Arbor region and across the country, our strike ended with little movement on our demands. However, the solidarity that we built during the strike laid the groundwork for future organizing and serves as a model for other campus organizers looking to win better conditions for students, workers, and community members.

The declining power of unions in the United States—from more than a third of private sector workers belonging to a union in the 1950s to a mere 6.2 percent today (Bureau of Labor Statistics 2022)—has meant that our generation has grown up without seeing what unions do for workers. As a result, we expended much of our organizing energy on communicating the importance of the very idea of a union. We had to initiate a fundamental shift in the way that many of our peers viewed themselves in relation to the university: they weren't just students but employees, and as workers they deserved a say in their working conditions. As GEO stewards ourselves, we served as the liaisons between GEO and the other graduate student workers in our departments. Stewards are the primary sources of knowledge and information for union members and thus are key to member mobilization. Michigan is a so-called "right-to-work" state, so graduate workers can still enjoy the benefits won by GEO without becoming members and paying dues. It's up to stewards to stress the importance of worker organizing.

But at an "elite" university like UM, the cult of meritocracy produces a competitive and atomizing atmosphere—one that is hostile to union organizing, and even to solidarity itself. Had all graduate students, GEO members and nonmembers alike, jointly refused to attend classes, university operations would have ground to a halt, providing GEO with crucial leverage. Unfortunately, students continued to attend classes, many failing to even consider that doing so crossed a picket line. And while some faculty were willing to articulate their support privately—and 712 faculty members signed an open letter to the university in support of the strike—few were willing to join our work stoppage by canceling classes.

Graduate students were on strike for demands that were intimately connected: a campus that was both safe from a deadly virus and from the danger—which disproportionately affects students of color—posed by the presence of militarized police. We worked from a different philosophy of union organizing: that of the union as a steward of the community. Our demands focused on the safety of those in Washtenaw County (where UM-Ann Arbor is located) as a whole. Not only does this approach build the power of the union by allying with other community members and organizations, it is also a model for winning *community* demands: the "bargaining for the common good" strategy. This was famously demonstrated by the Chicago Teachers Union in 2012, when twenty-six thousand teachers walked off the job—to considerable media backlash—to advocate for green spaces, more equitable class sizes, and coordinators for unhoused (Scott 2019). They went on strike *for their students*.

Unfortunately, as mentioned, the strike at UM ended with little movement on our specific demands. The university filed a court injunction against GEO, which, if granted, threatened to bankrupt the union, and so begrudgingly, we voted to accept a disappointing offer. But it would be a mistake to overlook the strike's very real, though less tangible, impacts. Most directly, we stood in solidarity with a separate organizing effort led by the Students of Color Liberation Front—an umbrella group representing several underrepresented minority student organizations—to fight the use of local police in the university's COVID response. As a result, the program was altered to reduce police presence and then canceled entirely. During the strike, GEO also saw a spike in membership, making up for the backslide brought about by remote teaching. Organizers began to identify political education as a critical precondition for activating peers and realized that effective political education requires a groundwork of strong personal relationships. By strike's end, nearly all departments' vacant steward positions were filled. This critical boost in organizing power was felt across the university, with increased labor organizing and activism on campus. A collective action of this scale has a unique power to motivate the unactivated to mobilize, and more fundamentally, can play a crucial role in undermining the deeply ingrained university culture of competitive individualism and self-reliance.

Finally, we disrupted business-as-usual: we activated more than one thousand members to walk off the job for a safer and more just campus. Dining workers, resident assistants, and construction workers stood in solidarity with us. We boosted our profile—citywide, statewide and even nationally—and in the months after the strike, campuses across the country reached out to GEO to seek guidance on their own campaigns.

We didn't win. But an abolitionist strike on a university campus may have rebuilt our union—and strengthened intersectional solidarity across campus and our region.

Note

A version of this piece was first published in *Waging Nonviolence*.

Works Cited

Bureau of Labor Statistics. 2022. Union Members Summary. Last updated January 20, 2022. https://www.bls.gov/news.release/union2.nr0.htm.

Scott, Dylan. 2019. "The Strike That Brought Teachers Unions Back from the Dead." *Vox*, last updated July 5, 2019. https://www.vox.com/the-highlight/2019/6/28/18662706/chicago-teachers-unions-strike-labor-movement.

About the Contributors

Sara Austin, PhD, (she/her/hers) is an assistant professor of English at AdventHealth University, where she teaches first-year writing and directs Writing across the Curriculum. She received her PhD in rhetoric and writing from Bowling Green State University and has a BA in Spanish for translation and an MA in English (both from Andrews University). Her research attends to writing transfer as feminist pedagogy, assessment, and first-year writing and has appeared in *College English Association Forum* and *Teaching Graphic Novels in the English Classroom*.

Khadeidra Billingsley, PhD, (she/her/hers) is an assistant professor of composition and rhetoric and writing center director at Jacksonville State University in Jacksonville, Alabama. At the time that she wrote this piece, she was a second-year PhD student at the University of Alabama, studying composition, rhetoric, and English studies. Her work has been published in *College English*, *Kairos*, and other book volumes.

Tessa Brown, PhD, (she/her/hers) is the CEO and cofounder of Germ Network, a social media platform. She was last a lecturer in the Program in Writing and Rhetoric at Stanford University. Her scholarship has appeared in *College Composition and Communication*, *Journal of Basic Writing*, *Community Literacy Journal*, and *Peitho*, and her fiction and essays have appeared in *Harper's*, the *Los Angeles Review of Books*, *Hyperallergic*, and elsewhere.

April Cobos, PhD, (she/her/hers) is a lecturer in the English Department at Christopher Newport University, where she teaches rhetoric, professional writing, and writing for civic engagement. She received her PhD from Old Dominion University in rhetoric, writing, and discourse. Her recent work includes a chapter on the benefits of two-way communication in online classroom environments in *Supporting the Military Affiliated Learner* and an article in the journal *Writing on the Edge* about her experiences living abroad and teaching international and multilingual learners.

Anicca Cox, PhD, (she/her/hers) is an assistant professor at Methodist University. Her areas of scholarship include labor, community-engaged practice related to food security and justice, and institutional ethnography. She has worked as a non-tenure-track WPA and more recently a coordinator of graduate writing in a writing center and a GTA. Her organizing work includes being a contract negotiator for her graduate union at Michigan State University.

Samah Elbelazi, PhD, (she/her/hers) is an assistant professor (lecturer) of writing and rhetoric at the University of Utah. Her research interests include arts-based research, poetic ethnography, Muslim rhetoric, and multilingual studies. Her recent coauthored article for *Qualitative Inquiry*, "The 'Exotic Other': A Poetic Autoethnography of Two Muslim Teachers in Higher Education," discussed the experience of two Muslim teachers at a predominantly white institution.

Jaclyn Fiscus-Cannaday, PhD, (she/her/hers) is an assistant professor at Florida State University, where she specializes in feminist and antiracist composition theory. Her work has been published in *Composition Studies*, *Composition Forum*, and *Peitho*.

Adam Haley, PhD, (he/him/his) is the senior graduate writing consultant at Oregon State University, a writing coach at the University of St. Augustine for health sciences, and a freelance editor and dissertation coach. He earned his PhD in English from Pennsylvania State University in 2012. His current research focuses on the social, psychological, rhetorical, and institutional contexts of graduate student life, labor, and writing, toward the broader goal of building more robust structures and practices of graduate student support.

Alex Hanson, PhD, (she/her/hers) is currently the multilingual student support coordinator at Hamilton College. Her work on the experiences of single moms in higher education has appeared in *Writers: Craft and Context*, *Composition Studies*, and the *Journal of Multimodal Rhetorics*. She received her PhD in composition and cultural rhetoric from Syracuse University.

Andrew Hollinger, PhD, (he/him/his) holds a doctorate in technical communication and rhetoric and is currently the coordinator of First Year Writing at the University of Texas Rio Grande Valley. His work focuses on materiality, "quantum" rhetoric, publics and circulation, and genre. In addition to his teaching, scholarship, and published work, he is interested in maker rhetorics and is a practicing bookbinder and linocut artist.

Allison Hutchison (she/her/hers) is a senior lecturer in the Engineering Communications Program at Cornell University. Her work appears in *Computers and Composition*, *WPA: Writing Program Administration*, and *Transformations: Change Work across Writing Programs, Pedagogies, and Practices*. Her current research project focuses on communication and collaboration qualifications in engineering job advertisements.

Jonathan Isaac (he/him/his) is a PhD candidate at the University of Wisconsin–Madison, where he studies the rhetoric of labor, higher education, and workplace decision making. He has been involved with his union, the Teaching Assistants' Association (AFT 3220), for five years, including serving as its English department's steward and treasurer.

Jacqueline Kory-Westlund, PhD, (she/her/hers) is an independent scholar with the Ronin Institute, as well as a writer and artist. She is the author of a forthcoming book from Columbia University Press on thriving in graduate school while keeping a healthy personal life. She holds a PhD from the MIT Media Lab and a BA from Vassar College.

Charlotte Kupsh (she/her/hers) is a PhD candidate in English composition and rhetoric at the University of Nebraska-Lincoln. Her research interests include ecocomposition, place studies, and writing transfer. She has published in *Writing on the Edge* and *Reflections*.

Zoe McDonald (she/her/hers) is a PhD candidate in English at the University of Nebraska-Lincoln with specializations in rhetoric and composition and women's, gender, and sexuality studies. Her research interests include ethics, democratic pedagogies, and writing instructor feedback practices.

Megan Mize, PhD, (she/her/hers) is the director for ePortfolios and digital initiatives in the Office of Academic Success Initiatives and Support (ASIS) at Old Dominion University (ODU). In this role, she facilitates the development of engaging digital assignments and programs, with an eye towards fostering integrative learning and digital literacies. Currently, her research interests include digital ethics and ePortfolio composition, extended reality (XR) use as an emerging high-impact practice, and GIFs as cultural and rhetorical artifacts. Her work appears in *AePR*, *Peitho*, *Field Guide*, and *In Media Res*.

Kelly Moreland, PhD, (she/her/hers) is an assistant professor of rhetoric and composition and director of first-year writing at Minnesota State University, Mankato. She earned her PhD in rhetoric and writing from Bowling Green State University in 2019, and her research can be found in publications such as *Peitho* and *WPA: Writing Program Administration*.

Talinn Phillips, PhD, (she/her/hers) is an associate professor of English at Ohio University in Athens, Ohio. Her research interests include graduate writing development, multilingual writing, writing centers, and writing development across the lifespan. Her books include *Supporting Graduate Student Writers: Research, Curriculum, and Program Design* (coedited in 2016 from University of Michigan Press, *Teaching with a Global Perspective* (coauthored with Dawn Bikowski in 2019), and *Approaches to Lifespan Writing Research* (coedited with Ryan Dippre in 2020). She is currently co-chair of the Consortium on Graduate Communication.

Anis Rahman (he/him/his) is a PhD candidate in the rhetoric and composition program at the University of Wisconsin-Milwaukee. He completed his MA in rhetoric and writing at St. Cloud State University.

Meagan Gacke Reed (she/her/hers) currently lives with her family in North Texas. She works remotely as a study start-up specialist for a clinical research organization. In this role she blends her academic interest in writing and reading comprehension with her professional interest in protecting human subjects in clinical research trials.

Matt Sehrsweeney (he/him/his) lives in Washington, DC, and works for the Natural Resources Conservation Service. His writing about climate justice has appeared in the *Progressive*, the *Chronicle of Higher Education*, and the *Nation*. He has master's degrees in environment and sustainability and public policy from the University of Michigan, where he was a department steward for the Graduate Employees Organization (GEO), Local 3550.

Elliot Shapiro, PhD, (he/him/his) is a senior lecturer in the Knight Institute for Writing in the Disciplines; the Knight Foundation Director of Writing in the Majors; and director of the Faculty Seminar in Writing Instruction. He regularly teaches the Writing in the Majors Seminar; a first-year writing seminar titled "Jews on Film: Visible and Invisible"; and "Jewish Films and Filmmakers: Hollywood and Beyond." Publications include articles on multiethnic American literature, American film, and the teaching of writing.

Paul Shovlin, PhD, (he/him/his) is the director of composition at Ohio University. He has worked as a liminal WPA for twenty years, helming writing programs, a writing center, and a WAC program. His research interests include writing program administration, support for first-generation students, and the broad intersection of computers and writing.

Kalena Thomhave (she/her/hers) is a Pittsburgh-based freelance writer and researcher on poverty and inequality. Her work has appeared in the *American Prospect*, the *Progressive*, and the *Nation*, among other places. She has a master's degree in public policy from the University of Michigan, where she was a department steward for the Graduate Employees Organization (GEO), Local 3550.

Megan Titus, PhD, (she/her/hers) is an associate professor of English at Rider University, where she teaches a variety of courses in composition, rhetoric, creative writing, and gender and sexuality studies. Her work has appeared in *Praxis: A Writing Center Journal*, *WPA: Writing Program Administration*, and the *Journal of Teaching and Writing*. She is currently examining the impact of embedded tutoring on first-year writing classrooms.

Alma Villanueva (she/her/hers) is a doctoral candidate in the English Department at Texas A&M University finishing her dissertation, tentatively titled "Photographing Mixed-Race Bodies: An Artistic and Scientific Visual Culture."

Xueshuang Wang, PhD, (she/her/hers) is an associate professor at the School of Education (Physical Education Teachers College), Beijing Sport University, China. Her research areas focus on higher education, and international and comparative physical education. She received her PhD degree in international and comparative education at Beijing Normal University.

Martha Althea Webber (she/her/hers) teaches and writes in Goleta, California, where she is a lecturer (and proud UC-AFT Local 2141 member) in the Writing Program at the University of California, Santa Barbara. She received her PhD in English with a concentration in writing studies.

Sarah Welsh, PhD, (she/her/hers) holds a doctorate in rhetoric and writing from the University of Texas at Austin. She is a freelance writer, and her writing explores the social dynamics of new media.

Weiyan Xiong, PhD, (he/him/his) is an assistant professor at Lingnan University, Hong Kong. He also serves as the program director of the MA in International Higher Education and Management (IHEM) and MSocSc in Organizational Psychology and Education Management (OPEM). His research interests include comparative and international education, indigenous education, liberal arts education, faculty professional development, and education for sustainable development. Dr. Xiong received his PhD in higher education management from the University of Pittsburgh and master's degree in higher education at the Graduate School of Education at Peking University.

Huiyuan Ye, PhD, (he/him/his) is a research fellow at Duke Kunshan University (DKU), a Sino-American joint venture liberal arts and sciences university in China. His research focuses on the internationalization of liberal arts education in mainland China. In particular, his studies seek to creatively untangle the often-ambiguous relationship between interdisciplinarity and learning outcomes. Prior to joining DKU, Dr. Ye was a visiting scholar at Boston College Center for International Higher Education (CIHE) as well as a researcher of competency-based education at Southern New Hampshire University. Currently he is an associate editor of the *International Academic Forum (IAFOR) Journal of Education*. Dr. Ye holds an EdD degree in higher education management from the University of Pittsburgh.

Index

Abram, Michael E., 277
academic freedom, non-tenure-track work as an infringement on, 21, 79, 182, 270, 272, 286
adjunct instructors. *See* non-tenure-track faculty
administrators, 1, 17, 29, 31, 36, 49–52, 73, 93, 95, 112, 114, 168, 182, 193, 200, 250, 265
   graduate student organizing in response to actions of, 11, 14, 243–244, 250–260
advising and advisors, 7, 11, 31, 35, 48, 102–103, 106, 108, 188, 198, 200
   dissertation committee, 55, 69, 196
   exploiting student research, 130–131
   importance of, 50, 73, 170, 176
   importance of, to Chinese international doctoral students, 221–229
   misunderstanding the academic job market, 121, 133, 194
   as responsible for giving recommendations, 130–131
   suggestions for, 103, 180, 201, 230
advocacy. *See* benefits; union organizing and collective bargaining
agency, 93, 95–97, 104–106, 109–110, 112, 157, 160, 181, 184, 186, 192–193, 197, 199–201, 252, 261
alt-ac, 19, 86, 88, 89. *See also* internships
alumni networks, 3, 230
American Federation of Teachers, 274–290, 299
Anyon, Jean, 121

apprenticeship model of graduate education, 60, 62, 209, 249, 270
   as a labor misclassification, 14, 193, 246, 270
austerity. *See* neoliberalism
Austin, Sara, 9, 19, 127, 194

Barad, Karen, 58
"bargaining for the common good," 17, 259, 292. *See also* union organizing and collective bargaining, solidarity model
Benderly, Beryl Lief, 214, 229
benefits, 1, 3, 4, 7, 10, 15, 17, 30, 81, 272, 281, 292
   childcare, 7, 76, 264, 266, 278, 281
   healthcare, 208, 210, 279, 283–285
   housing, 7, 281, 291
   parental leave, 208
Berlin, James, 8
Billingsley, Khadeidra, 6, 18, 106, 209, 242, 271
Black Lives Matter, 259, 284
Bousquet, Marc, 9–11, 13–14, 16, 17, 29, 246, 249, 268, 269, 271
Brandt, Deborah, 7, 164
Brown, Tessa, 52, 62, 75, 130, 175, 193, 217, 241

California State University system, 20
   paying to teach at, 237–239
Canagarajah, Suresh, 139
Cassuto, Leonard, 120, 131, 132
Caterine, Chris, 176, 177
Chaput, Catherine, 248, 256
Chicago Teachers Union strike, 259, 292

City University of New York, desegregation of, 16, 18
Cloud, Dana, 260
Cobos, April, 19, 34, 190
collective bargaining. *See* union organizing and collective bargaining
Columbia University, 241, 242
Combahee River Collective, 18
community, 34, 38, 41–53, 90–94, 106, 110, 169, 270, 291–292
community college, 3, 37, 132, 237
compensation for graduate student labor, 63, 75–76, 78, 198–199
    as below the living wage, 11–12
    compared with other academic workers' compensation, 5, 120
    data on, 5
    for supplementary work, 210, 239
    tuition waivers as, 129
composition studies, 2, 6, 19, 37–52, 60–82, 179
    First-Year Composition, 15, 142–163, 237–239
    invention of, 8
    labor practices of, 8–9
corporatization. *See* neoliberalism
Cost of Living Adjustment (COLA), 11–12
Cottom, Tressie McMillan, 4
coursework, 6, 13, 30, 34, 60, 71, 74, 93–99, 112, 142, 162, 167, 171, 176, 187, 225, 230
COVID-19, 10, 90, 96, 161
    diversity and, 18, 228, 291, 293
    effect on graduate student work conditions and organizing, 1–2, 11–12, 17, 19, 52, 74, 135, 209, 242, 258–259, 273, 285
Cox, Anicca, 5, 16, 20, 193, 242
CV (curriculum vitae), 93, 127, 131, 134, 168, 178, 181, 208, 210, 211

degree conferral, 2–4, 7, 11, 16, 30–31, 71, 89, 129, 185, 194, 196, 209, 221, 238, 249, 272

disability, 17, 44
    services for students with disabilities, 113, 266
    See also mental health
disciplinarity, 9–10, 141–147, 161, 178–179, 184–186, 188–204, 229
discourse. *See* graduate students, mythologies around; neoliberalism, discourses of
dissertation, 35, 37, 46–49, 55, 75, 93–95, 104–105, 137–139, 170, 172, 175, 191, 225
    "All But Dissertation" status, 89
    producing identity, 186, 193–199
    See also advising and advisors
diversity, 16–18, 20
    first-generation students, 50, 238
    LGBTQIA+, 15, 31, 37, 44–45, 50, 54, 167
    racial, 4, 15, 167
    religious, 37, 44–45, 54–56
    women of color, 4, 54–56, 168–169
    See also COVID-19, diversity and; international students; multilingualism and linguistic bias
diversity and inclusion, 54, 90
Downs, Douglas, 141–146, 161–162, 165–166

Eaton, Adrienne E., 30, 229, 270, 272
education policy, 4–6, 213–214, 216–223, 247
Elbelazi, Samah, 19
embodiment, 24, 42, 168
emotional labor, 2, 18, 19, 29–30, 39, 43, 48, 51, 57, 95–97, 105–109, 112–113, 187, 189–191, 198, 209
employability, 20, 108, 213–230
    critical thinking and, 223–225
    definitions of, 215–216
    graduate students' efforts to cultivate, 219–230
entanglement, 57–59

excellence, 8, 14–16, 245. *See also* graduate students, mythologies of; neoliberalism, discourses of
expertise, 1–2, 74, 102, 208–211, 274, 279
   dissertation as developing, 191
   teaching to develop, 141–162
exploitation, 1–22, 33–34, 39–40, 51–52, 58, 62–63, 75, 96, 109, 128, 182–183, 190, 192, 229, 237, 245–246, 253–254, 258–260, 268, 272, 280, 285

fees, 3, 20, 239, 241–266, 279, 284
   histories of student fees, 245–249
feminisms, 17, 18, 19, 167–169, 211
Ferguson, Roderick, 10, 16, 18
First Year Composition, 15, 142–163, 237–239. *See also* composition studies
Fiscus-Cannaday, Jaclyn, 20, 202
Flannery, Kathryn T., 34

Gacke-Reed, Meagan, 19, 271
Garcia, Ofelia, 139
Gee, James Paul, 166, 180, 181, 183, 187
GI Bill, and graduate school, 244
gig economy, 10, 15, 286
graduate school
   diversification of, 15–16
   history of, 213–215, 269–270
graduate student organizations (non-union), 265
   unpaid labor and, 93–95, 110–111
graduate students
   the average graduate student, 4–6, 130, 225
   Chinese, in American graduate programs, 215–232
   data on, 3–5, 29, 31
   as entry-level academics, 13, 22, 33
   international, 17, 29–20, 23, 54–55, 137–140, 214–232, 242, 247–250, 257, 262, 278, 280, 283, 284, 291

   mythologies around, 7, 9, 14, 57, 59, 171, 201
   place and migration of, 21, 33–50, 105–106
   prospective, 1, 22, 35, 41, 51, 140, 179
   reasons for choosing graduate study of, 218–219
   See also graduate student workers; graduate school
graduate student workers
   as administrators, 19, 55, 57–58, 60–85, 109
   doing research, 30, 120, 128–134, 184–191, 222–225
   as essential or frontline workers, 2, 11, 14, 17, 20, 91
   incorrect job descriptions for, 61–78, 129–130
   as misclassified as students, 1, 8–9, 270, 281
   preparation of, for teaching, 69, 72, 142–162, 237–239
   as teachers, 2–21, 29, 42–43, 57–75, 98–99, 117–169, 215, 237–239, 258, 268, 281–282
groundedness and placelessness, as a feature of academic life, 19, 33–52

Haley, Adam, 9, 20, 31, 247, 266
Hall, Stuart, 180, 181, 184, 193
Hanson, Alex, 20, 34, 172, 271
Harvard University, 3, 8, 133, 242
Hollinger, Andrew, 6, 19, 29, 122, 172, 242
Horner, Bruce, 9, 139
Hutchison, Allison, 20, 202
Hyland, Ken, 179, 183, 184, 186, 196, 197

identity formation, 29, 39–43, 178–201, 273, 277
ideology, 12, 195–198, 272–277, 281–286
international students, 17, 29–20, 23, 54–55, 137–140, 214–232, 242, 247–250, 257, 262, 278, 280, 283, 284, 291

internships, 19, 86–89, 230
Isaac, Jonathan, 5, 20, 193, 237, 270, 281

Jaffe, Sarah, 7, 175, 177
job market, 10–11, 20, 33, 29–40, 81, 83, 88, 132, 175, 185, 197–200, 208–211, 215, 221, 244, 230, 249. *See also* advising and advisors, misunderstanding the academic job market
Jordan, June, 16, 18

K–12 education, 238, 278
Kahn, Seth, 9, 122
Kamler, Barbara, 183, 191, 195
Koch, Paul L., 12–15
Kory-Westlund, Jacqueline M., 20
Kuebrich, Ben, 248
Kupsh, Charlotte, 9, 19, 106, 176, 215

laboratory-based research, 20, 21, 134–135, 170–172
language. *See* multilingualism and linguistic bias
Latterell, Catherine, 61, 76
liminality, 9, 195
  for graduate student writing program administrators, 60–79

Mantai, Lilia, 188, 190
materialism, 9–10, 34
McAlpine, Lynn, 189, 192, 195–196, 201
McDonald, Zoe, 9, 19, 106, 176, 215
mental health, 16, 52, 93, 210
  anxiety, 29
  fatigue, 57–58
  joy, 208–210
  loneliness, 40, 43
Mewburn, Inger, 188–190, 198
Mize, Megan, 19, 34, 190
Moreland, Kelly, 9, 19, 127, 194
multilingualism and linguistic bias, 54, 137–140

Napolitano, Janet, 11–12
National Labor Relations Board (NLRB), 241, 270–271
  New York University case, 241
  primary purpose test, 270
Negra, Diane, 168
neoliberalism, 4, 10, 15–16
  discourses of, 167, 180–182, 241–260
  effects of, on the academy, 199, 271–273, 286
Newman, Kathy, 243, 246
New York University, 133, 241, 242, 271, 272
non-tenure-track faculty, 1–5, 7, 8, 15, 21, 33, 60, 63, 73, 77, 86, 120–121, 134, 210, 211, 214, 231, 237, 239, 242
Nopper, Tamara K., 18
Northwestern University, 242
Nzinga-Johnson, Sekile, 168

offices, 7, 55, 65, 70, 81, 83, 167, 171
Old Dominion University, 91
orientations, 51, 68–69, 137, 239, 282, 286

parenting, 18–20, 57–59, 168–169, 170–172, 264–266
  pregnancy, 56
  single parents, 167, 264
  See also benefits
Pemberton, Michael, 60–61, 76
Phillips, Talinn, 19, 109
precarity, 4, 58, 106, 112, 120, 182, 189, 209, 246, 268–271, 282–287
privilege, 7
  economic, 171, 175, 210
  racial, 266
professionalization, 20, 88, 91, 104, 176
  professional identity and, 197–201
  research and, 209, 223–225
  role of advising in, 225–229
  See also job market
publishing, 7–8, 10, 88, 128, 132, 134, 135, 172, 198

race. *See* diversity
Rahman, Anis, 19, 242
Reid, Shelley, 142–144, 162
remote graduate school
   and COVID, 134, 291
   in a hybrid doctoral program, 90–114
   suggestions for program
      management, 110–114
research. *See* graduate student
   workers, doing research;
   professionalization, research
   and
Restaino, Jessica, 142, 161
Reynolds, Nedra, 41–42, 48–49
rhetoric and composition. *See*
   composition
Rhoades, Gary, 269, 285
Rhoads, Robert A., 269, 285
right-to-work states, 270, 287, 292
Rodríguez, Yanira, 248
Rogers, Sean E., 30, 270–272

Savio, Mario, 261
Schell, Eileen, 9, 10
Sehrsweeney, Matt, 17, 20, 259, 260
service , 10, 113, 120, 132, 135, 168,
   210–211
sexuality. *See* diversity, LGBTQIA+
sexual misconduct, 17, 17, 271, 283, 284
Shapiro, Elliot, 19, 141, 258
Shovlin, Paul, 19, 109
Slaughter, Sheila, 244
solidarity, 20, 242, 260, 268, 272–275,
   284–286, 291. *See also* union
   organizing and collective
   bargaining
Spelman College, 17
Stanford University, 3, 17

teaching, 2–21, 29, 42–43, 57–75, 98–
   99, 117–169, 215, 237–239, 258,
   268, 281–282. *See also* graduate
   student workers, preparation
   of, for teaching; tenure,
   undervaluing of teaching in
   securing

Teaching Assistants' Association (TAA),
   243–261
tenure, 175, 182
   decreasing numbers of tenure-track
      positions, 3–5, 38, 176
   undervaluing of teaching in
      securing, 199–122
THE General Body, 16
Thomhave, Kalena, 17, 20, 259, 260
Thomson, Pat, 183, 191, 195
Title IX offices, 266, 270. *See also* sexual
   misconduct
Titus, Megan, 19, 109
tuition waivers, 129. *See also*
   compensation

union organizing and collective
   bargaining, 5, 75
   for bread-and-butter issues, 18, 269,
      272, 275, 281
   craft unions *vs* industrial unions,
      272–273
   disrupting "business as usual," 257
   grade strikes, 11–12, 246
   graduate unions engaging in, 209,
      241–261, 291–293
   history of graduate unions, 269–274
   history of unions, 291–292
   improving universities, 280
   relationality in, 276–284
   solidarity model of, 20, 242, 260,
      268, 272–275, 284–286, 291
   See also specific strikes
University of California–Berkeley, 261,
   264, 269
University of California–Santa Cruz,
   graduate student wildcat strike
   at, 11–14, 242
University of Chicago, 242
University of Colorado–Boulder, 242
University of Georgia system, 17, 245
University of Illinois system, 242, 257
University of Michigan, 110, 242
   GEO wildcat strike at, 20, 259,
      291–293
University of Nebraska–Lincoln, 35–50

University of Pennsylvania, 264
University of Wisconsin–Madison, 20, 241, 269
    TAA campaign against fees at, 243–261

Villanueva, Alma, 19, 34, 266, 271
Villanueva, Victor, 59
Voos, Paula B., 30, 229, 270, 272

Wang, Xueshuang, 20, 108, 187, 271
Wardle, Elizabeth, 141–146, 161–162, 165–166
Webber, Martha Althea, 20, 242
Weisbuch, Robert, 120, 131–132
Welch, Nancy, 36, 246
Welsh, Sarah, 20, 21, 31, 122, 193, 247

Wright, Allison Laubach, 14–15
writing. *See* composition; dissertation; groundedness and placelessness
Writing About Writing (WAW), 141–162
writing centers, 9, 77, 237, 239
writing program administrators (WPA), graduate students as, 19, 57–58, 60–85, 109
writing studies. *See* composition

Xiong, Weiyan, 20, 108, 187, 271

Yale University, 242, 271
    1995 GESO grade strike at, 246
Ye, Huiyuan, 20, 108, 187, 271

www.ingramcontent.com/pod-product-compliance
Lightning Source LLC
Chambersburg PA
CBHW030607230426
43661CB00053B/1884